Practicing Lean

I0390408

Learning How to Learn How to get Better... Better

Mark Graban

Practicing Lean

Learning How to Learn How to get Better... Better

Mark Graban

ISBN 1520202679 (paperback); 1733519483 (hardcover)

Leanpub

This is a Leanpub book. Leanpub empowers authors and publishers with the Lean Publishing process. Lean Publishing is the act of publishing an in-progress ebook using lightweight tools and many iterations to get reader feedback, pivot until you have the right book and build traction once you do.

Also By Mark Graban

The Mistakes That Make Us

Lean Veterinary Practice Management

Measures of Success

Contents

Welcome to the Book!

This book is a collaborative project that took shape over time, with different authors contributing chapters and essays about the early days of their Lean journeys. That includes people with experiences in Lean manufacturing, Lean healthcare, Lean Startups, and other settings.

As the editor, I wrote Chapters 1 and 2 as a way to inspire others to share their stories and their honest reflections about their own personal Lean journeys. As the subtitle says, this is all about "Learning How to Learn How to get Better, Better." How have we learned about Lean through our own practice? Have we gotten better at how we help others get better? This is a book of those stories and reflections.

I asked people to contribute chapters that are first-person stories, with the emphasis on mistakes and honest reflections, not a chapter about how great they are with Lean.

This book evolved over the course of a year, with submissions being added to the electronic book through the LeanPub.com[1] platform. Those who bought the book early received updates as chapters were added over time.

Now, as of February 2017, the book has been released as a Kindle eBook and a paperback book.

I'm really excited that this book now contains chapters by 16 authors from different industries (healthcare, manufacturing, services, government, and consulting) and from different countries (the U.S., England, Canada, and Scotland). Some contributors are published authors of books and some are sharing reflections for the first time in this form.

All author royalty proceeds are being donated to the Louise H. Batz Patient Safety Foundation[2], a Texas-based non-profit that does excellent work in educating patients and hospitals about patient safety

---

[1]http://www.leanpub.com
[2]http://www.louisebatz.org/Home.aspx

improvement. Their publications, like the Batz Guide for Bedside Advocacy[3] are really making a difference in the lives of patients and staff. Over \$1000 has been donated, as of December 2016.

If you'd like to donate, please visit their website[4].

Thank you for reading! If you reflections you'd like to share, please email Mark@MarkGraban.com

Mark Graban[5]

July 29, 2015 Updated February 11, 2017

Update April 18, 2017 – this book is also available in audio book form (at least the first half of the book is available now). Learn more or buy it at www.leanpub.com/practicinglean[6].

Update July 1, 2018 – this book has raised over \$4,000 for the Batz Foundation!

---

[3]http://www.louisebatz.org/patient-education/the-batz-guide.aspx
[4]http://www.louisebatz.org/
[5]http://www.MarkGraban.com
[6]http://www.leanpub.com/practicinglean

Chapter One - Mark Graban

Originally written in 2015, edited December 2016
   Note - Some of the Lean Blog posts referenced in this chapter are included in Chapter 19 of this book

Mark Graban is the author of the Shingo Research Award-winning book *Lean Hospitals: Improving Quality, Patient Safety, and Employee Engagement*[a] (now in its third edition). Mark is also co-author, with Joe Swartz, of *Healthcare Kaizen: Engaging Front-Line Staff in Sustainable Continuous Improvements*[b] (also a Shingo Research Award recipient) and *The Executive Guide to Healthcare Kaizen*[c]. His latest book is titled *Measures of Success: React Less, Lead Better, Improve More*[d]

He is a board member for the Louise H. Batz Patient Safety Foundation, which is receiving all proceeds from this book.

He serves as a consultant to healthcare organizations through his company, Constancy, Inc. and is also the vice president of innovation and improvement services for the technology company KaiNexus[e]. He has focused on healthcare improvement since 2005, after starting his career in industry at General Motors, Dell, and Honeywell.

Mark has a B.S. in Industrial Engineering from Northwestern University, an M.S. in Mechanical Engineering and an M.B.A. from the Massachusetts Institute of Technology's Leaders for Global Operations Program. Mark and his wife live in Texas. He is also the founder of www.LeanBlog.org[f]. You can find him on Twitter as @MarkGraban[g].

---

[a]http://www.leanhospitalsbook.com/
[b]http://www.hckaizen.com/healthcare-kaizen/
[c]http://www.hckaizen.com/executive-guide-to-healthcare-kaizen/
[d]http://www.measuresofsuccessbook.com/healthcare-kaizen/

Identifying Problems is only the First Step in Improvement

It's sometimes easy to find fault in what others are doing with "Lean." Sometimes, we criticize because we don't recognize what they describe as "Lean" in their organization. Maybe it's natural for an experienced Lean thinker to identify problems, as we're prone to want to fix things and coach people, even if we have to speak hard truths.

For example, we might see process improvement leaders (or trainers) who focus only on Lean tools (or just a particular Lean tool, such as 5S). Or, we might get frustrated when we see people just chartering a few projects or pushing pre-determined "solutions" on others, while not even working on changing their management system and culture.

If you dig deeper, you might find that their limited or ineffective approach to Lean is due to ignorance, a lack of experience, or a lack of proper coaching. Can you blame people for what they don't know? You can't blame somebody if they were taught the wrong things, but you should challenge somebody who doesn't make the effort to educate themselves after declaring that Lean seems "simple" or just a matter of "common sense."

It could be that you have good people who are trying but are working under leaders and executives who don't support the idea of changing the culture (or they're not aware of the need or the possibility). Or, the leaders and executives are the ones who don't understand Lean (and sometimes, don't even try).

We, too often, hear about executives who use Lean as a cost-cutting tool. They lay off employees, which destroys morale and hurts customer service, doing so while collecting big bonuses. It's likely these senior leaders don't share the same Lean values that we appreciate and they, quite possibly, never will. The idea of a transformative "Lean journey" might be a pipe dream, if the senior leaders see employees as a "bunch of warm bodies" who are just a cost on the P&L statement instead of viewing them as human beings to partner with and develop.

Or, we read (in major business publications like the Wall Street Journal[7], no less) about a company's Lean office that has a self-proclaimed "5S cop" who does audits to make sure employees don't hang sweaters on the back of chairs and don't have any personal items on their desks. We read about another organization that bans "inactive bananas"[8] from employees' desks as if that does anything to improve the company's performance.

Employees in these companies are understandably annoyed by clumsy attempts at 5S. Unfortunately, they come to hate the idea of Lean instead of seeing Lean as something that provides job security and allows them to feel pride and joy in their work. When Lean is just about putting tape outlines around staplers on individual desks, then Lean rightfully becomes a punch line. That makes things harder for the rest of us.

Inexperience and Ignorance or Incorrect Knowledge?

There's inexperience, which we should probably be more tolerant of, and then there is flat-out ignorance or misinformation, which we should stand to correct. It's tempting and easy to criticize a "Lean Six Sigma Master Black Belt" who has such little understanding of Lean that he would actually say[9], in a presentation on stage, that applying Lean to a quality problem would somehow "speed up your quality issue and make bad stuff faster."

It's unlikely that any of the people in these stories are stupid or

---

[7]http://www.leanblog.org/2008/10/this-wsj-article-and-many-organizations/

[8]http://www.leanblog.org/2007/02/bad-lean5s-hits-uk-media/

[9]http://www.leanblog.org/2014/05/run-fast-if-you-ever-hear-this-phrase/

evil. They just don't know any better or they've been taught things that are untrue and harmful. We can criticize what was said – without personally attacking the individual. There's no room in Lean for terms like "toolhead" or "concrete head," if this is supposed to be all about "respect for people"[10].

> The false construct that "Lean is for speed and Six Sigma is for quality" has been taught to countless Lean Sigma students after it was the theme of the book *Lean Six Sigma*[a] by Michael George. Thinking that Lean is only about speed is an incorrect idea that's unlikely to go away with more "Lean Sigma" experience. But, it might go away if Lean Sigma students read books by Taiichi Ohno or Shigeo Shingo (or modern authors like Jeff Liker and Jim Womack). They would learn that Lean and the Toyota Production System have two main pillars - "just in time" flow and "quality at the source." Of course, Lean has something to contribute to quality improvement!
>
> ---
> [a]http://amzn.to/1DeOJ7z

It's easy to find fault with beginners while forgetting one's own early mistakes. I've been studying, practicing and teaching Lean for over 20 years in different settings. Whether you have 20 years of experience with Lean, ten years, or even five, you have experiences and life lessons that probably make you a better Lean practitioner than a beginner (or the willfully ignorant senior leader or "Lean Sigma" whatever belt who chooses to not even learn about real Lean).

Lean Means Always Learning

These years of experience hopefully make you a better Lean thinker than your own earlier self. That's because learning and mastering Lean isn't as simple as reading one book or taking one class. Heck,

---

[10]http://www.leanblog.org/2013/02/toyota-respect-for-people-or-humanity-and-lean/

given some of the mistakes and misunderstandings that seem to be common out there, you'd wonder if some of these "Lean professionals" have even read a book or taken a class. Maybe they just read one. A little bit of knowledge can be a dangerous thing.

The best Lean practitioners are continually learning. We're reading new books, re-reading old ones, attending webinars and conferences, listening to podcasts, and doing everything we can to better understand Lean and the Toyota Production System. We're also learning by doing, putting knowledge and theory into practice as we work with staff and leaders, getting better at teaching and coaching, bettering ourselves and practicing our craft. We reflect on our successes, our failures and those times when things were just OK. We challenge ourselves to think better and act better, continually improving what we do, practicing what we preach.

I recall a time back in 2003 when I was visiting Johnson Controls, a major auto supplier in western Michigan. During a large meeting, people around the room were introducing themselves to the group. Early in the introductions, an older gentleman stood up and said, with the raspy voice of a long-time chain smoker, "My name is Jim Pell. I've been learning Lean for 25 years." That was it. Then, he sat down.

Of course, all of the Johnson Controls people in the room knew who he was. I think all of the visitors knew who he was. Pell was the SVP and GM of global operations for the company. He chose those words carefully. He set an example for all of us in the room. We're all still learning... don't get too high on yourself. That was a powerful message.

If We Keep Practicing Lean, We'll Get Good At It

Lean concepts might seem simple, but Lean is not an easy craft. Being an effective Lean leader, facilitator or practitioner requires more than books and classes – it requires people skills, judgment and wisdom and other things that can often only be developed over time.

It's probably not realistic to expect people or organizations to be really good at Lean right away. It requires practice. Does a child (or an adult) sound good the first day they are playing a new instrument? Probably not!

> If you're not doing, you're not learning. Everybody makes mistakes. It's what you do with them that counts. – John Wooden (1910-2010), Hall of Fame Basketball Coach

I think that word – practice – is important. Attorneys get to "practice law." Physicians are allowed to "practice medicine." Think about that if you're a lawyer's first case or a surgeon's first procedure. Try not to think of the sound of an awful, screechy violin being played by a new student.

There are many imperfect words that get used to describe a person or an organization that is utilizing Lean methods and mindsets:

- "Doing Lean" (which incorrectly implies it's just action and not a different way of thinking)
- "Lean Thinking" (which implies action isn't necessary)
- "Implementing Lean" (which mistakenly implies that you'll be done at some point)
- "Getting Lean" (which also suggests there's an endpoint or that it's just about the results)
- "Leaning Out That Organization" (which sounds like something that's done to the employees instead of done *with* them)

One of my earlier healthcare clients pretty much banned everybody from using the word "implementation." I resisted that at the time, but I now see their point. That word bothers me more now than it did then. I'm progressing. I'm getting better… I hope.

I'm practicing.

We're all practicing Lean.

If we keep practicing Lean, someday we'll get good at it. Or, each day we'll hopefully be better than the day before. Each year, we'll be better than the year before.

In my own early days of learning and practicing Lean, I had a lot of misunderstandings and I made a lot of mistakes.

- I was taught a number of tools, so I tended to think about implementing tools.
- While I had mentors teaching me some of the mindsets, I didn't have the opportunity to work in a true Lean culture… it was always in companies in transition toward Lean.
- I didn't always involve front-line staff, as I was encouraged to come up with answers and solutions as an engineer.
- I was too focused, at times, on *doing* instead of *teaching* others.

During those various attempts, I had the best intentions. I was trying to improve quality and safety while creating a better workplace and aiming for long-term success for the companies I worked for and their customers. I was trying my best, but I sometimes failed others in the process.

I think we can reflect and admit mistakes without beating ourselves up. I know I'm not alone in lamenting past Lean mistakes. I've heard or read luminaries in the Lean world admit some of their own past mistakes. I admire their openness and honesty. That gives me the courage to write this chapter.

For example, at the 2015 Lean Healthcare Transformation Summit, Jim Womack made[11] a parallel between healthcare and Lean. Womack, one of the most prominent people in the Lean world, told the audience, "You can treat a patient with drugs, but drugs don't get at the root cause." Womack admitted that he had, in the past, been a "drug pusher" for Lean tools. Womack now realizes that organizations need to think more systemically and change the way we manage instead of just doing more Kaizens and using more Lean tools.

In his outstanding book *On the Mend*[12], Dr. John Toussaint reflected on the early days of Lean at ThedaCare, when he was CEO.

---

[11]http://gembawalkabout.com/2015/06/12/best-conference-ever-till-next-year-2015-edition/

[12]http://amzn.to/1U9uw5A

Today, ThedaCare has been practicing Lean for 13 years and is considered one of the world leaders in the use of Lean to improve patient care and reduce costs. However, in the early days, ThedaCare relied exclusively on weeklong Rapid Improvement Events. Toussaint wrote:

> We were frustrated because the transformation seemed to be stalling or rolling backward in some areas. Sustaining the gain was a constant struggle and it did not seem to matter that our staff knew the lean tools and were pressing forward with RIEs (Rapid Improvement Events) and PDSAs.
>
> Finally, some brave soul said to a senior executive, "How are we supposed to change when you keep managing the same way?"

To ThedaCare's credit, they used the Plan-Do-Study-Adjust mindset to "study" how things were working. They "adjusted" by supplementing their RIEs with a process they call "continuous daily improvement." More importantly, they also created a new management system that would help change the culture in a more meaningful way, as described in the book *Beyond Heroes*[13], by Kim Barnas.

Virginia Mason Medical Center, also considered a world leader in Lean healthcare, reported that, back in 2004, they had "backsliding" after 60% of their Rapid Process Improvement Workshops[14]. This meant it was too "easy to slip back into old ways of doing things if there is a lack of accountability and follow-through." They only sustained their new practices and results 40% of the time. But, by practicing Lean and getting better, Virginia Mason has improved its sustainment rates over time. By 2011, 90% of its projects showed sustained results after 90 days, but, still, only 50% held results for six or 12 months.

Jim Womack is, of course, one of the people who originally coined the term "Lean Production"[15]. ThedaCare and Virginia Mason are

---

[13] http://amzn.to/1IO51Vv

[14] http://www.leanblog.org/2010/10/consulting-case-studies-need-statistical-validity/

[15] http://www.leanblog.org/2013/09/the-term-lean-production-is-25-years-old-my-thoughts-on-the-original-article/

great organizations. But, they've all gotten better with Lean over time. Nobody is perfect at the beginning, not even the world leaders in Lean. That's an important point to keep in mind.

Is it Lame to Call Situations L.A.M.E.?

On my blog, I've been outspoken about criticizing incorrect or misguided things that have been said or done in the name of Lean or the Toyota Production System. My intent has been to educate people and to defend what I think Lean is all about. My criteria for "Real Lean" are the things that Toyota does and says or what respected Lean luminaries say, do and write. I run the risk of coming across as a know-it-all. I certainly don't know everything. But, I know enough to know when something is factually correct instead of being merely a differing opinion.

A few years back, I went so far as to create a really awkward acronym, "L.A.M.E."[16], which stands for either Lean As Mistakenly Explained or Lean As Misguidedly Executed. A union publication responded to one of my posts by saying the acronym, to them, stood for "Lean As Mostly Experienced." Touché.

If a company is using Lean to layoff lots of people, many will criticize Lean, often quite publicly. They're really criticizing the company's actions, and probably rightfully so. We can explain that the company is not really keeping with Lean principles or practice... it's L.A.M.E. instead. Or, if an organization is forcing employees to adopt a new "standardized work" method without involving them in the improvement process, that's arguably L.A.M.E., as well. If a company is speeding up the work to the point that employees are getting hurt, that's not very Lean. I think we have an obligation to those who came before us to call that out as L.A.M.E.

Along similar lines, Bob Emiliani, the author and professor, uses the term "Fake Lean"[17] to distinguish bad practices done in the name of Lean from "Real Lean." If an organization is just doing occasional

---

[16]http://leanblog.org/lame
[17]http://www.bobemiliani.com/back-story-real-vs-fake-lean/

Kaizen Events and isn't engaging people in Kaizen as the practice of ongoing continuous improvement, that might rightfully be labeled as "Fake Lean."

While it might be technically correct to label something as L.A.M.E. or "Fake Lean," is it kind or nice to do so? Upon reflection, it probably is not. Is it necessary to speak out? Maybe. Is it respectful to call out bad practices? I'd argue it is respectful if we're trying to help those who are being harmed or jeopardized by L.A.M.E.

Instead of just criticizing, is it better to take the patient tone of a coach or mentor? I like to think I'm a constructive mentor with people in person. I've never called a person or an idea stupid. But, I may have failed by shooting somebody a glance that might have suggested as such. We all have room for improvement.

By calling a scenario L.A.M.E., are we making the person involved in the story defensive, thereby possibly stifling their growth and development if they just retrench? What if the person who determined that employees shouldn't put sweaters on their chairs because it looks bad is a conscientious – but inexperienced – Lean facilitator who is trying hard to learn and practice Lean? How patient should we be?

There are times I have probably been too harsh in my online writing. It's easy to sit behind a keyboard and criticize. Maybe I should be more patient. Then again, perhaps some of the people behind these L.A.M.E. practices are choosing to be willfully ignorant of Lean principles. Does the criticism get through to them, or am I just preaching to the converted?

Let's Reflect

My hope for this book is that we'll celebrate the idea of practicing. I'm also hoping to inspire others to reflect upon being "bad" at Lean in our early days of practice and to get others to share their stories.

I'm hoping people will discuss questions such as:

- What did we misunderstand or not fully understand about Lean?
- What mistakes did we make?
- What do we wish we had done better?

- What lessons did we learn?

Sharing these missteps and reflections won't necessarily help prevent others from making the same mistakes. And, I don't think that's the point. We learn from our own mistakes, and it's probably necessary to go through that process. But, showing some humility and talking about our own mistakes might make others feel better about where they are at this point in their personal Lean journeys.

I'm certainly not perfect. I've made many mistakes, and I hope I've learned from them. I'm encouraging other contributors to this book to share their stories. My mistakes, from manufacturing and healthcare, are presented in Chapter 2. The chapters that follow will contain first-person accounts from others and their Lean journeys.

Chapter Two - Mark Graban

It has been over 20 years since I graduated from college and entered the working world. Graduate school took two years, with a six-month working internship in the middle, but let's say I've been working for 20 years. As of this writing in 2015, my career has had two very equal halves. The first ten years were focused on manufacturing, when my career aspirations included moving up through roles like plant manager, VP of operations, and chief operating officer in large companies.

Through happenstance, along with my own choices, I ended up spending the last ten years of my career working in healthcare. Thankfully, I was able to build upon mistakes and lessons from my time in manufacturing. But, being in an unfamiliar setting, I made a few mistakes as I started anew in hospital settings. So, I have two "first years of Lean" that I'll write about, from 1995 in manufacturing and 2005 in healthcare.

See One, Do Some, Teach a Bunch

There's a common expression that I learned in healthcare:

> "See one, do one, teach one."

That describes the traditional nursing mindset for how one progresses toward competence. First, you have to learn, whether that's from a book, a video, or a live instructor. Once you have some knowledge, you need to gain experience by trying – go and do.

In my experience, "learning by doing" is really only most effective when you have a capable coach or mentor. How many people keep doing something on their own - playing golf, for example - and end up just reinforcing bad habits instead of learning and getting better?

Once you've learned how to do something effectively, a great way to test for competence is gauging somebody's ability to teach what they've learned and done.

That's all a decent model, although I don't think "one" is the number that allows you to progress to the next step in that progression. Sometimes you need to see three before you can do (or try). You might need to do seven before you try to teach. It depends on the situation.

At a high level, I've gone through a similar progression in my Lean career. First I gained knowledge by reading books and from what my mentors taught me or they helped me see on my own. I've gone and done things, such as designing and implementing a kanban system for parts.

I think the ultimate level is the ability to teach others to understand Lean and to take action using Lean methods. An individual can learn and understand a Lean concept or method. You can only get so much accomplished by doing things alone, something I'll discuss later in this chapter. There's a great multiplier effect that comes from teaching and helping others see and do.

Take the Kaizen style of continuous improvement, for one. We can see Kaizen and then start to do Kaizen. However, improvement is limited if we don't then inspire others to see and do Kaizen themselves. We reach our peak by everybody doing Kaizen and teaching Kaizen to others.

Also, see, do and teach shouldn't be a one-time linear progression. Even teachers of Lean should continue learning new things and getting better at the things they do and the way they teach. See, do, teach should all include the cycles of continuous improvement that we should love as Lean professionals.

The progression also probably includes starting with seeing and learning individual Lean tools. Then, over time, we probably see how the pieces connect and interact - seeing Lean as a system rather than a tool. As an aside, the phrase "Lean (or Lean Sigma) is a toolbox, so grab the right tool you need at the moment" is like nails on a chalkboard to me.

But, now I'm talking about other people's mistakes (calling Lean a set of tools). Let me get back to my own mistakes and lessons.

My Early Days in Manufacturing at General Motors

When I started my career, I was bright-eyed and, like many, wanted to help make the world a better place. I was excited about doing that by improving how businesses run and helping the people who work in them. I'd like to think I'm still trying to change the world, now that I think about it.

Much of my formal industrial engineering education focused on technical methods, such as simulation, queuing theory and just-in-time inventory management and production principles. Northwestern University, my undergraduate alma mater, offered a class in organizational psychology that I took, but the emphasis was generally more on math than people, maybe to my detriment.

My father, who retired after working for 40 years as an engineer and leader at General Motors, attended one of Dr. W. Edwards Deming's famous four-day workshops at GM. This led to me picking up his copy of Deming's book *Out of the Crisis*[18] during the holiday break of my senior year. Yes, I read that book "for fun." That's appropriate, I guess, since Deming always said the goals of his workshops were to learn and to have fun.

Dr. Deming's approach to psychology and the human side of business and management really appealed to me. I decided that I wanted to work for a company that embraced those principles, even if the company wasn't perfect. It was just a couple of years after Deming's death, and he left quite a wake behind him in the American auto industry. He worked closest with Ford, it seems, but also spent some time at GM.

So, you'd think that I wouldn't have started my career at GM if I wanted to work in a Deming culture. I had actually found an opportunity that I thought would allow me to see Deming principles

[18]http://amzn.to/1LRs6ph

in action, taking an engineering job at the GM Livonia Engine Plant. GM recruiters talked about how the plant had a different type of contract with the union and embraced something they called "The Livonia Philosophy[19]," which was basically a rewording of Deming's key principles, or The Deming Philosophy. I thought this sounded like a great place to work.

As it turned out, the plant *had* previously embraced Deming's approach, but the Livonia Philosophy sort of died with Dr. Deming. Actually, the philosophy died when the plant manager who embraced Deming had been promoted (and eventually rose quite high in the ranks within GM). By June of 1995, when I started working at GM, there was a new plant manager and the philosophy was, quite ironically, nothing but slogans and posters on the walls.

Our plant was really struggling. Employee morale was extremely low and there was a very combative relationship between the union and management (something I didn't blame the union for). Our productivity was just about *half* that of a similar Toyota plant that produced similar V8 engines using similar technology. And, our quality was poor. We produced an engine that performed brilliantly under the hoods of Cadillacs and some Oldsmobiles, but the defect rate in the plant (and in customer use) was very high. We produced about 800 engines a day and anywhere from three to ten a week would fail or sort of blow up under the hood of these new cars, based on the weekly "field service incident report" voicemails that we were sent (we didn't have email yet).

The plant had managers that were decidedly "old school" in their approach to managing - I'd hate to call it "leading." Workers got blamed for problems and were lectured about how they either didn't care or didn't try hard enough to produce quality. I realized that, as Deming taught, the quality and productivity problems were quite systemic and were, therefore, management's responsibility. Without getting into details, I saw many management decisions that directly interfered with producing the best possible quality. You can read

---

[19]https://blog.deming.org/2017/01/the-failure-of-the-livonia-philosophy-at-my-gm-plant/

a blog post with one such story here[20]. For example, management wouldn't let workers stop the line to do scheduled maintenance or quality checks as the manufacturing plan mandated. Yet, workers always got yelled at when, predictably, machines or tools broke down or defects reached our internal customer, the Cadillac assembly plant in Hamtramck.

Thanks to all of that, morale was terrible. Moreover, I understood why when I heard production workers say things like:

- "They want me to check my brain at the door."
- "They hired me for my back, not my brain."
- "I want to stop the line to do my quality checks, but management says to keep the line running."

GM Powertrain corporate leadership wasn't happy, of course, with our poor productivity and lousy quality. Unfortunately, I'm not sure they believed that employee morale was an important problem to solve.

So, with a fresh degree and a youthful energy, I set out to try to make things better.

Some of My Early Mistakes and Lessons in Manufacturing

Looking back, I think I did some things well. I didn't know any better, so I think I had an intrinsic respect for the UAW members who worked on the assembly line. While you do hear many negative things about the union and so-called "lazy" UAW workers in the news growing up around Detroit, I think I spent more time talking to and listening to the workers in the machining departments that I was assigned to than did most people.

At the Gemba, but Doing What?

Another thing I did naturally was to spend a lot of time out of the office area, being out on the factory floor (what we'd call the "gemba"

---

[20]http://www.leanblog.org/2014/04/day-thought-get-fired-gm/

these days in Lean practice). While I spent time getting to know the men who worked in the area (and it was all men), I probably focused too much on collecting data, observing and thinking about the engine block line instead of collaborating with people. But, then again, I was already bucking the GM culture a bit so I probably shouldn't be too hard on myself.

I spent countless hours standing on metal catwalks above the engine block line timing the machines and automation that carved out metal from the aluminum blocks. I observed and tracked how much buffer inventory there was between each machine, often download-ing data from the computers that tracked a lot of this automatically.

With those observations and that data, I'd retreat to my computer in the office. That computer wasn't connected to the internet, so it was a pretty distraction-free environment. I'd sit and put data into the simulation models that I built to help make a case for how and why line productivity wasn't helped by keeping buffers of parts in between every single machine. That's the type of work I was expected to do in the old GM culture, so I had to do some of that. My mistake was spending too much time on that instead of engaging people in continuous improvement. But, again, the prevailing culture actively discouraged that sort of respect for and interaction with the line workers.

Going to the Gemba Isn't Good Without the Right Mindsets

Jumping ahead a bit to the year 2005... during my last year in my last manufacturing company, we had a vice president of Lean and Six Sigma who didn't really know much about either methodology. He was a finance guy, punching his ticket through a leadership rotation as part of his fast-track career.

Given his traditional management mindset, which including set-ting high targets and putting pressure on people, this caused many problems as some of us were trying to create a Lean culture. One day, my director and I wanted to take the VP down to the shop floor to see some improvements that had been made. This "gemba trip" had been scheduled pretty far in advance (it wasn't his style to leave the office area).

Knowing that the production area had some major downtime on a key piece of equipment, we tried setting his expectations that he wasn't about to see full production because the one piece of equipment was broken down.

He replied, "Well, maybe if we sent people home early, that would give them an incentive to keep the machines running." Wow. He didn't understand manufacturing at all. If anything, the employees did a great job of keeping the old equipment running at all. We tried to keep his gemba visit as short as possible since we were afraid he would say the wrong thing to the wrong person.

It was a great reminder that we have to be careful when we encourage leaders to "go to the gemba." If they're going to have the wrong mindsets, behave badly, and say the wrong things, it might be better if some of those "leaders" just stayed in their office.

Improving Ergonomics, but How?

In the first few weeks of my new job, I was excited to be sent to Lansing for a formal ergonomics class and certification. I think it was a full week's worth of time, an investment in my own engineering skills and, more importantly, in improving health and safety in the workplace.

With the blessing of the joint GM/UAW class, I was now considered to be fully capable of "doing" ergonomics improvement. I had seen examples in the classroom and I wasn't qualified to teach. My mistake was too much solo doing, working by myself, rather than engaging the employees.

In one example, there was an easily identifiable ergonomics problem at the end of the engine block machining line. As the completed, washed aluminum blocks were pushed to the end of the line by the powered rollers, a production worker's job was to lift the block off of the line, placing it in a stack on a pallet with special plastic dividers. I think the blocks were stacked six to a layer and the blocks were four layers high.

The workers had an overhead hoist to use, thankfully, since the blocks were heavy. (GM wasn't that bad, in case you thought they were lifting them by hand.) The ergonomic problem, one that I shouldn't have needed certification to see, was the bending and reaching. When the pallet was empty, the worker would have to bend down a lot to guide the block onto the first layer. After laying down the first three blocks, they'd bend and lean over to place the next three. Even the second layer was too low. When we produced about 450 to 500 engines in a shift and there wasn't a lot of job rotation, there was a lot of repetitive motion for anybody, yet alone guys aged 55 to 60.

Job rotation could have helped, but with union seniority and rules (and a "team coordinator" or supervisor who didn't want to be bothered), people generally worked the same job all the time unless there was an absence and need to fill in.

I was asked to solve the problem. I was motivated to do so because I believed strongly that proper ergonomics was a must. People might not have enjoyed coming to work, but they certainly shouldn't get hurt on the job. I wanted to help avoid injuries.

I came up with a solution, after getting guidance from some more experienced engineers and finding out what other plants did. The solution was to install two rotating lift tables that the pallets of blocks would be set on. The base for the tables would have to be set into the floor, which meant cutting concrete and digging big square holes to set those bases in. With the lift tables, the workers could push a button to easily raise and lower the height. That, along with an easy spin of the table, meant that bending and leaning would be eliminated.

My memories of this work are pretty clear in terms of identifying vendors, researching costs, drawing up the layout (leaving enough space so the tables wouldn't hit each other when rotating) and working with maintenance to schedule the work. What I don't remember is conversations with the workers about the solution I was getting installed.

Thinking back to the prevailing culture, there was nothing in the culture that would have encouraged me to get much input from the workers because, again, they were asked to leave their brains at the door. As an engineer, it was my job to design the equipment and to fix the ergonomics. I wasn't being coached to do any differently as I wasn't yet working with the internal Lean coaches.

I got the tables installed. It was a bit stressful because when you're cutting big holes in concrete, you have to be right rather than saying "let's Kaizen that." The tables worked as designed. But, the workers didn't really like using them. They didn't use the lift or rotate functions.

There was a certain macho mindset in the culture that valued being tough over working in an ergonomic way. If the employee input had been them saying, "We like it the way it is," that wasn't going to be an option for me or GM. We had to give them a more ergonomic workstation.

Reflecting on this, I should have talked more with the guys. I remember one of them went by the nickname "Bama," as he was, of course, from Alabama. He was part of the big wave of southern African-Americans who migrated to Detroit from Alabama and adjacent states to take auto industry jobs in the 1960s.

I should have talked with Bama more about the problem. I should have helped him understand the importance of ergonomics instead of being so stubborn about having to implement my solution. I probably should have asked him if he had his own ideas for improving the ergonomics of the job. That might not have helped achieve buy in, but I should have tried.

We went from a work area that had bad ergonomics to a work area where we had to police the workers, with the Team Coordinator having to threaten disciplinary action if the workers didn't use the lift tables to eliminate the bending. It was better, in some ways, but not ideal.

Pointing Out the Right Problems, the Wrong Way?

As I've said, I place a very high value on safety and ergonomics. In our machining line, it was pretty common to have grease on the floors, thanks to cutting fluid mist (a health and safety problem that others were trying to fix) and parts that had that mist and grease on them. Part of the strategy was using a hose to spray down floors, even though that wasn't fixing the root cause.

The hose was quite heavy, not quite a firefighter's hose, and it was on a retractable reel. At some point, the retractor was broken and glitchy. When a worker tugged on it, it often didn't retract. Or, at times, it would start suddenly reeling up and pull the worker. With the slippery floor, it was an injury waiting to happen.

I tried "speaking up for safety"[21], as current GM CEO Mary Barra has encouraged people to do. I formally reported the problem to maintenance. I saw another near miss. So, I followed up with the maintenance manager, Jim, a guy who had been there forever and was close to retirement. One day, the hose with its heavy brass nozzle went flying and almost hit a worker in the head. I was fed up.

I "escalated" the issue by leaving a very pointed and angry-sounding voicemail for the plant superintendent, telling him that I had repeatedly reported the near misses and nothing was happening. I needed help getting the maintenance manager to prioritize this issue.

After my call, the plant superintendent, Bob, must have yelled and cursed at Jim. That was Bob's standard approach, as I blogged about here[22].

Later that day, I was standing in the office area at another industrial engineer's desk with my back to the aisle. Out of nowhere, a pair of really rough hands was suddenly around my neck, gently squeezing me, with a creepy silence.

I turned and saw that the hands belonged to Jim, the grizzled old maintenance manager, as he slowly removed them from my neck and gave me a glare. Jim had told me before that I was being a pain about reporting that hose problem, but this time he didn't say a word as he walked away.

The hose reel eventually got fixed, but I sure wasn't making any friends. I never got thanked by anybody other than the UAW worker out on the floor who knew I was sticking up for him and his colleagues.

In my youthful zeal, I was trying to do the right thing but did so in a very clumsy way. I should have talked more with Jim and probably should have appreciated that he had a lot on his plate. My assumption

[21]https://www.linkedin.com/pulse/20140411234819-81312-my-new-program-speak-up-about-speak-up-for-safety-at-gm

[22]http://www.leanblog.org/2007/02/gm-got-gamed/

that he was tired and didn't care anymore might have been true. But, he cared enough to not appreciate being called out and yelled at by Bob. I should have handled that better.

There's No Such Thing as a Dumb Question?

In the name of improvement, Powertrain headquarters hired many employees away from Toyota suppliers and Nissan to learn about what was then called either "just in time" or "Japanese manufacturing methods." The term "Lean" was still relatively uncommon, as the book *Lean Thinking*[23] hadn't been published yet (although *The Machine That Changed The World*[24] was published in 1990).

With those external hires, we had a group of about ten employees who were meant to serve as internal consultants and coaches. That's a lot of people to work with a plant of 800 people. But, they were frustrated because local plant leaders really wanted nothing to do with them. "We're here from headquarters and we're here to help," is a statement that usually causes eyes to roll in manufacturing. The external hires were given an office area that was up in a mezzanine level, just about as far away from the plant manager's office as physically possible. They wanted to help but spent a lot of time playing cards and wondering why they had left their old companies (I wasn't the only one disappointed with the gap between the hiring story and working reality).

But, I was an eager student who was willing to learn from these mentors. I was caught in between the existing predominant GM culture and these Lean thinkers who were experienced, brilliant and kind teachers. The traditional GM culture wanted me to be a traditional engineer, which meant coming up with answers and solutions and implementing projects that helped improve productivity and quality. They were mainly concerned with productivity. I wanted to try to do things differently.

Although that team of consultants wasn't allowed to implement much of anything, they would do a lot of "waste walks" with me.

---

[23] http://amzn.to/2hX2bTj
[24] http://amzn.to/2icx4m0

They'd point out problems or things that weren't managed properly and they'd explain how it was different in a Toyota-style culture. We daydreamed about what we'd like to change and how things could be better.

Headquarters knew our performance was poor, but there were a few quality incidents that led them to bring in a new plant manager.

The product and process designers for our factory decided that our Northstar engine was so well designed and was going to be so well built (to aerospace tolerances) that our assembly line would not have a "hot test" station at the end of the line. The engines would be shipped directly to the car assembly plants, assuming good quality, and the first time the engine would be cranked up would be at the end of car assembly.

The assumption of built-in quality was a VERY BAD assumption. The GM engine plant had some very major quality "spills" where defective engines were caught at the end of the car assembly line. That meant more than 1,000 potentially defective engines were upstream in other cars and in our engine plant's finished goods inventory. That's a very expensive problem to fix, whereas a hot test station could have caught the problem much earlier.

Better yet would have been having process controls that could have prevented the error in the first place. Or, a management system that allowed workers to actually do their scheduled quality checks and to actually stop the line of a process was statistically "out of control." I had to argue once with Bob, the plant superintendent, about why being out of control was bad. Bob argued that the parts weren't "out of spec," so it was OK to keep the line running. Well, that caught up with us.

We finally got a new plant manager, Larry Spiegel, who was one of the first GM leaders to be trained at NUMMI, the legendary joint venture plant that was run by Toyota and GM (meaning it was run as a TPS/Lean management system). I finally saw what good leadership looked like. The internal Lean consultants were turned loose and they started training and coaching people. We started fixing the things that mattered - the management system and the culture. I learned a lot of great leadership and change management lessons... and I was hooked.

Larry spent the first few months spending a lot of time at the gemba, talking to everybody he could (and really doing a lot of listening). This was very different behavior from the previous old-school, imperial plant manager.

I was young and anxious for change and I asked Larry, one day when changes would be coming. (That's not the dumb question I refer to in the header above.)

Larry said something to the effect of "I know what the problems are and what the solutions are... but the people here don't know that yet."

He was building trust and relationships.

Larry had moved from a GM transmission plant to a GM engine plant. Dealing with the common complaint of "but, we're different here" was still an issue, but not as much as going from, say, manufacturing to healthcare.

I think Larry knew he had to "go slow to go fast," as we say in Lean.

So, here's the question I asked Larry that I'd now consider being a "dumb question."

Larry was in our department for a skip-level department meeting and he was taking questions from the hourly and salaried team (we were barely becoming a real team at that point). There weren't many questions, so I asked this:

> "I know our quality and productivity are much worse than
> our competitors. Which of those do we improve first?"

Larry looked at me patiently (instead of glaring at me for asking a dumb question). He said, basically, "We need to improve both. And we'll improve both at the same time through this new way of managing. It's not one or the other."

As I've seen play out in many settings, working together to reduce waste and improve processes leads to better flow, better quality and better productivity. It happens in manufacturing and it happens in healthcare.

That was a pivotal moment for me in my early Lean days. Even though Dr. Deming wrote about quality and productivity going hand-in-hand, I don't think I had heard anybody say so in the workplace.

Understanding WHY we were changing the management system and embracing Lean was an important thing to understand. Starting with why, then understanding our problems, are steps we must take before implementing tools.

I was fortunate to have mentors and teachers, early on, who emphasized some of the nuances of Lean that some people seem not to learn. Again, I think we should be patient, to a point, with people who haven't been taught something or haven't learned it yet. We probably shouldn't be infinitely patient with people since there's so much good information about Lean available for free online or in inexpensive books.

Early Mistakes in Healthcare

I made mistakes during my remaining years in manufacturing, even after working at GM. As we practice Lean, we should get better over time, but we shouldn't expect to make a leap to being "perfect" (whatever that means) after our first year or so. But, to avoid boring you with other stories about what I would have done differently in different settings, I'll jump ahead to my transition to healthcare in 2005.

When I had my opportunity to move into healthcare, I did so by taking a position with ValuMetrix Services, a consulting group that was, at the time, part of Johnson & Johnson. Hospitals are a very different setting than manufacturing, of course, with lots of new terminology and acronyms and things to figure out.

In some ways, my first year of Lean healthcare felt like another first year of Lean. Based on my previous experiences in manufacturing, there were some things that I did better during my new start in healthcare, such as:

- Starting with problem statements, goals, and "whys" instead of tools
- Building teams of front-line staff to teach and coach instead of "doing Lean" things myself

- Creating elements of a Lean management system, such as a daily Kaizen process, and coaching managers instead of just doing projects

That said, I think the biggest mistake I made in that first year was relying too much on examples and stories from manufacturing. I saw parallels and similarities between these different settings, in the sense that a process is a process. A hospital laboratory is very much like a high-tech factory in that you have automation, skilled employees and important time-sensitive work to do well. But, stories about factories, even if they are stories about people and leaders, don't resonate with people in healthcare.

Some of that, I think, comes from an ignorance about manufacturing. Most people in healthcare have never set foot in a factory. So, they think manufacturing is archaic, dirty or unsafe, or that people aren't expected to think. Those things aren't true (not in a Lean factory), but biases against manufacturing often get in the way of people learning from that industry. I can bemoan that fact all day long and wish it wasn't so, but it was more important to adjust my approach.

I sometimes still use lessons learned and stories from manufacturing, but generally just with managers or executives. When I tell a story about somebody "gaming the system" because they're under the brutal pressure of a single performance measure, that's not just a "factory story," that's a "people story" that many can relate to. But, I'd probably offend a medical technologist if I compared him or her to a high-tech factory team member.

As I worked in healthcare, I started to accumulate stories that were more relevant. Medical technologists were more comfortable hearing about stories from other labs and I could illustrate Lean with examples from those settings. But, I also learned that nurses didn't want to hear about stories from labs and pharmacists didn't want to hear stories from nursing units because - well, they're different.

Were there times in my early days of healthcare when I could have better engaged more people? Of course. Even with just over ten years of Lean experience under my belt (not a "black belt," by the way), I still wasn't perfect. I was still practicing.

I'll continue practicing. I'll probably make more mistakes. I do intend to continue learning and reflecting – and I hope you'll do the same.

Chapter Three - Nick Ruhmann

Nick Ruhmann is the Director of Operational Excellence for Aon National Flood Services, Inc., a subsidiary of Aon plc, the leading global provider of risk management, insurance and reinsurance brokerage, and human resources solutions and outsourcing services.

Nick has been working in the insurance industry since 2012, however he began his career in manufacturing working for automotive supplier Tenneco Inc, and the medical technology company, Becton, Dickinson and Company (BD)

Nick has a B.S. in Mechanical Engineering from Southern Illinois University, lean manufacturing program certificate from the University of Michigan and a certification in "TRIZ" from the University of Kaiserslautern, Germany.

Nick and his wife currently reside in Montana with their two children. He can be found on Twitter as @Kaizen_Krazy[a].

[a]https://twitter.com/kaizen_krazy

Timing is Everything

I wish I could tell you I'm that smart, or that talented - but truth be told I really just feel like I've been that lucky. Lucky that other more seasoned engineers passed up the chance to attend Six Sigma training when it was offered. Lucky that management took a chance investing in a brand new engineer. Lucky that a new mentor and teacher who espoused behaviors key to be being a Lean manager decided to join the company, just as I was in the spotlight to catch her attention. Lucky that Toyota decided to get involved, just as I was beginning to question aspects of Six Sigma, and had ears ready and willing to listen.

I've heard it said that luck is where preparation meets opportunity, and I suppose there's some truth to that. But knowing that I wasn't always completely prepared, I'm extremely grateful that those behind the opportunities were patient enough to let me catch up. To all those people that have served as a teacher, model, and mentor in my career - thank you. I sincerely hope I've still proved I was worth the investment.

Starting Out with Six Sigma

"Tim wants to see you, Nick," were the words I heard just into my first full week as an Associate Design Engineer. I wasn't "brand new," having spent a couple summers at the same company (a Tier 1 Automotive Supplier) as an engineering intern in product development. Now I was there, full time, out of college, and just barely getting settled... what the heck did the Chief Engineer of North America want to see me about? Surely, I hadn't screwed up yet, I thought.

As I walked into the largest office in that area, I noticed not just Tim, but also my direct manager Scott seated at the small table in his office. "Nick...We've got an opportunity for ya," they said. That was June of 2000. By September, I was sitting in a large training room with about 20 other colleagues from around North America getting introduced to "Six Sigma." For a young engineer fresh out of college, this felt like a mighty big deal. Speeches from senior executives that I probably would have never met for years otherwise, expensive training, catered meals, brand new laptops with cool stats software... who wouldn't be impressed?

Six Sigma was a big thing for us for several years... and I'd gotten pretty good at it. I managed to be the first in my class to get that coveted "Black Belt," won our first "CEO" award for a project I led and got to hobnob with folks in the company well above my real experience and grade level. Now to be fair, I wasn't nearly as arrogant as that might make me sound - or at least I hope not. Being a farm kid who was taught to respect my elders (regardless of my title) probably saved me a whole lot of headaches early on, and likely bought me some patience from those on whose shoulders I rode. But then again, I don't think it's ever possible to be too humble. Luckily, that viewpoint would serve me well later on, but I didn't know to what degree yet.

After two or three years, the shine of the Six Sigma deployment had started to wear off. The company had trained about 100 of us "Black Belts," maybe half of which had completed certification, but we had no strong sense from leadership regarding what we should be doing - other than saving money. Internally, a backlash grew against the new cadre of "experts", fueled by special attention, bonus plans, and the confirmation of a rumor that the Black Belts were getting company cars.

Actually, no one ever took a car to my knowledge - the backlash from the rumor getting out kept that horse in the barn. But it was true, we were offered our choice of three different black convertibles or a one-time payout of $10K upon hitting a major cost savings target. Talk about breeding "elitism," they were making it hard to be humble and not have it come across as a total act.

Cost reduction was the name of the game. So much so that, even after a bit of time, it pained me to see some people using those fancy statistics to justify a cheaper supplier over the other or a cheaper material over the other. These suppliers and materials were not on equal terms, but those making the choice played a game of "showing no difference" by selecting small numbers of parts. Sample sizes that weren't being contested, as there were attractive dollar signs associated with them. We soon outsourced part after part to lost cost suppliers in China, India, Mexico... all on a piece price savings basis.

Many times, engineers worried that switching suppliers might cause problems, but we had savings goals to hit. We'd pair suppliers against one another, find the "equivalent" part at the cheapest price and put in the change order. The OEM's were often happy to approve such changes, 5 cents per vehicle after all was 5 cents per vehicle. They had targets to hit too. Thankfully, years later we'd see nearly all these changes undone, as we'd finally do what W. Edwards Deming[25]

---

[25]https://deming.org/theman/overview

had been calling for the industry to do decades earlier. We'd eventually build long-term relationships with select suppliers, often local suppliers. We'd even train them, work together on improvements, and let them keep the cost savings - knowing that a healthier supplier was a better partner for us in the long term. I'm happy to say that some of my students from that time include those from our supply base - suppliers still in use by the company today. But I digress; we weren't there yet.

A healthier approach was still years away. At this time, the pressure to deliver the almighty standard cost accounting dollar was king and a slight twinge of pessimism had started to creep into the ranks. Many of us thought - is this it? This can't last... this isn't making our company stronger for the long haul. This wasn't healthy cost reduction; it was cost cutting.

Now, I don't know how we got so lucky, or who was smart enough to hire her, but in about the third year, the company hired a new Director of Six Sigma - we'll just call her Barb. Barb was well known in the old guard of Six Sigma originators, had been a part of the Allied Signal launch, a partner of Six Sigma Qualtec, and had led other well-known deployments prior to ours. But, what many of us didn't know was that Barb was also a quiet promotor of what you might call "real Lean," having been exposed to Lean cultures at Akebono and Bosch before ever hearing of Six Sigma.

Due in large part to the pessimism in the company that had developed by that time, I wasn't expecting much to come of our new director. I was, thankfully very wrong. Barb's leadership turned out to be a blessing I never expected. I didn't know much about Barb at first, but what I would find out, and what I would learn over the next five years, still surprises me to this day - and continues to inspire me to keep learning.

Barb had officially come on board right around the same time that I won an award within the company for a project completed in a Nebraska manufacturing plant, a plant I had asked to relocate to from corporate. When I was selected, I found out there would be a grand ceremony and presentation of awards from our CEO at a company symposium. I approached the plant manager (a great guy named Terry) and together we agreed: the entire project team needed to go; I didn't want to be "that" guy that stood up there alone taking all the credit for the good work others had done.

The plant ponied up the money to fly or bus the entire team (about 30 people, mostly hourly employees and a few engineers, because in reality, it was three projects spread over three departments) out to Chicago for this global symposium. It was there that I first spent a significant amount of time around Barb and I was impressed. She was inspiring, smart, and, most importantly, the most sincerely humble person I think I've ever met. After my presentation, I remember someone telling me, "Barb's got her eye on you. She was very impressed with you, and that you brought your entire team." Time went on, and eventually, Barb did ask me to join the corporate Six Sigma team - I, of course, said yes.

Bucking the Trend

In 2005, I joined Barb's team as a "Master Black Belt," though not certified as one yet, as Barb had a very specific process and set of requirements for that. One basically had no chance of earning that certification without having actually performed the role for a couple of years. Barb made sure not to put that stamp on anyone who hadn't earned it.

Most Master Black Belts will tell you they received specific "train the trainer" courses, additional finance courses, project management training, etc. Much of which would be akin to MBA style academics. But these approaches don't always focus on becoming a better teacher, or a better leader, especially a "Lean leader". Barb's approach was to learn by doing. We had to actually DO things, learn new techniques, teach each other, experiment, and actually apply what we'd learned. We were constantly reminded that we were a team of "servant leaders," with lots of responsibility, but almost no authority. If we wanted people to come along for the ride, we'd have to earn their trust. There was no "command and control" option for us.

"Servant leadership" - Barb introduced me to this principle for which I am forever grateful. I don't remember a team meeting that didn't start or end with a discussion about leadership. For example, we'd often discuss a chapter of the latest John Maxwell book Barb had bought and given to us all, or how our greatest impact was through developing others. We embraced the idea of a leader who could influence others, in any organizational direction. We had to practice what we preached within our own group, a safe place to fail. We would get assigned topics to learn about that weren't our strengths and prepare training courses for our peers (imagine being asked to learn advanced multivariate analysis techniques well enough to teach a dozen other Master Black Belts and hundreds of Black Belts). We didn't have individual goals; we had a team goal. We either all met the goal, or none of us did. Whether a teammate was out for the birth of a new child, or an overdue vacation, the rest of us stepped up and supported divisions that weren't "officially" ours. To this day, it was one of the most cohesive, most supportive and most talented teams I've ever had the pleasure of working within. Individually, none of us were that special, but together we strived to set the example. They were, and have continued to be my friends, mentors, and a source of inspiration.

So within my "official" support structure was about six facilities totaling approximately 4000 employees spread across North America. Initially, my role was to support and train their "Six Sigma" personnel. At this point, we were still working within the basic project management style of continuous improvement with everything being a project, having ROIs, charters, timelines, etc. Within the formal structure of Black Belts and Green Belts,, we still followed that, with defined processes, approvals, and the Six Sigma DMAIC process. But, I found myself often bucking that trend when asked to visit plants that were having problems. Which coincidently, must have been working as I got the reputation of being "one of the plant guys" corporate could send and not catch flack for. Truth be told, I enjoyed the manufacturing plants much more than being stuck in a corporate office, so I'm sure it showed through when I was visiting a facility. There is something about looking like you actually enjoy and appreciate where people work and what they do that automatically ingratiates you to them - funny how that is.

For example, one fall I was asked to visit a plant that was having problems correcting what was a common defect for the parts we made, and the cost of sorting labor and scrap was totaling in the tens of thousands of dollars a month. When I arrived at the plant, the engineer for the area met me and proceeded to explain how they needed a completely new machine, as the current one was just "flat out not designed to do this type of weld." I suggested we visit the manufacturing line and, after a while, the engineer in question had a scheduling conflict and had to leave me on out the line by myself. That is what I was after in the first place, as I had realized not a single employee had been willing to approach me while this engineer was in tow. Something was terribly wrong here.

After about 15 further minutes of watching the welder, I noticed a maintenance technician start to make eye contact. I smiled and approached the gentlemen, introduced myself and noted that I'd been hearing a lot about the problem, but wanted to come and see the issue firsthand. Within minutes, the technician unloaded on me that he'd been trying for weeks to get someone to listen to him about how to solve the problem. They didn't need a new machine, he said, just a small change to the angle of the welding guns. I listened and asked a few questions:

1. **Who have you already suggested this to?**
   - The engineer had been told but hadn't been interested
2. **Has there been any attempt to test your theory?**
   - Not that he was aware of, it seemed all attention had been on getting a new machine
3. **What would it take to test your theory?**
   - A little overtime after the shift and we could create some control parts, alter the process, run test parts and return the machine to the current state before the next shift.

By this time, I'd already learned that, success or not, I'd earn this gentlemen's trust if I could arrange for the test to be carried out. It didn't matter if he was right or not. What mattered was that he trusted me to accept the possibility that he *could be right*. Testing it was the only way to know, and the only way he and I could learn together. Even if it did fail, I'd need this man's trust and expertise regardless.

I excused myself and headed straight for the plant manager's office. The plant manager was a surly older gentleman, a guy who had literally grown up in the plant, had no formal education but came from the days when you could actually start out on the floor as an hourly employee and advance. He'd become stuck at the plant manager level mostly due to the current day requirements of "needing a degree." But, he commanded a vast amount of respect, both from his employees and his superiors at corporate due to his experience.

After humbly asking if I could get a couple minutes of the plant manager's time, I explained the situation to him. I said I didn't know if the idea would work, and that it might completely fail, but that we could confirm the potential overnight. He agreed, but with some obvious reluctance. I sensed he felt almost guilty for not going to the source himself, rather than accepting an engineer's explanation and proposal at face value.

Here's a key point about engineers: simple solutions don't show off engineering prowess. I'm an engineer myself, and I can say without hesitation that, many times, engineers will almost always go for the new technology, the new machine, or the wildly complex solution. Why? They have a lot of skill they're dying to use and dying to display to the world. Engineers want to solve big problems. Small continuous improvement can be a tough sell to some engineers, but they're also very data-driven people. Sometimes, you just have to get them to agree to "try" something, even if it means convincing them to try, just so they can prove you wrong. So what if they do prove you wrong? What you learn together will be invaluable, and will improve your relationship far beyond what any verbal conversation can. You do an experiment with an engineer, and you're sharing an engineering experience with them - whether you are one or not.

So I did just that with the engineer in question. It was his area after all. Even though I'd already received the OK from the plant manager to carry out the experiment, I made sure to have him withhold that news until I had spoken with the engineer in question. When I broached the idea, I got the response I expected, "That won't work, it's still not right even if it helps."

"Fair enough," I replied. "But you have technicians that think it will, wouldn't it be a good learning experience for them to try and see the results for themselves?" Needless to say, we carried out the experiment that night.

They made parts, and I helped test them to failure, and we recorded the results. The results were pretty striking. The new configuration wasn't perfect, there would still be some defects, but the defect rate was reduced by a huge percentage. So much so, that the ROI of a new and untested machine would be flat out almost impossible to justify since the defect was entirely containable when it occurred. Not only was this engineer surprised at the results, but the trust between him and his technicians was instantly improved. They had learned something together. All I did was get them to try - they did the rest.

The next day, I was making changes to my flight plans to return home early. There were no charters that needed submitting, no timelines to update, just a quick report on the results and how a technician's idea had avoided a large capital expenditure. One of the Black Belts in the plant had commented that I was welcome back in the plant *anytime, in any role* - although time would prove they didn't need me near as much as corporate office often thought they did. They just needed to go and see and LISTEN to their employees. There was plenty of brainpower on site if they'd just tap into it, which they did.

Leaning Out of Six Sigma

After another year or so, the company had finally managed to get a few contracts with Toyota and Lexus. This was a pretty big deal, as our sales had previously been so heavily concentrated with the "Big Three" that as GM and Ford went, so did we. Their "blame first, fix later, squeeze you for cost reductions always" attitude was so prevalent that it permeated our own culture at times, even when we knew better. Around this time, Barb had also managed to bring the

"Lean" people and the "Six Sigma" people under a common banner in the company. Those terms had been formally replaced with an overall "Global Production System," with our team in a supporting role under the guise of the Global Process Excellence Team. The Master Black Belts were being teamed up with Lean Directors, and we started working together, and learning from each other rather than trying to outdo each other. Of course, we still had problems and one day, one of those problems escaped to Toyota.

"Nick, I need you to make travel plans to Tennessee. We're having weld spatter defects, and it has caught the attention of Toyota. Another member of the Process Excellence team will be there as well as our director of quality, and head of operations. It's all hands on deck."

A few days later, we sat in a conference room watching a presentation on the issue from our internal folks. My peer, John, and I sat, mostly quiet until the presentation was completed. We were itching to get out of the conference room and out to the floor, but politics meant there were PowerPoint slides to see first. The more senior managers made their expectations understood and excused themselves. Eventually, by midday, John and I made it out on the manufacturing floor. Time could be clouding my recollection here, but I believe we found the issue within a matter of minutes - or rather, the employees showed us the cause by their actions.

We watched the process, this time a manual "MIG weld." Now I don't remember who noticed it first, but between John and me, we noticed something on the welding gun just didn't look right. Where a shield should have been, to direct the inert shielding gas over the weld, it was instead just cut off. The lack of shielding gas over the weld... well, that can certainly cause weld spatter.

John and I approached the individual performing the weld and asked politely about the shield...he agreed, "Yep that's the reason", but proceeded to show us that he couldn't access the area to be welded with a shield in place due to the acute angle of the parts. "Surely this isn't a new problem for a MIG weld, have you mentioned this to your supervisor?" we asked. "Yes," he replied, "but we were told to make do with what we have".

John and I then approached the area supervisor and inquired

about the lack of shields. "Won't do no good," he replied sharply. "We tell them to put the shields in place and they either cut them off or pull them back. Can't get them to do what they're told, so I'm tired of trying."

John and I weren't so easily dissuaded. The employees wanted to produce good welds, but they had to actually make a weld first, and they couldn't with those shields. Thirty minutes later, John and I arrived back at the line with a box full of narrow gas shields designed for tight spaces that were already in stock - in the plant's parts crib. Almost immediately upon trying them, the weld spatter disappeared.

Sometimes, listening isn't enough. Listening and asking questions goes hand in hand. The supervisor had "heard" their complaint, but had resigned himself to enforce the standard rather than question it. Unfortunately, this wasn't a problem of non-adherence to a standard. The standard itself was wrong and the employee's reaction of removing the shield was symptomatic of that.

When the news and updates reached Toyota, from what I understand, the response was quite abrupt:

"Why must you fly in experts to solve your problems, when you should be teaching your people how to solve their problems themselves?"

I can't say for certain if that was the epiphany all by itself, or if it just happened to occur around the same time, but I couldn't help but agree. Why did my peers and I keep getting asked to fly to this plant or that plant "to fix some issue" when most of my visits just confirmed what Toyota was saying? They didn't need "experts", they just needed someone to go and see, listen, ask questions and arrange for some experimentation. The big problems got attention, but they almost always began as a small problem, one unworthy of a Black Belt's attention with their small ROI. In reality, rarely were the answers beyond the reach of the employees if someone offered just a little assistance and an ear.

By 2007, there was a definite "air" of change in our internal culture. Along the way, we'd changed CEOs and a significant part of the senior management team. I had since completed my Master Black Belt certification and accepted a role leading Quality, Engineering, and

Process Excellence in one of our larger plants. Barb had been working with Toyota personnel from TSSC (Toyota Supplier Support Center) to get our company involved in the Bluegrass Automotive Manufacturers Association, or BAMA. BAMA is a group of Toyota suppliers that agree to learn from one another under the guidance of TSSC mentors. That involvement led to one of our sites being selected as a learning site, a place where our TSSC mentor, Jamie could mentor personnel from our company as well as other Toyota suppliers on our actual processes. For the first round, Barb made sure I got an invitation to attend, with the rest of the class being made up of plant managers from around our company and other suppliers.

That week was titled "TPS for Executives," but it could have been called "The Lean you've never been told about." No standard work, no kanban, no value stream maps, nothing you'd ever seen in the dozens of commonly available courses, classes, or books about Lean at that time.

Jamie explained that TPS or Lean was entirely about our ability, as management to: * Design work to expose problems * Solve those problems using the scientific method * Share what we learn with others * TEACH the organization to do the first three

We'd cover a little bit of a concept, then go out onto the floor to observe. We'd make changes to the process to better expose problems, make note of those that occurred, and do quick dirty experiments to test ideas. Jamie would tell us:

"If you can't tape it, hold it. If you can't clamp it, tape it. If you can't bolt it, clamp it. If you can't weld it, bolt it. "

We didn't waste time welding up a new stand for parts. We grabbed the stand and held it for a few cycles to get instant feedback from the team members...too high, too close? Let's move it... better? Let's put a block under it and try it a little longer. We tried tiny, small experiments before making permanent changes. Sometimes, we collected data, and sometimes we just tried things for a few cycles to see if it was obviously better or obviously worse. Did we improve the processes? Sure, but, most importantly, we learned... A LOT. The employees got to see their leadership out on the line, learning with them. Respect was being transferred, both ways.

It was an exhilarating week and we left with the task of keeping a journal about our coaching and teaching others the same process. I kept a close ear and eye to whatever Jamie and team were working on, including the work towards adding enough teachers, at all levels to make these concepts viable.

Jamie said "If you can't get your team member to team leader ratio down under 10 to 1, then we might as well just stop right now. You don't have to add labor cost to do it, just problem solve your way to it so it's labor neutral."

This was the stuff... this was the piece and the thought process that I knew was missing, but never "saw" in action. This was how we could get away from the "white knight" syndrome I seemed to be continually cast in. I needed to make the transformation from being one of those "experts" to being a teacher, someone whose value wasn't measured in the problems they solved, but in the *people* they were able to improve. Why limit our problem solving to 100 experts? We had 25,000 employees who just needed a little help, a little guidance in solving their own problems. It was really just that simple. Everything else would come if we stuck with it.

The plant manager of the facility that had the weld spatter issue was on hand to speak to the rest of the group. They had been actively problem solving and freeing up labor in their plant to get to an employee to leader ratio of 5 to 1 or 7 to 1, per Jamie's guidance. The results were startling: Every single metric the plant was measured by had improved by 30-40% and showed no sign of stopping. This same manager, who had been defiant, untrusting, and downright belligerent two years earlier was now the happiest, calmest, and most humble person imaginable when describing what Jamie and Toyota had helped transpire at his facility. It wasn't easy, but now he truly **enjoyed** his job.

Since that time, I'd say I restarted my Lean education from a fresh slate. Sure, all the technical knowledge of statistics, analytical techniques, calculating kanban levels, takt time, value stream mapping, and standardized work charts is handy, but I realized it's not the key. In fact, I think knowledge of those tools can be a heavy burden if not taken with a very healthy dose of humility. After all, everything we know now as a "tool" or "technique" is just the outcome of hundreds or thousands of small experiments that someone else did, someone else's countermeasure to a problem they faced that they learned through the application of the scientific method. If we accept them all at face value, are we really practicing Lean - or are we missing the point entirely? If we are done learning, and all that's left is choosing the right tool from the toolbox, then we are truly not practicing lean.

Perhaps "Lean" is about nothing other than the humility to accept that we have more to learn and that we'd better get on with it, one tiny experiment at a time - *together.**

Chapter Four - Michael Lombard

Michael Lombard, MBA, PMP, is a seasoned leader in Lean Health-care, currently serving as Chief Executive Officer of Cornerstone Critical Care Specialty Hospital of Southwest Louisiana.

He has a track record of helping hospitals and other care providers radically improve performance through continuous improvement. His specialty is enabling leaders, from the front-lines down to the c-suite, to develop strong Lean Management habits through proven coaching techniques.

Above all, Michael is a lifelong learner, always looking to apply lessons learned at work and home as a father and husband. You can find him on Twitter as @MikeLombard[a].

[a]https://twitter.com/mikelombard

Into the Learning Zone of Parenting

"I'm just going to let you find out for yourself."

That was the answer given to me by a great mentor of mine, Mike Rother[26], when I asked him if he could share any lessons learned from raising his daughters. This was in mid-2014, about one month prior to my first child, Isabella, being born, and I was quite curious as to what I should expect from parenthood. Upon hearing his coy response, a smile of satisfaction came across my face and I thought to myself, "Enjoy the learning zone."

Enjoy the learning zone? What is that, and why did I think of it at that moment? Shouldn't I have been a bit frustrated by Mike's inconclusive response?

[26]http://www-personal.umich.edu/~mrother/Homepage.html

Well, at any other time in my l life, I might have been. But because of my lessons learned from practicing Lean the past ten years, I realized Mike was actually doing me a huge favor. But before I explain, please allow me to go back in time to eight years before this conversation...

2006-2010: Discovering Lean, Practicing L.A.M.E.

The first time I had ever heard about Lean was in early 2006 while I was working as an executive trainee in a manufactured housing factory. The general manager of the plant handed me a copy of Jeffrey Liker[27]'s book [The Toyota Way](http://amzn.to/1kXCN0o), informed me that he had enrolled me in a 3-day Lean training course, and told me to come back in a month ready to teach Lean to the entire leadership team. We figured we'd be able to "roll-out" Lean within a few months or so.

Yes, please feel free to chuckle now.

As adorably naïve as we were with this endeavor, reading Dr. Liker's book was actually a life-changing experience for me. Even as a recent graduate of a decent business school, I had never once even heard of Toyota's incredible success story, must less anything about the Toyota Production System. But the principles and philosophy espoused in this book resonated with me deeply, way down in my bones.

With my mind sufficiently blown, I went to the 3-day training and learned all about the tools of Lean. Newly armed with all these Toyota Way principles and a Lean toolbox, I was excited to get back and teach it to all the folks back home. Everybody's going to love this stuff!

This was when my first great Lean lesson was learned:

The fact that something is self-evidently awesome doesn't mean that anybody will care.

When I returned to my factory I put together a pretty darn good training course, successfully delivered it to every leader in the organization, received great feedback, and even facilitated a few successful 5S events right after the training. Like many Lean newbies,

[27]http://liker.engin.umich.edu/

we thought training with a simulation was a great way to "get people fired up" and whatnot, and we thought 5S was the obvious right way to get started because it's fairly easy, inexpensive, and visually impactful.

Unfortunately, training and 5S are meaningless without purpose.

In our haste to get started, we failed to take the time to understand the overall direction in which we were headed with Lean, or to communicate the link between practicing Lean and achieving our top business challenges. Perhaps we just thought that if people were exposed to such a powerful and obviously awesome concept such as Lean, our leaders would naturally jump in with both feet.

That didn't happen.

Instead, most members of the leadership team only participated in Lean activities when participation was mandatory. Some actively and even loudly resisted it (I can neither confirm nor deny that there may have been a shouting match or two about Japanese vs. American pick-up trucks). Only one or two leaders really saw the potential of Lean.

But even those few early adopters were just using Lean as a point solution for specific issues on the shop floor. Even though we achieved several pockets of success with 5S and other shop floor countermeasures, we always struggled to translate those localized wins into results that made a difference at the strategic level. This made it really hard to build a case for Lean to be the way we ran the business. What was the purpose of Lean?

But here's the kicker...

When the corporate head of manufacturing visited our factory one day, he liked what we had done with 5S so much that he promoted me, at the age of 27 and with exactly one year of Lean experience under my belt, to be the corporate head of Lean deployment.

Are you chuckling again?

As one might imagine, I was a bit overwhelmed. Not really know-ing what to do, I stuck to what little I did know I could execute successfully...that's right: good old Lean training and 5S! We hired a professional trainer this time and delivered an awesome 4-week educational program to all of our Lean managers companywide. Then, we established a requirement that all 14 of our factories had to implement 5S in every department by the end of the year. Uh oh. I traveled non-stop for a year doing training and facilitating 5S events, but it felt more like pulling teeth.

And it was mostly for nothing.

Again, we had failed to understand the overall direction or challenge that Lean was there to help us achieve. We were once again hoping that people would magically love Lean once they experienced it for a minute or two. The only difference was that, this time, we had support for the initiative at the senior-most level of the company. That helped initially but ultimately didn't make much of a difference.

This led to a modified version of my first Lean lesson learned:

Even though something is self-evidently awesome, and even if the boss-man makes it a requirement, that doesn't mean that anybody will care. We have to understand the direction and challenge that Lean can help us achieve for it to mean something to us.

No matter how much senior leader support we have for Lean, if Lean is just viewed as a shop floor solution, it will always be relegated to afterthought status when it comes to how we run the business.

Now, I've been pretty hard on myself with this example. Even though we were fairly clueless, we did achieve some pretty awesome (albeit short-term) results:

- We reduced the # of safety incidents in the 5S areas (this by itself made it worthwhile)
- We achieved multi-million dollar inventory reductions
- We equipped our 14 Lean managers with valuable professional skills

So, it wasn't all bad. In fact, this experience was a critical first venture into the "learning zone" that I mentioned earlier. More on that later...

2010-2012: Getting Clinical with Lean

When the U.S. housing market collapsed in 2008, I knew my days in manufactured housing were limited. So, I began looking at options for how I could apply my lessons learned with Lean to other industries. The editor of this book, Mark Graban, suggested I consider healthcare. So, at his urging, I went to work for a wonderful pediatric, academic medical center in Texas.

I went from building trailers to helping transform hospitals. That's a natural progression, right?

I figured that since I knew exactly nothing about healthcare, maybe I'd be assigned an easy first project far, far away from any clinical units. You know, perhaps implementing a kanban system in the supply warehouse? Or hey, maybe another 5S event in the break room! Alas, that was not to be my path; my first assignment was to work with physicians, nurses, and a wide range of other clinicians to completely redesign the value stream for the highest-volume pediatric emergency room in the country. No sweat.

Fortunately, I had done a lot of reflection on my earlier days practicing Lean and learned from my first Lean lesson. I knew that if we jumped in first with training and Lean tools, we'd never get to the higher purpose of Lean. I knew that we had to first understand our overall direction and establish the business challenge that we wanted to achieve with Lean.

On this project, we achieved this by first engaging the entire ER leadership team in mapping out the ER value stream. We wanted to understand how we delivered care, from the patient/family's perspective. We wanted the constancy of purpose that comes from putting aside individual priorities and short-term departmental goals, and focusing on the needs of the customer.

Once we had mapped out the value stream, the challenge started to come into sharp focus. We had identified a tremendous amount of waste in the form of patients waiting for hours on end, nurses and other staff walking miles upon miles to get what they needed, and communication errors being made by clinicians working in silos. We decided to cut that waste in half by the end of the year, and we identified a small handful of metrics to help us measure progress. We had identified a challenge that was measurable, big enough to require strategic thinking, and important to all the leaders of the ER. We now had alignment and direction.

But, would having alignment and direction create "pull" for Lean? Would the leaders of the ER engage in Lean activities to tackle this value stream challenge, or would they resort to other methods? In this one isolated example, the team did start pulling for Lean.

In fact, we actually achieved a surprisingly high level of engagement with a wide range of ER leaders and staff. For example, we conducted several multi-day workshops over the course of a few months that were heavily attended by numerous physicians, nurses, administrative leaders, and many others. These events were highly effective for both tackling complex process issues in the ER and for promoting team building amongst the participants. The fast-paced and exciting nature of these events made it easy for our people to want to stay engaged in the process. We had a unifying challenge, we had Lean activities to help us achieve that challenge, and the team was on-board. We were happy with our level of engagement; understanding the overall direction or challenge created the tension that we could relieve with Lean practice.

However, our approach was still flawed. While the event-based approach was great at engaging the big ER team, it wasn't so great at helping us learn what would actually work in the ER. We were coming up with a lot of ideas and plans that looked amazing on the surface, but we didn't know if they'd actually work in the ER. Our workshops, while meticulously planned and flawlessly executed by several Lean specialists, just weren't great for testing our ideas and assumptions.

This led to my second great Lean lesson learned:

Batching leads to waste, whether working on a production line or doing improvement work.

Anybody who's ever read a book on Lean or attended Lean training has been taught that batching is bad. We even hear that overproduction is the fundamental waste because it leads to most or all of the other wastes. Batching hides defects and creates buffers that allow unreliable processes to hide, etc. Instead of batch and queue production, we instead seek to flow value at the pull of the customer. Any Lean practitioner knows this.

However, we don't always apply this core principle to our own work as Lean coaches. When we were facilitating the ER workshops, we were creating big batches of improvement work. We were coming up with dozens of improvement ideas over the course of a few days, vetting them right there in the workshop with our large team, and then coming up with action items and implementation plans to execute those ideas. Sounds good, right? Efficient, right?

However, just like on a production line, this efficient batching led to hidden defects and delayed detection of defects—in this case, many of the defects were in the form of bad assumptions about what would work in the ER. When we went out in the ER to begin trying to implement the ideas the team came up with, we immediately began getting bogged down.

We were a bit confused as to why we were struggling. It's not that the ideas the team came up with during the workshops were impractical. We had all the right people in the room to make informed decisions and achieve broad consensus. We had meticulous change management plans complete with a communication matrix, training modules, town-hall sessions, etc. But we were still at risk of a veritable quagmire.

As we tried to implement the team's ideas, we ran up against all sorts of unexpected obstacles and started uncovering bad assumptions that we had made during the workshops.

Eventually, we realized that we needed to stop trying to implement and start testing. We kind of stumbled our way into doing a series of rapid Plan-Do-Check-Act (PDCA) cycles to test every key assumption we had made during the workshops. The moment we switched to this more scientific approach (and let's be honest, a more humble approach), the obstacles began getting resolved quickly and we were back on track.

Side note: One would think that in healthcare, an ostensibly scientific industry, the need for the Scientific Method (i.e., PDCA) would have been obvious from the onset of the project. However, in my experience in healthcare, we're great at applying the Scientific Method to our practice of medicine, but not so much to our practices of business or Lean. Lean specialists are some of the biggest offenders too, as we often fail to practice what we preach.

By the end of the project, we had delivered some excellent results:

- Reduced the average ER patient length-of-stay by 30 minutes
- Reduced the left-without-being-seen rate from 12% to <1%
- Increased Press Ganey ER patient satisfaction scores to 99th percentile nationally
- Reduced staffing costs by $1 million annually without layoffs

We were happy with the results, but I was personally more satisfied by the insight I had gained about not batching improvement work.

This led to a modified version of my second Lean lesson learned:

Batching leads to waste when doing improvement work. Whenever possible, do improvement work in small, rapid cycles so we can test assumptions and flush out unforeseen obstacles.

I didn't realize it at the time, but this lesson learned was perhaps the most pivotal for me, as it opened the floodgates for future lessons learned in my practice of Lean. This was when that "learning zone" mentioned earlier first started to feel like home. It would become an even cozier place over the next few years.

2012-2015: Practice Makes Permanent

Once I developed a bias for one-piece flow for my own improvement work (e.g., opting for small, rapid cycles of PDCA instead of big workshops whenever possible), it triggered a period of rapid learning for me. This was when I began to understand the power of learning-by-doing, and it coincided with me reading my mentor Mike Rother's book, *Toyota Kata*[28].

Upon first reading, the idea that stood out the most was that we don't always know, and often can't know, the path that we'll have to take when doing improvement work. This was eye opening for me. For my entire adult life, I had taken comfort in being a good planner and knowing the entire playbook in advance. I was a trained project manager, and I was taught in my training to always produce a meticulous project plan before ever getting started with the execution of a project. If I were to get caught off guard on a project, like on the

---

[28]http://amzn.to/1kJOxFm

ER project discussed earlier, I would attribute it to not doing a good enough job during the planning phase. More planning! Better action item lists! Better status updates!

But, having gone through the struggles of the ER project, when many of our assumptions were proven wrong and the ideas we developed in these workshops were proven ineffective in the ER, my mindset had already begun to shift. I had started to see the difference between technical change and adaptive change.

Ronald Heifetz[29] of Harvard University teaches us that there are different types of challenges. Some endeavors, such as changing a hard drive on a computer, are "technical" in nature. For this type of work, we know the path from A-to-Z because we have a proven process for doing the task. If we have the right tools and skills, we should be successful the vast majority of the time.

Other endeavors, such as transforming the value stream of a pediatric emergency room, are "adaptive" in nature. For this type of work, we don't know the path from A-to-Z, even if we like to act like we do sometimes. We may have done an ER transformation at another hospital in the past, and are thus tempted to think that what worked there will work here. This is rarely the case, especially in the overwhelmingly human-centered field of healthcare, because of the significant amount of adaptation required of our people and the difficult-to-detect differences between one location and another.

On the ER project mentioned earlier, I began to see that, sometimes, no amount of planning is enough to predict all the obstacles that will arise when doing adaptive change. Not until we started doing the rapid PDCA cycles were we able to test our assumptions and flush out unforeseen obstacles. Doing more workshops wouldn't have helped. More testing and experimentation, earlier in the process, is what was needed.

In *Toyota Kata*, we are taught that when it comes to adaptive change, we are **not** better off doing more planning, better action item lists, or better status updates. Instead, we are encouraged to establish a "target condition" that we want to achieve, and then pursue that target condition, iteratively, by navigating through the

---

[29]https://www.hks.harvard.edu/about/faculty-staff-directory/ronald-heifetz

"gray zone." Think of the "gray zone" as the space between where we are currently and where we want to be, and that space is filled with obstacles we can't see (hence the term "gray"). That gray is like a fog that covers those obstacles. But, through rapid cycles of experiments (using PDCA or whatever scientific framework works best), we can work our way around, over, or through those obstacles.

We end up zigzagging a lot as we're navigating through this gray zone, and that can feel quite discomforting to folks like me who take comfort in certainty. But eventually, through enough PDCA cycles, we **learn** our way to the target condition. That's right, we learn our way to producing results.

This was my third great Lean lesson learned:

If we can learn fast enough, we can overcome adaptive challenges.

After seeing how effective the rapid PDCA cycles were on the ER project, I knew that breaking big adaptive challenges down into small bite-sized chunks was effective, but I didn't understand why. After reading Toyota Kata a second and a third time, then attempting to apply the concepts at the hospital where I was working, I began to understand why.

It was because of the learning.

This only became apparent to me after I had done literally hundreds of coaching cycles with dozens of hospital leaders using the Toyota Kata approach. Getting so many repetitions and being exposed to the improvement efforts of so many leaders allowed me to notice things I wouldn't have otherwise. Working on a limited number of big improvement projects per year just doesn't have the same effect.

What I started to see was that the people having the most success on their improvement endeavors were not the ones with the best ideas or the most well thought-out implementation plans. Rather, it was the ones who were the best at trial-and-error. And by that, I mean the ones that didn't get discouraged after a trial produced an error, because they were curious and interested in learning, regardless of whether the outcome was what they expected.

When I realized this, I began modifying my coaching technique to be more focused on encouraging the hospital leaders to run experiments for the sake of learning. When I did this, people were much more likely to stick to it and not give up after one or two cycles. It was amazing to see people liberated from their fear of failure.

After a few hundred more coaching cycles with a dozen or more additional hospital leaders, I finally realized that this concept of learning experiments applied just as well to me as a coach as it did to the folks I was coaching. I realized that my own coaching technique needed to constantly undergo adaptive change and that I would need to navigate through my own gray zones. Fortunately, my neurons had already been trained through repetition to focus on the learning, so I was able to cope with my many, many failures my attempts at coaching produced.

That led me to a modification of my third great Lean lesson learned:

If we can learn fast enough, we can overcome adaptive challenges. Becoming an organization of rapid learners requires a mindset shift that we can achieve through lots and lots of repetition.

Repetition.

Not classroom training, which, although useful in the right situations, is just batch-and-queue production applied to learning. Not "see one, do one, teach one," which implies that new habits will form just because a new skill has been attained. Not participating in a kaizen event, unless you're having one on a daily basis (bless your heart if you are). None of these activities, even if they are useful for other purposes, provide the repetition necessary to rewire neural pathways and form new habits that lead to new ways of thinking. Think of the adage: "It's easier to act our way to new ways of thinking than it is to think our way to new ways of acting."

Once I realized that repetition was the key to creating rapid learners who could tackle any adaptive challenge, the whole calculus of Lean changed for me. I began seeing opportunity in the smallest of improvement endeavors. I began looking for any excuse I could find to engage a leader in running a rapid experiment for the sake of learning. I started seeing how coaching people to think this way was not just a core competency for a Lean coach, but a fundamental behavior of leaders in general. A chain of coaches and learners running experiments daily at multiple levels of the organization can even be viewed as the nucleus of a Lean management system. If we have this nucleus, this DNA, we can arrive at the rest of the Lean organism.

That's why, when Mike Rother told me "I'm just going to let you find out for yourself" about raising daughters, I thought to myself, "Enjoy the learning zone." He knew that my learning how to be a parent was going to be tough and fraught with mistakes, but that some of the things I had learned by practicing Lean were going to aid me in parenthood. That made me happy and gave me confidence. That also pointed out to me the true value of practicing Lean—it can help individuals and organizations eagerly tackle and overcome whatever challenges may arise. But it takes practice.

Chapter Five - Paul Akers

Paul Akers describes himself[a] as an "entrepreneur,business owner, author, speaker and Lean maniac." Paul is founder and president of fastCap LLC[b], based in Ferndale, WA. fastCap is an international product development company founded in 1997 with over 2000 distributors worldwide.

A prolific inventor, Paul holds U.S. and international patents. His company fastCap, launches approximately 20 new innovative products per year and has won the business of the year award in 1999 and 2010. Paul and his wife, Leanne, have built fastCap from their garage into a multi-million dollar company in 13 years.

In 2011, Paul wrote his first book about Lean Manufacturing, 2 Second Lean[c]. In 2015, Paul published his latest book Lean Health[d], which you can download as a free PDF.

Read his full bio online - PDF[e].

[a]http://2secondlean.com/
[b]http://www.fastcap.com/
[c]http://2secondlean.com/books
[d]http://2secondlean.com/books
[e]http://2secondlean.com/bio

Every Day is a Massive Revelation

I've been doing Lean for 17 years and every day is a massive revelation as to how much better I could do everything.

You'd think at some point I'd have it figured all out, right? ....not a chance.

I always tell people that becoming a lean thinker is like stepping into a perpetual Edison's laboratory. I'm just experimenting... doing the scientific method, over and over again. You plan, you do, you check, with extreme emphasis on the "you" part you have to get your hands dirty you have run endless experiments... and discover what works and what fails. Skip the theory bullshit, as it will lead you down a rat hole that will rob you of all the real joy and satisfaction that lean bestows.

Studious and Creative

Sakichi Toyoda

That's really all Lean is experimenting with every facet of life. I'm constantly analyzing, learning "What is this? What's going to happen here? What's going to happen there?" I am basically a problem magnet and a problem solver.

Mark Graban asked me to write a chapter in a collaborative book he was writing with other Lean leaders asking the same question.

The Question? What would I do differently if I did lean all over again with all the knowledge and experience I have today?

The funny thing is, just minutes earlier, I was in line at Starbucks and I opened an e-mail with the same thought-provoking question from someone who had read my book, *2 Second Lean: How to Grow People and Build a Fun Culture8[30].

Being the Lean maniac that I am, I didn't wait to think about my answer.

Steaming coffee in hand, I simply pulled out my iPhone, leaned my Phone against my wife's coffee, and begin to muse.

You can go to YouTube and see me give my answer in living color[31]. For those of you reading the book, here it is in black and white, in a slightly edited form.

For those of you reading the book, here is my answer in black and white, plus a little editing for good measure.

In order to properly answer this question, I have to transport myself back to my small little cabinet shop in 1986.

What would I do if I was starting over and just learning about Lean? I think it's a really good question. I don't think anybody has ever asked me that before. So I'm going to take myself back in time for just a minute.

I am putting myself in my small little one-man 2,400-square-foot cabinet-making business. I'm going to ask myself that question. What would I do? I'm just starting out and I just learned about Lean.

---

[30]http://amzn.to/1lCkjTl
[31]https://www.youtube.com/watch?v=KJfRRWI3Yqk

Paul in his shop

1. Understanding the Eight Wastes

I think the first thing is I would need to have a keen understanding of the 8 wastes. I have a very basic understanding of waste. I certainly didn't understand all the nuances and how the eight wastes interacted with one another. I understood excess motion, but I didn't really understand overproduction.

I didn't understand that transportation and inventory was really all just waste. I thought they were just part of every process and you just had to live with it.

Then, there was all the over processing from reworking all the defects I created.

If I really had a deep understanding of these concepts, I would have systematically gone about trying to reduce them in "every breath I take and every move I make," as the song so aptly states.

8 Deadly Sins of Waste

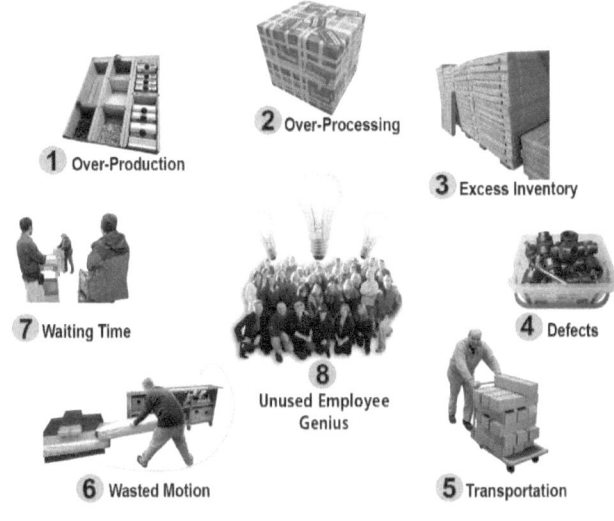

8 Wastes

8 Wastes, Animal Style

2. Eliminating Batch Work

I would have tried to eliminate batch work, refine every process so they were quick to set up. If I had done this, I would have only needed to produce what I needed to produce at the moment.

Back then, I always said to myself, "Hey, let's just make 30 of those." Then, when I needed some, I'd just grab some off the shelf instead of wrestling with the time-consuming process of resetting up machines to make what I needed. They key was to leave the raw material in as raw a state as possible so that it was just as flexible as possible.

I was a master at batch work and had no clue what one-piece flow was

3. Understanding Variation

I think the next thing is I would have a solid understanding of the role that variation has on everything we do.

I would have realized that every time there was something different going on, I had to stop and readjust. I would have realized that variation was not just a variation, it was actually producing mountains of waste and slowing me up and denigrating my productivity and the quality of my product.

Worst of all, variation was sucking the emotional energy right out of me and diminishing my productivity because I was constantly having to stop and start.

4. The Importance of Standardization

I wish I had a really keen understanding of standardization.

Back then, I really tried hard to standardize things. I standardized the way I built my cabinets, as my top and bottoms were identical. I used the same screw most of the time but made plenty of exceptions instead of trying to focus on standardizing absolutely everything.

I did not have a high-level understanding of standardization and, as a result, my non-standard ways produced a lot of variation.

The lack of standardization make me want to choke myself!

Today, standardization for me is almost a religious experience, as we basically have one cleaner that cleans 98% of everything in our facility, Windex. We use one kind of paper towel and the list goes on and on.

I remember when I first had the standardization epiphany. We were trying to standardize our bathrooms when we had at least 15 different cleaners that people had acquired over the years to maintain our bathrooms. Needless to say, this was sheer craziness we cut that all down to Windex and Comet.

Here's an example of how a toolbox was improved and standardized:

Before

After

5. The Need to Emphasize Quality

I think if I had understood quality back then a little differently, I would have felt entirely differently about the quality equation. Often, I bought drawer guides and hinges based on what was a good deal... everyone loves a good deal!

I know when I had problems with one drawer system, it was less expensive and it seemed like it would work okay. I remember having to go back and replace a bunch of drawer guides that I had implemented this new system on. Twenty years later, I still get calls from customers asking me if I have replacement drawer guides and I have not been in the cabinet business for 17 years.

Quality = Trust!

If I would've just made quality the first criteria for my decision-making, I would've saved myself much heartache. Today, the first question I ask about any purchase is quality. Price is way down the list.

6. The Power of Kanban

From an organizational standpoint, Kanban rocks! I didn't understand what a Kanban system was, let alone how it worked. I just kind of created a pseudo-reorder system. I'd see a hinge getting low and I'd say, "I'd better reorder some of those." Like many people, I'd order a whole bunch more then i needed so I didn't run out of them again... right?

I built my inventory up to ridiculous levels. I wish I had a simple limit Kanban system, a card that said reorder when I hit 20 hinges. This little card would tell me all the critical info, vendor, how many I ordered last time, and a history of the reordering, so I can make thoughtful decisions about what the best levels would be. This simple card system would allow me to order 50 instead of 500 and make my cash flow a whole lot better.

I had way too much inventory!

I remember one time my banker visited me when I was a young startup business owner. My hardware sales guy was delivering boxes of hinges because he gave me a smoking deal. I think I paid $1.50 a hinge when they were normally about $2.50.

So I said, "Just give me a thousand," about a 6 month supply. He pulled up in his hatchback car with huge box of hinges. We were both unloading these hinges on my workbench when my banker stopped by. "Wow," he said, "You need that many hinges?" I said, "I got a good deal on them." The banker replied, "Don't you know inventory is really expensive? You got to be careful with how much inventory you carry."

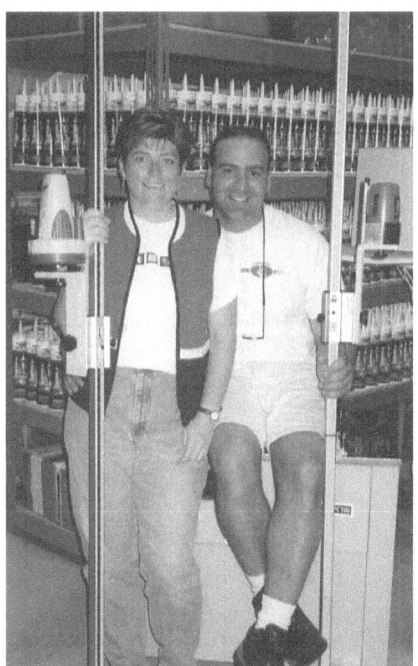

Man, did I love my inventory

I looked at him like he was crazy, that he didn't know anything about manufacturing or anything about the time it took to stop and reorder everything. He was right and I was clueless!

If I had a Kanban system, I would have never had that problem. But instead, now my garage had to get bigger and everything had to get bigger to house the thousands of hinges that I bought that I didn't need. The next thing you know, instead of buying ten boards of melamine, I was buying 50 boards of melamine. It was cheap and it lasted me a long time, but everything had to start getting bigger and then I was managing my new bigness! I had to walk further to manage everything. It was insane.

If only I would have understood kanban. It would have been so powerful.

7. Wheels!

I would have definitely understood the whole concept of wheels. I was into wheels back then, I had a lot of my stuff on wheels, but not because I really understood the flexibility that wheels brought to an operation.

I had my edge-bander on wheels, a massive machine. I had to be able to roll it out of the way to perform different operations because I had very limited space in my small little shop.

I kind of understood the flexibility thing, but only from the standpoint of needing to move it because I was in such a small confined space. It was forced flexibility instead of really understanding designed-in flexibility.

Our morning meeting. Notice nothing in the photo is fixed... everything is on wheels.

8. The Shop Layout

You asked, "How would you lay out your new shop?"

If I was doing it again, I would not build anything in, just watch FastCap Lean Tour video[32], which has over 190,000 views.

---

[32]https://www.youtube.com/watch?v=jYby_HczyDA

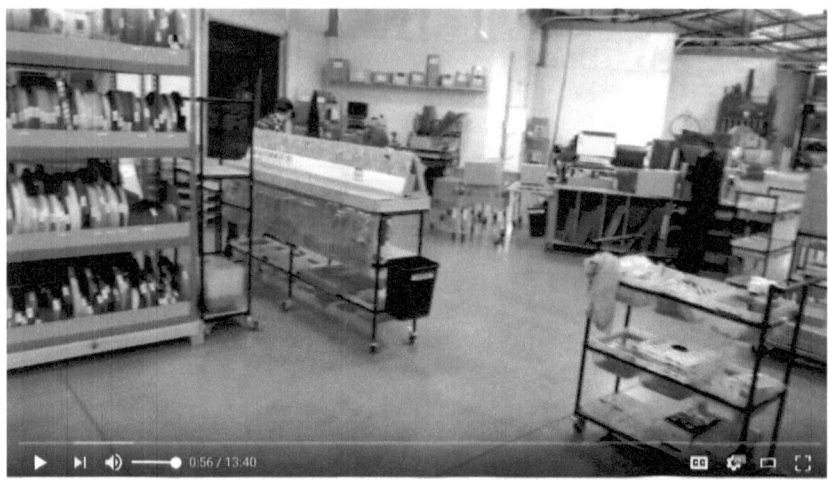

You'll see we built nothing in. Everything is just open and almost everything is on wheels. Everything is very simple, our desks, our carts it is all on wheels and easy to move and change at the drop of a hat. We make everything out of our FastPipe system[33].

When you understand standardization, standard work. quick setup time, Single-Minute Exchange of Dies (SMED), Kanban, flexibility, and building nothing in... gosh, it's just a magic system. I don't know what to say, It's magic!

9. Cut It In Half!

There's a saying that I learned from Toyota that says, "Don't approach anything unless they can cut it in half." If I would have understood the power of this concept, I would have viewed every process completely differently.

If I was cutting parts or building a base cabinet or drawer bank, I would have constantly challenged myself. If it takes me an hour, I would have asked, "How I can do it in 30 minutes?"

I know, for sure, these kinds of gains are totally possible. I mean I don't even question it, It's absolute for sure, everything can be cut in half.

Here are two great examples:

When I was in Kazakhstan, they were building the World Expo

---

[33]https://www.fastcap.com/estore/pc/FastPipe-p44266.htm

Center, and they were putting up one window upright a day. I said, "You can do way better than that," and within two weeks they were putting up 15 a day.

My good friend Nick Kocelj, President of Walters & Wolf, was manufacturing approximately 30 windows a day and I challenged him to get it up to 50 a day. He looked at me like I was crazy. Today, six months later, they're doing 110 a day, and the new target is 200 a day.

10. Lean Culture

Because I was a one-man shop, I didn't really have to deal with the cultural aspect. I didn't have employees.

Fast forward to the early days of FastCap, with new team members multiplying like rabbits, I would've done everything different regarding the cultural aspect of Lean.

For the first five years practicing Lean, I essentially failed on the culture, because I viewed Lean as a management tool to more effectively run my company.

The reality of it is Lean is all about people and tapping into their boundless capacity. It wasn't until I realized that Lean was a people-orientated concept that I finally broke through and began to successfully build a Lean culture.

> "The Toyota style is not to create results by working hard.
> it is a system that says there is no limit to people's cre-
> ativity. People don't go to Toyota to work, they go there
> to think." – Taiichi Ohno

Essentially, a Lean culture is a learning culture were management focuses on the relentless training, teaching, and elevating of its people to become world-class problem solvers.

We accomplish this by the implementation of two basic concepts before we worked each day:

1) 3s-ing our facility and everyone making a small improvement.

2) A morning meeting where we teach our people about everything from the products that we make to the U.S. Constitution. When I started focusing on the daily development of my team members, everything changed. People don't believe in you until you believe in

them, they really believe in you and will work super hard for you when you first invest in them.

In Japan, all the children clean and 3S their classroom and school every day - no janitors

What I'm saying is a bit counterintuitive for a lot of leaders. Spending money, on a daily basis, developing your people will be hard to see on the bottom line, but, it will be clear as day in the productivity and team atmosphere that is created from creating a Lean learning environment.

This is true long-term thinking at its best.

Lean is the craziest system in the world. I wish I knew it all back then, but I know it now. I often say to myself, If I learned Lean when I was 20, oh my gosh! I could not even imagine where I would be now. I feel like I have the best life in the whole world. I attribute 90% of that to my understanding of Lean, because it has turned my life into a rocket ship ride.

It just keeps getting better. Everything just keeps getting better.

Lean Thinking – It Never Ends!

Today, when I ordered my coffee, I used a very specific process for telling them exactly what I want. I hold my fingers in a certain way so they clearly understand and they don't screw it up. I try very hard to be thoughtful about everything I do, then that result is total clarity, less variation, I get what I want the first time, and the quality of everything I do is always improving.

Something that frustrates me is when I brush my teeth in the shower. I like to put my toothpaste on the toothbrush, but if I'm in a hotel, sometimes it will roll over. So, I put a little suction cup on the bottom of my toothbrush so it would stick to the wall and not roll over. No variation.

Sometimes, on a vertical surface, the toothpaste always seems to drip off before I use it, so now I changed the process. I squeeze the toothpaste into the bristles so that it can't drip off. It's a simple process improvement that saves all that mess and hassle. And, when you think about it, the maid at the hotel has less to clean up, as well.

When you create a deep understanding of Lean, the ideas just goes on and on, and on, and the benefits never end.

What would I do if I started over? I'd become a Lean Maniac first and foremost.

Get hooked on Lean!

www.paulakers.net

Check out Paul's books at PaulAkers.net[34]

---

[34]http://www.paulakers.net

Chapter Six - Jamie Parker

Jamie Parker practices Lean and is passionate about learning and sharing Lean leadership. She has 15 years' experience in operations management/leadership across retail, service, and manufacturing environments.

Jamie serves as an internal coach to her organization's operations managers across the country while supervising P&L and operations management responsibilities for six commercial print plants. Jamie expresses a passion for helping leaders break the habits of traditional management approaches to create environments primed for team member fulfillment.

Connect with Jamie on LinkedIn[a].

[a]http://www.linkedin.com/in/jamievparker

Bike Ramps: Crashing and Burning

Growing up, I lived on a cul-de-sac, and most of the neighbor kids were boys. Fittingly, I liked climbing trees, playing football, and riding bikes - this tomboy was just one of the guys! My buddies and I built bike ramps using any random thing lying around the neighborhood, which meant each one was often more elaborate and risky than the next. We would launch our bikes from the driveway of a house atop a wicked hill to get as much speed as possible before hitting our daredevil creation. Our goal, of course, was to log the most time spent airborne without ending in a bike-bending, bone-breaking crash.

One memorable ramp emphasized extra thrills overstability as we gathered all sorts of odd-sized items in an effort to outdo ourselves with the biggest, baddest ramp yet.

A courageous pal went first and promptly crashed and burned. Badly.

I was up next. Inwardly nervous and outwardly bold, I started my downward approach but had to come to a screeching halt when the ramp began tumbling over. The boys put the ramp back together while I climbed up the hill to give it another shot.

You can guess what happened, but I didn't see it coming. I absolutely could not understand how I ended up with the same outcome as the first kid: I was bruised, had a serious case of road rash, and a big dose of wounded pride. I was in tears and did not see one bit of humor in the situation.

That was then. Thankfully now, knowing my body and my pride fully recovered eventually, I can look back and laugh whenever I tell this story. What on earth were we thinking? The ramp was literally wobbling from the get go, and the first kid demonstrated what we could expect as our results. Then, on my turn, I couldn't complete the first try because the ramp fell apart without any weight on it. Yet, somehow I thought my magical powers of awesomeness would prevent the ramp's collapse. Now, I look back and can see that we were doomed to fail. But at the moment, I couldn't see it. None of us could. We were too engrossed in seeking thrills and neighborhood fame to see all the evidence of pending doom right in front of us.

That's how I feel about my first few years of practicing Lean. At the moment, we had some pretty brilliant ideas. Even when we didn't think they were brilliant, we still thought they were darn good given our circumstances or constraints. At the moment, our mistakes were painful, figurative road rash all around. There were warning signs telling us the idea was going to collapse like that old ramp did, but we were often too engrossed in the Lean-seeking moment to heed those warnings. I had to go through the experience and come out the other side to truly learn and appreciate the failure - and be better as a result.

When I visit for the holidays, my brother and I like to tell stories like the famed bike ramps and other ridiculous stuff we did as kids. Stuff that was challenging or scary or just plain painful at the time, but now we can laugh at and think of how we might have done it better (with an occasional probably-shouldn't-have-tried-it-to-begin-with). That's what I'm going to do here. I'm going to share my stories, and my hope is that my lessons learned, my skinned knees, may help you see the warning signs so you can adjust accordingly.

Diving in Head First... in the Shallow End

After ten years in operations management in one area of our organization, I transferred to a different department while staying in an operations management role. My new department was a fairly independent group within the company. There wasn't much structured support from the corporate office, but that also meant there wasn't much corporate oversight either. We had 18 plants across the country, and I was one of three regional managers. We often had to figure things out and do things ourselves, learning from our mistakes along the way.

Shortly before I joined this network, they had begun practicing Lean. The plants rearranged equipment to be in what we called "cells" and had started doing what we referred to as "one piece flow." As the new girl, I jumped right in and began talking with authority about such things. As instructed, I read *The Gold Mine*[35] by Freddy and Michael Balle, so I understood some of the concepts of flow and takt time.

Unfortunately, my new region wasn't stable, which meant I didn't have enough time to truly immerse myself in the Continuous Improvement and Respect for People foundations of Lean. I was in firefighting mode, with my efforts focused on trying to stop the bleeding from jobs done wrong or late. So instead of getting my bearings and taking the time to truly understand the core principles of Lean, I just dove in head first. Unfortunately, with my Lean knowledge being shallow, it wasn't the best of moves.

Now I know that the things I was saying weren't always accurate. We didn't produce using one-piece flow, and we didn't have cells or cellular workflow. Now I can see that the meaning of other Lean terms just wasn't what I was trying to make them be.

[35] http://amzn.to/1mONI9y

On the other hand, there were things that I got right. The analogy of the lake and the rocks, for example, has stuck with me since that first reading of *The Gold Mine* years ago. Certainly, we did get better through the process. But it would have been less confusing and less painful for our team members if I had taken time to be more knowledgeable about Lean. Of course, I didn't need to be an expert on any tools, but the study of Respect for People early on would have enabled me to better serve my team.

The Hammer or the Screw Driver

In Chapter Two of this book, Mark Graban mentions how much he dislikes the concept of Lean being presented as a toolkit that practitioners pick and choose from. While we didn't formally present it as such, this is absolutely how my practice of Lean began. It was part-time. When we ran across a problem that we thought a Lean tool would be helpful for, we tried to apply that tool and then went back to business as usual.

Actually, in the interest of full disclosure, it was more often the case that we found a tool we thought was cool and then tried to use it without even understanding "what problem are we trying to solve" or how it fits into an overall system or culture. Whom am I kidding? An overall system or culture wasn't on our minds yet.

It is painfully clear today that what we were doing wasn't good. At the moment, though, we thought we were "Doing Lean." I mean, we had corners and labels in our plants and an elementary Kanban system and andon lights and some plants even had Huddle Boards. We were making progress on this journey!

What made our toolkit approach even worse was that sometimes we really misapplied the tools. Nails and screws are used for different purposes. Using a hammer to beat in a screw can cause some serious damage because it's a misapplication of the tool. So, too, does this happen with Lean.

Mark Graban created an Office 5S Gone Wrong parody video you can watch here.[36] This video generally elicits chuckles or even out loud laughter. While it is an extreme parody, the chuckles and laughs occur because there is an element of truth that many of us have experienced in our misapplication of Lean tools.

One part of this parody video goes like this:

> Employee: "Why would I have to put tape around my monitor?"
>
> Supervisor: "So it does not get lost. We will always know where the monitor is. You will not waste time looking for it. Now our office will be more efficient."
>
> Employee: "Has anyone in our office ever had a monitor go missing?"

And so went our first attempt at 5S. Our areas were all shared workspaces, so there were real problems with things going missing or with motion waste as team members looked for supplies or tools. However, we didn't keep our eye on the problem; we only used the artifact part of the tool. Let me explain.

On conference calls, a few of our plant managers discussed what supplies and tools each plant needed. They made labels and outline stickers for the tabletops, floors, and shadow boards and then shipped a "5S Kit" to every plant. In addition to many other outline labels, these kits included rectangle outline labels for the phones and keyboards. Has anyone in our office ever had a phone or keyboard go missing? (The answer is "No" if you're unsure).

We sent pictures of what the plants were supposed to look like and set a date for all plants to be in compliance. We gave a verbal overview of the steps in 5S, but we didn't teach those steps or actually do those steps in our plants. We gave a lot of top-down direction and rules about what was allowed and what wasn't allowed.

So not only was this a tool-focused approach, but it was a misapplication of the tool altogether. The teams didn't actually perform the steps of 5S. They didn't make decisions to make abnormalities visible. They didn't develop their capabilities in any area. Why? Because we

---

[36]http://www.youtube.com/watch?v=t8IfQp4A4ZI

didn't let them. We treated this as a top-down push for a compliance activity.

This was the very first time our team members heard the word "Lean". As you can imagine, it didn't go well. And the damage to trust was felt for a long time.

After making this type of mistake a few times, we changed our approach and continued to learn over time. A few years later we were finally ready to develop our team members' capabilities to use 5S to make abnormalities visible and to reduce process waste. This time, we had weekly 45-minute group sessions with all team members. In each week's time, we taught 5S, one step at a time. We showed them video content explaining the concept of the step and facilitated discussions for better comprehension. We led experiential activities such as the 5S Numbers Game[37] or the Pen Building Activity[38] to better appeal to adult learning styles. Also, team members worked in groups to apply what they learned and practice the steps in small areas of the plant, one step at a time. At the end of the time period, each group stood up in front of the rest of their peers in the plant and delivered a report-out on what they did in their area of the plant. We had them walk through the decisions they made in each step of the process and share before and after photos.

As you can imagine, this was a much more successful approach. Our team members actually learned how to use 5S to make their jobs easier. Their results were much better than what we pushed to them years before and sustainability was viable for the first time. Most importantly, though, they developed their capabilities as communicators, presenters, collaborators, and problem solvers. A team member swelling with pride as she presents to her peers how she helped make their workplace a little bit better gets to go home with greater confidence and fulfillment and carry that forward to her family and community. That is the real prize!

---

[37] http://www.lean.org/FuseTalk/Forum/Attachments/5SGAME.PPT
[38] https://www.youtube.com/watch?v=ILIqVxN8WyI

Standards for Standards' Sake

Our department has 18 plants across the United States, and many of our customers have employees spread across the country as well. So, one of the value drivers we provide our customers is to use our distributed network to create product for the customer near the end user, greatly reducing speed to market and shipping costs for the customer. This means that we have to deliver consistent products, services, and lead times across all 18 plants. Our customers define this as valuable to them. In order to accomplish this, we have to execute on consistent production standards across all plants. We didn't start here initially, and we've worked many years at incrementally getting there.

However, our desire for standardization crossed the lines of what was truly necessary. Remember how we first tried 5S - sending pictures of what every plant needed to look like and sending a list of rules to follow? We used that approach for quite a few things. At one point, we made our first attempt at a Leader Standard Work program across all plants. There was a project team of several managers who collaborated remotely to develop this program, and there were checklists for every leadership level and a visual control board to try to make the results of those checklists visible.

It was a complete flop.

We couldn't get any level of execution. Even after we solicited feedback and made adjustments to the program based on that feedback, we still visited plant after plant and saw that they just weren't doing it. There were several reasons for this. First, we didn't have a culture of discipline in our plants yet. Second, we had inconsistent execution of our shift huddles to engage team members in closing the loop and solving the process problems we were observing. And third, we didn't have buy in or even understanding of the purpose of the program from the people that had to execute it day after day.

We were working on standardizing our shift huddles around the same time of this flop and were about to launch a program to address the second problem listed above. We had approached it the same way: a project team of several managers collaborated remotely to develop the shift huddle program. The program dictated the timeframe in which huddles had to occur, who would lead them, who would participate in them, the agenda minute by minute, and a standardized huddle board to use during the huddles.

I'm thankful we didn't launch this program. A colleague and I attended a Lean conference that caused us to rethink this approach. In learning from other practitioners, we realized that releasing these programs that required strict adherence to every detail wasn't respecting our people. All we were doing was teaching (not very effectively) our team members to execute a program or follow a checklist. We weren't engaging their brains and respecting how they could effectively run their business. We were making standards for standards' sake.

While there were certainly key processes that had to be standardized to deliver the consistency our customers defined as valuable, the nuances of exactly how shift huddles were executed or exactly how leaders monitored processes didn't have to be standardized across locations.

So we actually abandoned the Leader Standard Work program. We just weren't ready for it yet. We did have feedback from our team members that they weren't receiving the level of communication necessary to effectively do their jobs and improve their jobs. So we moved forward with shift huddles but in a different manner.

We set some basic parameters. Shift huddles had to happen every day. All team members had to attend shift huddles. Huddles had to cover our five pillars: Safety, Quality, Delivery, Cost, and Morale. And plants had to make their huddle content visual on some sort of display. Everything else was left to the local teams to decide. As a result, our team members were more engaged in shift huddles. We respected the value of our team members' brains and gave away decision making.

A year later, Eric Kulikowski[39] from Dare to Be Amazing shared with me the phrase "Global Consistency with Local Implementation." This is a good description of the lesson we learned. Standards are very important. And each plant could absolutely create standard work for their huddles. But our need for standardization of everything across

---

[39]http://www.daretobeamazing.com/MeetEric.en.html

18 plants was just taking it too far and suppressing the creativity and engagement of our team members.

A Five Letter Word

Trust. It's a pretty important five letter word. In the lessons I've already shared, you can probably imagine how the mistakes we were making early in our practice of Lean hurt the level of trust our team members had of the organization and of us as leaders. When we first started practicing Lean, we presented it as a way to increase efficiency and cut costs. Combine that with the connotations of the word "lean" itself and we had a problem. Then, add in our misapplication of tools and top-down push of Lean initiatives and the problem only got worse. We created a sense of fear and resentment among many of our team members.

To course correct, we actively worked on changing that by investing in our team members and giving them more opportunities to create change. At one point, we trained our team members on the basics of continuous improvement and focused that effort on what we called daily improvements. Paul Akers of FastCap, author of Chapter Five, calls these "2 Second Improvements." Essentially, these are improvements that team members can make in their work environment and processes. We created "Improvement Walls of Fame" in each plant where team members could document and share their improvements. It was a great way for them to get recognition and to learn from each other.

However, we had to approach these daily improvements differently than we had started in our practice. We couldn't focus on efficiency or cost cutting as the primary goals; we had already learned that many of our team members viewed that as a way for "the big man upstairs" to make more profit without sharing any of it with them, and some of them were even afraid they would improve themselves out of their jobs.

Shigeo Shingo is quoted as saying, "There are four purposes of improvement: easier, better, faster, and cheaper. These four appear in the order of priority." This became our rallying cry.

We repeated over and over and over to our team members that we wanted their help in making their jobs easier and better. That's it. Those are the first two priorities for improvement and the only thing we asked for. It wasn't just a "flavor of the month" either. Two years later, this remains our rallying cry.

This paradigm shift had a tremendous positive impact on rebuilding trust with our team members. It wasn't about efficiency or costs. It was about making their jobs easier and making their plants a better place to work. Of course, their improvements did make things faster and cheaper, too. In fact, team members regularly made improvements that lowered our costs. I think that's mostly because we didn't ask for it and instead trusted them to make the improvements they found value in. And they trusted us in return.

I only wish we had started this way and not put ourselves in a hole to climb out of, to begin with. Skinned knees!

West is Best

Indulge me while I take a trip back to my first ten years in operations management before I was ever introduced to Lean. Our organization conducted Voice of Customer (VOC) surveys to get direct feedback from customers on their experiences. Each location's VOC scores determined part of the incentive payouts for all team members in the location, including the manager, which was me for my location. Even more than that, first quartile performance or "number one" performance in a particular district or region was highly celebrated, and the culture included a high emphasis on stack rankings. So much so that throughout my tenure there were times when fourth quartile performances in some metric were punished - either by mandated formal disciplinary action or by having to attend horrific conference calls from your office weekly on Fridays at 5 pm.

I had been promoted to manage a location that was ranked last in the company. I was using my traditional management style (I didn't know any better yet) to dramatically improve that ranking. One month, our VOC scores were so high they were second in the region to only one other location. I was thrilled, but apparently, this just wasn't good enough for me.

During the last days of the month, I constantly checked Voice of Customer scores to monitor results. I clearly remember thinking, "I hope the #1 location gets a bad survey so we can take over the number one spot."

What??!!??

Yes, I genuinely wanted a customer of my company to have a bad experience or get a job late or wrong so that I could move up in the rankings. The recognition given to achieving "number one" status was so high that I went there. I guess I could have argued that I didn't want a customer to have a new bad experience, but just one that had already had a bad experience to take the survey. I'm not sure that makes it better.

Fast forward to moving to this new department that had just started practicing Lean. Stack rankings were very important here as well. In fact, your stack ranking was almost how you justified your value to the organization. As I studied Lean and, more importantly, as I learned from a new director hired from outside our company how dangerous it was for our plants to aggressively compete against each other, I devalued stack rankings. Eventually, we were able to remove stack rankings from all of our scorecards and metrics reporting so that our managers could focus on improving their own performance against their history. The problem was that this culture was so ingrained in my belief system and the belief system of our plant managers that it was difficult to change.

In fact, right after we removed stack rankings, I noticed that my plants were rerouting a lot of their volume to other plants. What really irritated me about this was that that work was being rerouted to plants in a different Region. I vividly remember getting on a conference call with my plant managers and in no uncertain terms dictating that they would, collectively, figure out how they would keep that volume in our own West region. Why would I say such a thing? Not because it increased shipping costs for the company or had some negative impact on our customers. It was because losing that volume decreased my region's metrics while improving the metrics of my peers' regions. Remember, my boss was the new director who didn't value stack rankings, so this being a big deal was all a figment of my imagination, or more accurately of my experience.

As I was learning Lean, I was beginning to question this methodology even more. In a one-week period, I had two great mentoring experiences - the first was a lengthy email exchange with Kevin Meyer[40] of Gemba Academy[41] and the second was a lengthy phone call discussion with Steve Kane[42] of Gemba Academy. During these interactions, I found myself sharing the culture I was in and repeating back some of these types of stories. As the words were literally being typed by my fingers or uttered out of my mouth, I had mental, physical, and emotional reactions to what I was sharing.

What in the world is wrong with me? I'm part of the problem. Of course, I can't change this when I'm still leading this way.

That marked a major changing point in my belief system and leadership style.

I immediately began changing my dialogue with my managers and team members, and I started by apologizing for the way I had led them in the past. After two months of changing the dialogue, we were on a team conference call (my team was geographically dispersed, so conference calls were our reality). At the end of the call, one of my plant managers yelled out "West is Best" (we were the West Region). Before, it would have been music to my ears. But this time, it was like a knife through my heart. After two months, I clearly had not done enough to change this.

Over time, we continued to make headway in changing the culture. I knew we weren't there, but we were making progress. After nine months of this heavy dialogue and changing my behavior, we were leading an activity with all of the plant managers and department managers in each of the three regions. In the activity, the groups were split into teams with the task of building a contraption out of packing materials to protect an egg that was kicked across the parking lot. One

---

[40]http://kevinmeyer.com/bio
[41]http://www.gembaacademy.com/
[42]https://www.linkedin.com/in/steven-kane-6250b56

team's egg survived and their contraption had the lowest cost. During the ten-minute time when they were assessing and building another contraption for a second round, one of the members of this team approached another team and asked: "Do you want to know what we did?"

The other team shrugged him off and turned around to continue its own activities. My peers and I watched in disbelief. During this activity in each region, we also heard comments like "they're cheating" or "don't try to steal our ideas." It was painfully clear that, despite the attempts for change over the last nine months, the drive of internal competition instead of collaboration was still very much alive with our teams.

Of course, there is value in understanding how comparable business units perform. It helps a manager identify someone who is performing better and collaborate to learn what is causing that gap. And some friendly competition can be fun.

But the culture of extreme internal competition - of winning by "beating" another business unit within the same company - is unhealthy. We need to redefine winning in these cases. We shouldn't be asking ourselves "what will make my individual business unit's numbers the best?" We should be asking "what is best for our team members? What is best for our customers? What is best for our company?"

In reality, it's not the fault of our managers or team members that they have this mindset. They are only emulating what they were taught and what the culture encouraged, just like I was when I was in the other department.

We continue to make progress in this area. But, I wish I had this realization sooner. And, I wish I had been more aggressive in helping our teams make this transition as well. That is my mistake. I have a responsibility to lead them differently. It remains a work in progress.

Beliefs Drive Behavior

As you have probably gathered, we started with a results-only culture that celebrated results, no matter the method. The partner to this is that when failure happened, people were blamed. In fact, it was not uncommon for the first question asked of a manager after a high-profile failure to be "who is at fault and how are you holding them accountable?"

The flip side to this type of culture was a celebration of people going "above and beyond." Keep in mind that going above and beyond often meant deviating from the standard process. Productivity was valued, even when completely achieved by overburdening our team members.

That was our history and the culture we had when we first began practicing Lean. And realistically, probably through the first two years of our Lean practice as well. As we continued to learn about and practice Lean, we began to better understand Respect for People. We started talking this language because as senior leaders in the department, we genuinely believed it, and most of our leadership style with our plant managers emulated it.

But, we came to realize that what we were saying was not aligned with how our plant leaders were behaving, and it wasn't their fault. They had years of managerial programming to behave a certain way, and we weren't doing a very good job of giving them the development, coaching, and time necessary to behave any differently. In fact, while we believed and often practiced it, we were still torn on delivering to company expectations while trying to change our collective leadership behaviors, especially because this often comes with a short-term dip in performance. Of course, you get all of it back in the long-term by engaging your people, but, in the short-term, the time and effort it takes to develop people and improve process may result in a dip in performance.

We did respond in one way that was extremely impactful. We led our managers through a Lean Leadership Series that was introspective and challenged their current beliefs on their roles and responsibilities as leaders. It used content from thought leaders and practitioners like Simon Sinek, Bob Chapman, and David Marquet to put our leaders in a different frame of mind.

Of course, we had some leaders who didn't respond. And, the reality is we had to spend some one-on-one time with those leaders to understand the gap and to figure out what to do. But, many of our leaders changed their beliefs based through this series.

One plant manager said, "Lean Leadership teaches us to be openly fallible and to give our team members the respect of fulfilling their potential as human beings by becoming active members of the improvement process," which was a fundamental shift in this manager's belief system. A plant manager talking about his responsibility to engage team members to help them fulfill their potential as human beings? That's huge.

I attended a Lean conference and heard a talk by Libby Gill[43], author of You Unstuck[44] and other books. Gill declared "belief drives behavior." In that way, this Lean Leadership Series was a success because it changed the beliefs of our leaders. We wanted our leaders to behave a certain way, but their beliefs were counter to that. Changing their beliefs was a critical step to enabling them to change their behaviors.

Where we failed, though, was in not acting to help them change their behaviors. I understood the first part, the belief part, after hearing Simon Sinek's Leaders Eat Last[45] talk at a Lean conference and then doing my own research. What I didn't know, though, was how to help our leaders change their behaviors. In fact, I often found myself succumbing to task overload and not properly prioritizing, even after having a major change of heart in my beliefs. I jumped in helping our managers change their beliefs but wasn't prepared for the next requisite step in the process.

This is a recent mistake of mine and one that I am currently working to correct. I'm not sure if I would have done anything differently, as I don't think delaying the change in beliefs would have been any better. I should have been better prepared for what's next. Instead, I

---

[43] http://libbygill.com/about/
[44] http://amzn.to/1mORRdI
[45] http://amzn.to/1I3V86j

allowed myself to get consumed with stuff and stalled the progress of our leadership development.

The Tortoise and the Hare

I love the idea of a road trip. Wind in my hair, music blasting, experiencing the sites and the people from different places. It's like a symbol of freedom. But there's a problem: I'm a planner. I like to have every detail mapped out: where we're going, our route, where we're staying, every detail of the trip. When I experience the inevitable gaps in my plan, I get frustrated. Whether it's traffic, road construction, advice for a different stop, or heaven forbid a wrong turn (keep in mind, most of my road trips were in my 20's, before the proliferation of GPS-enabled devices).

Any of these obstacles and bumps in the road caused me frustration and, in turn, frustration for my companions. So much so that at some point they just stopped inviting me on the road trips.

Our Lean road trip has been similar. Once I studied enough that I had some confidence in mapping out the trip, that's exactly what I did, but the actual road trip was taking much longer than what I had mapped out.

It turned out that what I thought would take one year to accomplish, actually is taking three years to accomplish. At first, I was frustrated by the slow pace because I just wanted to get there (I know there's not an end destination, but I at least wanted to get to my milestones by my original plan). Go. Go. Go. Go.

By slowing down, what actually happened is that we didn't slow down at all. Instead, we learned. For each concept we were studying, we understood and applied it more effectively than we would have had we kept to my schedule. We progressed at a pace that was right for our journey. There are countless Lean principles or tools that we don't practice... yet. We are by no means experts. In fact, you might classify us as beginners still.

Every time we slowed down, we learned something. When something I planned to accomplish in three weeks instead took eight weeks, we studied our culture, our leadership, our execution. We learned about where we were and what gaps existed. We adjusted accordingly. When we were deficient in an area, we took time and invested in that area before moving on to the next one.

Through that process, we learned to better see the yellow flags. We learned how to listen and recognize when there was misalignment between our team members and leadership. How to identify when we were being too controlling or too top-down. How to see when our plan was a plan for plan's sake and wasn't really aligned with our high-level goals and values. How to heed and correct when our ramp was wobbly and probably wouldn't hold up when we rode the bike over it.

What I had to learn about road trips was that the value isn't in the destination. It isn't in seeing the sights and crossing them off the list. The value of a road trip is in the experience itself. It is in the hours upon hours of driving while sharing great laughs and delving into the depths of my companions' personalities while also sharing things I never thought I would share with another human. The value is in unexpectedly stumbling across the 90-year old couple who had grown up in Anytown and shared the amazing history that most people in this world will never get to hear. The value is in the experience.

In order to find value in the experience, we have to go at the right pace. This is generally the slower, tortoise pace. So maybe it takes us longer, but when we travel at the right pace, we find the hidden gems along the way. We practice better. We learn better.

Chapter Seven - Harry Kenworthy

Harry Kenworthy has authored articles on the topic of Total Quality in the magazines Quality Progress and Purchasing, as well as several articles in Government Finance Review: "Getting Started with Lean"[a], "A Guide to Starting the Lean Journey"[b], and "Blending Agile and Lean Thinking for More Efficient IT Development"[c].

He worked previously in several manufacturing organizations, serving as process engineer, general foreman, operations manager, division manager, group vice president, and lastly as vice president of manufacturing. Harry has worked in industries including copper and brass rolling, tube and bar mills; printed circuit boards; custom plastic molding; and his last tenure was 26 years at Rogers Corporation which served a variety of markets and technologies. He was responsible for the Rogers worldwide Lean Six Sigma effort and left to devote full time to his consulting firm in 2004.

His consulting organization, QPIC, LLC[d], focuses on clients implementing Lean Management Systems in over 20 states with state government agencies, counties, cities, and large K-12 school systems.

Harry has a B.S. in Materials Engineering from Rensselaer Polytechnic Institute (RPI), and an M.B.A in Finance from Syracuse University. Harry and his wife Elaine reside in Connecticut. This chapter is excerpted from his book: *Lean Government Now - We Can Do This!*[e]

[a]http://www.gfoa.org/getting-started-lean-government-projects
[b]http://www.gfoa.org/guide-starting-lean-journey

[c]http://www.gfoa.org/blending-agile-and-lean-thinking-more-efficient-it-development
[d]http://www.leangovcenter.com/
[e]https://amzn.to/2ThaJ9T

My First Job - Trial by Fire

I joined Revere Copper and Brass after college as a process engineer. This facility in Rome, NY, was an integrated facility with separate rolling, bar/rod, and tube mills and it employed 2000. I was able to work in all three mills as my introduction to process engineering, and it afforded me the opportunity to work with many different supervisors and managers. After an 18-month tour as a process engineer, I was asked to become a first line supervisor in the bar/rod mill. I was "the experiment," as previous first-line supervisors had been promoted through the union ranks. Since I had the technical skills in engineering, the thinking was that I could make better process decisions on the shop floor. Learning the necessary management and leadership skills to work with people was left up to me. There were no role models to draw from other than the other supervisors who had worked in the "system" for years; also there were no individuals with mentoring or coaching experience for me to draw on.

So on the job training and trial by fire ensued. It was a challenging production environment. An early lesson learned was my visibly getting angry with an employee on the shop floor and blowing my cool. A floor argument in front of others never pays off and created permanent scar tissue. I learned quickly that once things are said in anger, they can't be retracted and people don't forget. That was the last time I lost my cool at work. I learned that addressing the situation at hand calmly and with respect to the employee(s) involved paid dividends in building relationships and subsequent employee respect. "Fair, firm and friendly" became my mantra.

So, my mindset went from thinking people were trying to screw the company, to shifting my thinking to believing that folks really did want to do a good job, with very rare exceptions. It was clear that the system everyone worked in was owned by management. The comments heard were things like "what good does it to raise problems and issues when nothing happens?" and "why should I provide any ideas when nobody listens?"

My team had frustrations and ideas on how to improve production. These ideas had gone unheeded by past supervisors. After all, the previous supervisors had come up through the ranks and learned to live with a defective system before they were promoted to the role of supervisor. It was extremely hard for them to break the habit of status quo and mill management was in the same rut.

It took three or four months to build a better respect level on the shop floor. Folks knew that I was in a new role and there was always the tendency to test the new supervisor. I began to spend more time listening to understand the issues and problems my team was facing in doing their job. We started to make a few changes in team participation, especially on equipment changeovers, without knowing anything about Lean and achieved some good results. My credibility level was increasing.

Leaving Revere after 3 years to pursue my M.B.A. was one of my key goals. What amazed me in my two-year M.B.A. program (albeit mid-1970s): there were no required course offerings in managing or leading people or managing change (this has since changed in M.B.A. programs). Learning the technical side of finance was there in spades. Learning the cultural aspects of how to effectively manage organizations was essentially absent.

Learning on the Next Job

After my M.B.A., I worked for a small 40-employee custom printed circuit board company as operations manager, involved with all aspects of the business, including outside financing to generate working capital. The owner of the business was not a manager and wanted to just be presidential in his office. He always wanted to engage with customers and receive new prototype prints, however, the rest of us had no clue what he was doing. After several customer phone follow-ups to check on the status of their orders, he threw everything to me and I had to now talk to the customer and come clean that we hadn't even started their order. In the meantime, the customers were very upset. This cycle constantly repeated itself during my 12-month tenure with the firm. Many of the negative actions and behaviors in this environment by this company owner developed my clear sense of what not to do. I learned big time how to treat and respond to customers since I was being handed the customer when they were already upset about any lack of response by the owner. I learned a lot about customer focus. Given the breadth and depth of learning from this experience, I felt this job was the equivalent of a Ph.D.

Connecting with a Great Mentor

My next tenure was at a custom plastic molding company, Diemolding Corporation. The president of the company was Donald Dew, Jr. He was the first and best mentor in my career. Don was very disciplined, principled and focused on learning and coaching to develop his people. He was always challenging my thinking to consider alternatives and options to solve problems. I was a plant manager, yet he seldom made a decision for me in my area.

The sequence he used was:

1. Spend the necessary time identifying what is the real problem. To him, this was the most important point. I learned not to jump quickly to solutions, as several times I hadn't done a good job of identifying the real problem.
2. Once there is a clear understanding of the problem, then what alternatives or options did I develop as potential solutions?
3. Which one did I propose to try? Don would listen and then offer some questions to test my and his level of understanding of the situation. Invariably he would only say "give it a shot" rather than coming up with the answer and telling me what to do. Once in a

great while, if he thought that I was really going down a wrong path, he'd ask me to take another look.

Under Don's coaching, as plant manager, I became more and more knowledgeable about all aspects of the plant I was running. I never knew what questions he would ask me, so I continued to anticipate, learn, and be better prepared for his open-ended questions. The United Auto Workers represented my plant. Union leadership was solid, and relationships continued to get better. Trust and respect were high for management.

Don also used phrases that stuck with me throughout my career, such as:

"You get what you expect, inspect, and enforce"

This instilled making sure that expectations were clearly communicated and followed through to ensure successful outcomes. The "enforce" part was focused on having good discipline to complete the cycle, not for the purpose of penalizing or embarrassing people.

"It's not what you say, it's how you say it; it's not what you do, it's how you do it; and timing."

This sequence is gold. The learning was to instill a five-second delay between what my brain was thinking and what words came out of my mouth. It's amazing to see politicians and others totally violate this sequence. "Foot in mouth disease" is all too common.

Really Learning about Union Relations

My tenure at Rogers Corporation started in 1978 and ended in 2004. I started as operations manager in a plant that was a key automotive supplier. Union relationships were poor. Union leadership was disrespectful to management and the union president openly verbally abused supervisors.

Needless to say, discipline on the shop floor wasn't good, complemented by alcohol and substance abuse issues. The period from 1978 to 1980 was a challenging period, as I re-established management's ability to manage the facility while also removing several supervisors. During these two years, I dealt with over 100 step three grievances (step one of the grievance process was handled by the local supervisor, step two if the grievance wasn't settled, by the manufacturing manager and step three by me). I spent time on the shop floor every day talking to people and building my trust and credibility. Staying in my office was not an option.

This was when I learned to listen even better. Previous union relations were more based on adversarial approaches by both sides. Contract negotiations were seen as trying to overwhelm the other side with your point of view, to create win-lose outcomes.

So, I learned to reduce adversarial approaches. When grievances were submitted, I evolved my approach into what is one Dr. Stephen Covey's 7 *Habits of Successful People*[46]: "Seek first to understand and then to be understood," without knowing Dr. Covey's work at the time.

When grievances were presented, I followed this process (after learning from my mistakes).

1. Asking the union committee or group to help me understand what the grievance was all about. This was amazing. As one person presented the issue, others would pipe in and correct him or her. This would go on until a consensus was reached with the group on what was the real issue and it was captured on a flip chart or whiteboard for all to see.

2. This helped show that I really wanted to understand the real issue. This also helped diffuse emotions, as usually, the meeting would start with union members being upset with the perceived issue at hand.

3. With emotions defused and the problem clearly understood, listening skills increased for both sides. This resulted in a broader understanding and a less confrontational approach to grievance resolutions.

4. Many times, going through this process resulted in discovering no real contract violation existed, making the grievance invalid. Over time, the union committee developed the ability to do a much better job of vetting out grievances before submitting them.

---

[46]http://amzn.to/1OzbAIr

Learning about Accountability and Getting Stuff Done

Back to my first job at Revere, I had several agreed to annual goals. What this meant is that there was no urgency until month 11 or 12. Everyone else saw it the same way. As my career evolved to higher leadership levels, I learned that having agreed annual improvement targets with my direct reports was a non-starter and we shifted to quarterly targets. This just shifted the urgency to the end of the quarter. The next step was to break down the quarterly targets to monthly agreed to targets, and weekly targets, if necessary.

When it came to getting things done, having a team or group with agreed improvement targets was not that effective. Team members could always say: "we would have gotten this done, but one team member didn't come through" or "we were going to have a team meeting to get this done, but the meeting had to be re-scheduled and we're late," etc.

So, as my learning evolved, I came up with this approach that worked very well when something needed to be accomplished:

1. WHO - This is the person that has stepped up as the acting individual to bring a task or action item to completion. It should be their commitment and not an arbitrary assignment. Individuals must have accountability, as this is the best way for things to get done. They can be part of a team or head up a team or group; however, accomplishments happen much more effectively when one person has it and can draw on others to help, as needed.

2. WILL DO WHAT - This is a specific accomplishment goal. Specific metrics are important, rather than fuzz balls, to shore this up better. On a larger goal, it should be broken down to smaller monthly (or weekly) pieces. Break a larger goal down so it can be able to be accomplished in one month, or less. A Kaizen newspaper action item would be a good example. If a % completion is given it must relate to the specific action items that were laid out along with a valid measurement system.

Arbitrary calls of 50% or 75% are not acceptable.

3. BY WHEN - The specific date must be agreed to by the WHO and, once again, not arbitrarily assigned by someone else. "Ongoing" has no place here. "Ongoing" translates to potentially never-ending. The results are reported out on or before the agreed date. There are two acceptable outcomes:

- A. The task is done by the specific commitment date and reported on accordingly - great!
- B. There is a recognition beforehand that the due date won't be met and the WHO contacts the project or process owner to make them aware. This may result in an acceptable new date or a re-arrangement of priorities to still meet the original date.

The unacceptable outcome:

- C. The date is missed without any early communications, the task is not done, and follow up with the WHO has to occur - in Lean, spending extra time to do rework to follow up on something that should have been done is known as WASTE.

Instilling the discipline of this simple sequence enhanced my organization's accountability, effectiveness, and productivity.

My Experiences with Dr. Deming

Rogers started a joint venture in 1983 with Inoac, MTP, a major Toyota supplier, based in Nagoya, Japan. I visited Japan numerous times, including being on the JV's Board of Directors for nine years, creating great learning experiences about the Toyota Production System (TPS).

I met Dr. W. Edwards Deming, author of *Out of the Crisis*[47], in 1981. Beyond the famous Dr. Deming four-day seminars, MIT's Dr. Myron Tribus sponsored a series of two-day sessions from 1983 to 1985.

Dr. Deming covered his 14 points on day one and a series of industry participants presented on day two, talking about how Dr.

---

[47]http://amzn.to/1OzegpF

Deming's 14 points were being applied in their organizations. I was honored to have been selected to present at five of the day two sessions. Numerous trips to Japan were coupled with Toyota factory trips and visits to Deming Prize-winning Japanese companies. As a Malcolm Baldrige National Quality Award examiner from 1989 to 1991, I knew Dr. Deming was revered in Japan and the Baldrige award was very prestigious. Japanese company leaders were very focused on status and protocol, so this paved the way to open doors to many excellent Japanese companies.

The quotes that I remember best from Dr. Deming that impacted me:

> "You either change management or you change management."

I viewed this as meaning you either have managers "get it" as to the new direction and help them get there or you need to get them out of the way. Having resistors staying in place undermines the change effort.

> "It doesn't matter when you begin as long as you commence at once!"

Stop procrastinating - make a decision and get on with it! I developed my own spin on this, which became: "80% right, 100% implemented." The 80% was the part where enough information was developed to try something, and the 100% was to make sure to follow through and implement thoroughly.

We can study things forever and make sure we've covered all of the options or alternatives, which may take a long time with no action. Moving decisively forward to try something ("trystorming") will uncover problems that were never anticipated and then adjustments can be made. This was about the same time I was learning more about PDCA (Plan-Do-Check-Act). Identify the problem, determine potential root causes, and then implement a countermeasure (Do / try) and see what happens - the scientific thinking process.

If I Only Knew Then What I Know Now

It would be great if much of my learned knowledge, through the mistakes I made, had just been given to me to start. I'm sure everyone else feels the same way. It's all part of our learning. Having a great teacher or mentor early in anyone's career would make a huge difference. Mentoring and coaching skills can be trained and encouraged as a key development goal for all leaders and managers.

Recommended Reading:

1. Juran, Joseph M. and Gryna, Frank, *Juran's Quality Control Handbook, 4th Edition*[48]
2. Bhote, Keki R. and Bhote, Adi K., *World Class Quality: Using Design of Experiments to Make it Happen, 2nd Edition*[49]
3. Warner, Dr. John, "Are Leaders Born or Made?[50]"
4. Liker, Jeffrey and Trachilis, George, *Developing Lean Leaders at all Levels: A Practical Guide*[51]
5. Liker, Jeffrey and Convis, Gary, *The Toyota Way to Lean Leadership*[52]
6. Rother, Mike, *Toyota Kata*
7. Collins, Jim, *Good to Great: Why Some Companies Make the Leap...and Others Don't*

---

[48] http://amzn.to/1Ym3ugR
[49] http://amzn.to/1PdeKpX
[50] http://blog.readytomanage.com/are-leaders-born-or-made/
[51] http://amzn.to/1Ym3Dkt
[52] http://amzn.to/1Ym3QUP

Chapter Eight - Bob Rush

Bob Rush has over 35 years of operations experience and has had over 25 years of Lean practice. His experience is in companies ranging from startups to Fortune 100 companies, and title levels that ranged from shipping clerk to VP of operations. Some of the companies he has worked with, and for, include Hewlett Packard, JDS Uniphase, and Idex Corporation. His journey includes ten years of consulting experience, where he had only himself to blame if things didn't work out.

His Lean journey started with World Class Manufacturing, which led to Lean manufacturing, where he was fortunate enough to learn kaizen events from the Shingijutsu Consulting group. He continues to work with a love of kaizen as a way of life and has led more than 500 kaizen events over the course of his practice of Lean. He has been trained that respect for people is the most critical pillar of Lean and he shows it with all people that he works with.

Bob lives in San Jose, CA with his wife and two of his four sons.

Connect with Bob on LinkedIn[a].

[a]https://www.linkedin.com/in/bob-rush-865731

Note from Mark Graban: I noticed Bob's posts on LinkedIn under the banner of "Lean observations from an old guy." The stories and tone completely reminded me of what we're doing in this eBook, so I asked him if I could edit the posts and share them here. Thanks, Bob!

Everyone is an Expert

After being in the Lean world since before the term "Lean" was used (and instead was referred to as World Class Manufacturing), I have seen a number of things over the years that just grab my attention. My sensei has told me numerous times that "There are no Lean experts, only people who have been at it for a longer time." I am now officially one of those that have been at it for a longer time.

I know exactly what he means now. In my new position, I am involved in Lean full time, not as part of my duties, but as my only duty. It is a different view when all you have to look for is waste and problems, yet have no authority to fix them. This reminds me of when I first went into production control, when planners had to get everything through the plant and yet had no authority over anyone. I feel I really became good at getting results by working with people, by helping them solve their problems, and by focusing on the results needed not the methods used. It's what I think Lean is about.

At my new job, I have had the pleasure of dealing with another sensei who prefers to be called friend, not teacher, yet he is clearly both. I have met numerous "experts" who can tell me what the word sensei means but can't tell me what it actually is. I have met people who call themselves "Lean Expert" or "Thought Leader" (or my favorite "Waste Guru"). I have been told by these people why the Japanese systems don't work, why Lean won't work here, no matter where here is, why this system works better or that system fails there, etc. All these statements are usually followed by the words "Here's what it's going to cost you to fix these problems".

One of the associates here took scrap material and used it as a weight to hold a cover in place, eliminating part of the scrap creation itself! The cost of the solution was minuscule compared to the scrap cost. He was not a Lean expert but he was a process expert and solved his own problem. He quickly followed that up by putting a piece of another scrap material in place to eliminate parts from jamming the machine. Was he an expert in that machine? He was as it applies to output. Who knew Lean better in this case, the doer or the experts? The world is full of people who can solve problems if they are allowed to.

Go to your gemba and listen to your experts, they already work for you! You can use outsiders for advice but listen to your own experts for the best results. If you have in-house Lean champions have them partner up with your in-house experts or better yet have them help identify those hidden gems.

I'm Now the Old Guy

As I explained, I have reached the point in my career where I am the old guy, so my observations are from the point of view of someone who has worked in factories and supply chains for well over 30 years now. In my new job, full time Lean, I am working with a wide variety of people, attitudes, educational backgrounds, and temperament. What a ride!

I find the vast majority of people here are looking for help, and in fact are actually now demanding that I help them, usually by teaching them something in the Lean tools. I have worked with associates who have been here one day, and I just got to work with someone who was here from the start of production. I have shown them how to do value stream mapping and root cause analysis. The "5 whys" is a big hit here, as are 5-day Kaizen events, an adaptation of the A3 process for quick fixes, and most importantly, gemba walks.

I am working with an Industrial Engineering Technician to VSM a critical process, and he has taken it over with me being simply an advisor. He just asks me questions now. We started out to just look at one station, and he took over and made it the whole line. He has started weekly gemba meetings to fix the worst station, has gotten buy in from a cross-functional team, and has moved the needle on improvements - just from a few talks and walks. He has fired me up so much that I am pushing for a 5-day Kaizen event in this area, with him as the team leader. We will get fantastic results I am sure, and I am just as sure that the sensei will be impressed by him as well.

I have been working with someone who actually got me this job, and he has taken the modified A3 process (we call it One Point

Lessons) and has his whole group turning in three to five of these per day. Savings are generated, 5S has come alive for these guys, his peers in the department have implemented it, and best of all the senior manager of the department responds on a regular basis with congratulations and with words of wisdom. The same senior manager did a gemba walk along with a group of people I invited to see the three areas in which we did our 5-day Kaizen events. He loved what his group had done, but then he did the coolest thing and that is he made those of us on the tour do something in the way of noise reductions for the associates in this particular area. This is a guy who clearly gets what Lean is about, and does something about it.

Before those of you who know me well try to figure out what happened to the old Bob, I can tell you that there are people here who talk a good game of Lean but then their actions fall well short of being Lean. We have people who are afraid of the factory, so they stay in the bullpen a mere 50 feet from the most exciting place on earth, our production line.

I have run across people that worked here when it was NUMMI and it is clear they just do whatever they are told to do without any of the spark I am used to from people who buy into the Toyota way.

My favorite incident, thus far, though is having an intern tell me why my way of doing time analysis was wrong because I include wait time and everyone knows the only thing that really matters is machine time. Then, he closed out with explaining to me that VSMs are obsolete, that nobody is doing them anymore, and, by the way, the visual factory will make my ways obsolete. Good thing I had a cold drink in my hand or I might have been heartbroken to find all this out. Hopefully, he'll get a chance to learn why I do the things I do instead of just hanging his hat on the process du jour.

Here's to the ones who want to change the way we do things, may they multiply!

My Firefighting Got in the Way of Progress

Those of you who have dealt with me on any Lean journey know that the "Respect for People" portion of Lean is at the heart of what I believe. I firmly believe that, without it, Lean of any consequence would not be possible. I have always said that respect is earned by being involved with people and helping them achieve better results than they could have gotten on their own. But what does that mean?

Respect for people in the way I was taught is that you are expecting more from the people than they do of themselves and that you are willing to coach them to that new level. It means you listen with your ears and mind, not with your mouth. It means you are willing to stop and talk to anyone at any time about any issue that bothers them and to then do something about it. It means, dear manager, that you are here to help the people, not yourself. It also means that they are not simply a number to be utilized.

In my first planning job. I had gone from a shipping clerk to an industrial engineer to a production planner at a very large (then and now) company and was successful in my new planning role. Or so I thought. Enter a new VP/GM who spent two weeks just talking with people and looking at how and where things happened. He quickly figured out that I was the main firefighter and, in my mind, was the reason we could pull off these "miracles" that beat our lead times being pushed through the factory by the sheer will of me. This was not the same thing that was in his mind. He called me into his office on Friday afternoon and told me I was being "loaned out" to another division a thousand miles away. But, what would happen to our factory if I wasn't there? He smiled and said that he thought it would be OK.

I spent six weeks in this different location and helped fixed a few small things from an IE standpoint, but nothing from a planning viewpoint. When I returned to my home plant, I discovered a lot had changed, locations had been consolidated, work groups had been formed, and physical walls had been torn down. The GM toured me through all the changes and explained what was going on, and oh, by the way, did you notice the factory is running a lot quieter and smoother? We ended up at the front lobby and he said quite plainly that I had a choice to make – be a part of this new way or find another job. Easy choice, since I had a small son at the time. He sat me down to explain why he offered me a choice and that was that he saw my potential to add value as much greater than pushing product through the plant. My next stop was at a class on World Class Manufacturing taught by Dr. Richard Schonberger, and the rest is history, as they say.

Lean Without Respect Isn't Lean and Will Fail

The next story took place in the last 18 months or so and involves a government agency and its attempt at implementing Lean. They received funding from their parent organization, and they received donated leadership time from a known expert in cultural change. I had spoken to their leader about Lean, and they had "committed" leadership. So far so good, but, as an outsider, they didn't have the one thing they should have had from the start and that is front line people telling them what the problems were.

They brought in consultants who taught them Lean tools, formed teams and started to do kaizen events, BUT they still didn't listen to the people actually performing the work, nor did this management team consider their customers in any variation of their attempts. The only results that I can see as an outsider is that the workforce is now totally demotivated, the Lean consultants quit and told this entity to not contact them again, and the local government spent thousands of dollars that could have gotten results if it was applied correctly. To get a consultant to quit on you takes a lot – we all love the money, right?

The root cause on this one is very easy. There was no respect for people ever considered by this management team. If I was brought in to lead a Lean implementation here, I would get rid of the anchor draggers, in this case, the management.

RESPECT IS EARNED BY ACTIONS NOT BY A TITLE. Just my opinion.

Learning From an Expensive Mistake

To my racing buddies, we always say you are either on the throttle or you are off the throttle. No race has been won by being off the throttle. Ted Lin, the founder of Lin Engineering, told us to "Play to win, don't play to not lose." Your efforts could have the same results, but the effort and the feelings about that effort are totally different. My sensei has told me repeatedly that there are lessons in everything you do, but the best ones come from a spectacular failure. I have done this as an employee and I have seen it as a Lean consultant.

Early in my career, I was moved around quite a bit in operations. Our VP of operations believed in cross training and in placing talent where it could have an impact. I moved from shipping clerk, to industrial engineer, to production planner, and then to buyer. This was in the days when MRP was first coming on the scene, but we were still on the Kardex system. Yes, that is how old I am. I had a need for a certain electronic component and worked the supplier for a price break and got it. I ordered $1 million worth of this product, and it was delivered as promised on time and to specification. Unfortunately for me, I had transposed numbers on my order and we received a product that was unusable for our needs.

Rather than fire me, the VP told me to find a solution and then to let him know when I did. It took me weeks, but I found a competitor that used this model AND they paid more for the product than we had. I gave them a 3% discount off of their regular price and we made 5% on the material. I more than learned my lesson from that and, to this day, I check numbers very closely.

I am always asked about what causes failures in Lean implementations and, in my experience, the biggest one is Management (with a capital M). But, not just from the lack of commitment, but from both micromanagement and from playing to not lose.

If a company bets their future on Lean, it is easier to try to not lose than it is to try to win. What happens is that the new people aren't allowed to do as much as they could, being limited to safe projects overseen by a manager and/or a Lean leader.

The new person gets micromanaged, I can just hear it now; NO! I said the "I" goes inside the inventory triangle on a VSM, or your data box has to look exactly like this, or here's what your VSM will look when you are done as the teacher draws it on a whiteboard.

If they make their VSM wrong or if the Kaizen event is not held to the exact standards someone else wants, does that make it any less successful? Not really and, if we are truly Lean coaches or champions, we will take these chances as a real learning time and show them where they went wrong or even suggest some solutions but we will let them make more mistakes if we want them to learn. One of the people I have worked with over 10+ years on Lean recently told me that he learned more when he failed and we talked about that failure then when he succeeded and had no idea why it worked. He is now a Lean coach and tells me of some failures he's seeing.

So, I say let your junior people go try something, anything and, if it doesn't work, have them tell you what lesson they learned from it. You can then work on helping them along their Lean journey by teaching them a better way.

The Gleam in Her Eye

I was recently asked to write some directions on gemba walks, and I have to admit I was surprised by the request. I remember my sensei's directions when I asked him about gemba walks: "You just put one foot in front of the other and open your eyes to what is going on around you." I have to admit that I followed the traditional route of looking for waste while on my walks, but I happily discovered that you can find all manners of things to observe, not just waste. Early in my Lean journey, I was told to "stand in circle" to observe a particular process. After 30 minutes, I had three observations and all three were about waste I saw. My sensei suggested I do the exercise over again, this time for four hours of observations. I did the 360 view and I found over 300 things to write about.

The process I had been observing had been through a kaizen event the prior month and there were a number of cool things going on that I noticed the second time. I noticed things upstream and downstream of the process I was observing, and I found one piece flow until a bottleneck on the next station that resulted in a huge buffer stock being built to work around the issue downstream, but the buffer was being supplied in one piece flow until the buffer was full. I saw the material handling and kanban replenishment being done in sync, but the builds were not in sync to the material flows. I saw andon lights that were all green for periods of 30 to 60 minutes but turned red regularly. The biggest lesson I learned was to watch the people, to talk to them whenever I could, and, most importantly, to listen to them.

Over the following year, we performed numerous kaizen events, taught many of the tools we all use to help out, and the plant became the top performer in this corporation's portfolio, going from an annual loss of 7% to net profits of more than 10%. Most important is that this plant supplied Lean champions to the rest of the company for the next three years and they spread the word of Lean. The biggest lesson I learned during this three year period was that Lean was not designed to eliminate waste, it was designed to enhance the value-added portion of these activities via the improvement of the people, processes, and flows through the use of positive tools, not negative tools. People are the main reason we do our Lean processes, they then add more value for our customers.

I very recently did a gemba walk with one of my fellow Lean practitioners, and we went through some of the areas I had held kaizen events in the two previous months. He liked what we had done, but his high point was one of the supervisors that had been involved in the earlier kaizen. This was her first time doing a kaizen event, and it came as a complete surprise to her, at that. Because of our schedules, we have shifts that start on days and hours that are not the normal 8 to 5, Monday through Friday routine. She started her workweek on Wednesday and had to take over the event midway through. She dug in and got herself up to speed quickly and, at the end of the week, her team was as far along as any of the other events. The following week, she made some more changes, and the week after that, and the week after that. She was assigned more processes to supervise and she started changing that area.

When we met up with her on our gemba walk, she asked for help quantifying some of the further work she had done. It was very clear she was enthused about this process, that she felt she owned this process, and that she owed it to her people to get them excited about it, as well. It was very fun stuff and, as we headed to the next area, my cohort told me, "Did you see how excited she was and the gleam in her eyes? How do we do that to everyone?" Indeed how do we do that for everyone?

Lean Champions

After all my years involved in Lean, my favorite title I have come across is "Lean Champion." It seems to encompass all the traits that are critical to the success of a Lean implementation. They have to talk to and teach all levels of an organization, from a trainee on the line to the CEO. They not only have to like that, they have to be excellent at communicating. They have to love working with people and they must know and trust Lean tools.

Of course, they need to know the Lean tools, but more importantly, they have to be able to apply them in many different situations, often at an extremely fast pace. They really need to have that hands-on experience of having done this for years, not just getting certified or taking a class, but actually having used the tools and having shown people how to use them. My sensei has told me that his generation (the first generation of Toyota consultants) believe that 30 years of experience is the mark of someone who can be a great sensei. In that vein, I believe that a great Lean Champion must have at least ten years of experience in all phases of Lean.

I think that kaizen experience as a team member, as a Lean coach, and as a team leader is critical to their success. The truly exceptional ones I have worked with learned from the masters of kaizen. My experience says that Shingijutsu-trained Lean champions tend to be stronger at kaizen than those trained by others, simply because kaizen is at the heart of the Shingijutsu way. I am not knocking anyone's training in kaizen, just noting what I have seen in my travels. The good ones know that kaizen is a way of life and that every day there are many opportunities to improve. When they get to a 5-day kaizen event, they handle multiple teams and get results in all of them.

I also have seen the truly great Lean Champions have worked their way up through an organization to learn various jobs and functions, and they have a solid understanding of how those functions interrelate and how they should mesh together. They can then combine that experience with their Lean knowledge to ask the right questions that will lead an organization to real change. The great ones I have been around got their ego satisfaction from the results of the TEAMS they are working with, not the individuals.

The final trait is that they all have the heart of a champion, they have to excel, they have to make people around them better, and they hate to lose at anything. When I've worked with groups that included multiple Lean Champions, they each wanted to get the best results and they drove their peers to higher levels of achievements. At one multi-plant company, we held synchronized events around the world and, every day at wrap up, the Lean Champions held their own conference call to compare notes, results, and more importantly, they shared what they had done that was different than what they had done before. At the end of the event, we discovered that the seven Lean Champions had bought something from the area of the world they were from and the one that they thought had come up with the most innovative solution was awarded the prizes. The CEO got wind of it and added three vacation days to all seven of their vacation pools as a way of saying "you guys' rock," his exact words.

My First Kaizen Event

I want to share some of the story of my first Kaizen event with Shingijutsu. I was a consultant to a supplier of one of Shingijutsu's biggest successes. I read everything I could on this kaizen stuff, which at this time was really not much, and studied hard. I stayed up the night before the event to make sure I got this stuff down pat because after all, you can learn everything from a book, right? WRONG!

The first day started at 8 a.m. and, by 8:15, I was pretty drowsy and managed to fall asleep. Keep in mind this is an event paid for by the CUSTOMER of my CLIENT. Oh man, I was embarrassed and knew I was in for real trouble.

Instead of yelling or screaming at me, the Sensei said, through his interpreter, "I hope you give discounts for the sleeping time." The room laughed, as did I, and then the sensei said it was time to pick up the pace and we would go to the gemba. The fun really started then and I discovered a whole new way of looking at things. We did things that the sponsor's people thought were impossible, we changed so many things, and I got to deal with all levels of their organization.

At the end of the week, I was hooked and have been on this path since. The sensei that week is still my sensei after all this time. I thank him for making my journey so interesting and so fruitful, although he will never read this (but his interpreter will). Sensei – I am giving back just as you requested and I am having fun just as I wanted!

How Did I Get Here?

I really never thought about giving back to the Lean community in this way, I really thought I would do it one on one and in person. In my training, it was made abundantly clear that Lean is a "pay it forward" environment and that I was more than obligated to help people understand Lean and the tools used in our journey to PRACTICE LEAN. Once again, I thank Mark Graban for changing my view from "implementing Lean" to "I now practice Lean," and I am attempting to get others to practice Lean as well.

Well, how did I get here? (with apologies to the Talking Heads)

When I was discharged from the military, I relocated to Silicon Valley and, at that distant time, it was just starting to be called that. I worked in construction and, during a layoff period over the winter, I went to work at a high tech company as a shipping clerk. Compared to construction, the electronics industry was easy and, in those days, hard work was recognized and rewarded. In a very short period of time, I fell in love with the work and the industry and, even back then, technology fascinated me, no matter how crude by today's standards.

All of the positions I held were as an individual contributor, so I really did just my job as I had been told or taught. There was no standard work at that time, but every now and then we would be told about "policy and procedures," usually when one of us had made a mistake that caused our manager some kind of aggravation. We all came to dread the "P&P" reviews that our boss held on a more and more regular basis as the company grew larger. It was during this time that I was lucky enough to attend a 5-day session with Dr. Richard Schonberger, who was teaching companies about "World Class Manufacturing" and I was hooked. It was a very simple process and, if you did it right, you would see results like a 40% reduction in WIP. What I didn't know at the time was that this was my first exposure to the Toyota Production System. I used these simple WCM methods to really work out some issues in production, but it really wasn't designed to work for the whole company. Along came a book titled *The Machine That Changed the World*[53] in 1990, and suddenly WCM looked like just the beginning.

What I didn't realize at that time was that this methodology would become my life's work and I was lucky enough to have managers that supported my experiments. I also had clients that had been exposed to this new thing called "Lean manufacturing" from their customers such as Boeing and Danaher. So, I was helping people get better at manufacturing while I was getting better at managing manufacturing improvements. As I sit here more than 25 years later, I can tell you that, for me, the two things I love the most about Lean are the relationships with the people and that you continue to learn every day about Lean and how it can work and fail.

I wrote earlier about my first kaizen event so I won't repeat that story, but it took me several years to really understand that Kaizen is NOT a 5-day event; it is an event that should be occurring every minute. I am fortunate enough to have had a sensei who saw something in me that I didn't see in myself, managers and companies that wanted changes for the best of both the people and the company, and when I started I truly didn't know what I didn't know so I went and did things that more experienced people said could not be done.

---

[53]http://amzn.to/1neZpua

I practice kaizen daily and I am starting to get others to do so as well.

One of my fights throughout my career has been that Lean "works for cars, but it won't work for XXXXX" with XXXXX being whatever product the company I was working with made, and I know that's not true. I've seen Lean work, and sometimes fail, in many industries. I've read about Kevin Meyer's journey at Specialty Silicone Fabricators, a medical products company that is successful even after his exit. I read Mark Graban's articles and blogs about healthcare, and again I see successes. At this point in my career, I don't know the limits of Lean, and I hope to see it applied in many more situations. In fact, I hope the next step of my personal Lean journey is into the great frontier of government! If you are in government and want some advice on Lean journeys, please connect with me and I will help in any way I can. Note that if you contact me the price of admission is that you have to know who your customers are and you have to give back to the Lean world freely.

I want to thank some people for their encouragement for my posts on LinkedIn. First, Keven Meyer and Ron Pereira from Gemba Academy who contacted me about a possible podcast and Mark Graban of KaiNexus[54] who encouraged me to write more, who asked me to participate in this book, and who has helped remind me to always be practicing Lean. All three have had an impact on the latest stage of my Lean journey and, in case I haven't said it before, try the Gemba Academy[55] training series of online videos and DVDs - they actually work. I used them at a small company I worked at and they worked there.

Thanks to all the people I am practicing Lean with now but, in particular, to the younger people I am helping out with their Lean journey. You guys make my days and keep me young. Now go out there and have some fun!

---

[54]http://www.kainexus.com/
[55]http://www.gembaacademy.com/

Chapter Nine - Samuel Selay

Samuel Selay is the Continuous Improvement Manager within his organization in the Marine Corps at Camp Pendleton. He has worked in the field of supply chain and logistics for the past 12 years. For the last six years, he has managed his organization's Continuous Process Improvement/Lean Six Sigma (LSS)Program. During this timeframe, he has facilitated/mentored 28 completed LSS projects or kaizen events. Additionally, he mapped and standardized 36 processes, conducted 90 process audits, and implemented his organization's Quality Management System, resulting in a 20% reduction in shipping defects.

Along with project leadership, he has instructed and certified 481 employees as LSS Yellow Belts and 121 employees as LSS Green Belts. He is a certified Lean Six Sigma Black Belt from the University of San Diego, a certified Logistics Technician (CLT) from the Manufacturing Skills Standards Council, and a certified ISO 9001:2008 Internal Auditor from the World Wide Quality Network. He holds a BS in Management Studies from the University of Maryland University College and an MBA in Management and Strategy from Western Governors University.

Sadly, Sam passed away in 2018. We miss him deeply. Read more[56]

Learning Continuous Improvement: Reflections on Practicing CI in the Marine Corps

Over the last six years, I have had the great privilege and opportunity to learn and practice continuous improvement within the Marine

---

[56]https://www.leanblog.org/2018/10/thinking-of-samuel-selay/

Corps. The Marine Corps has an umbrella approach called Continuous Process Improvement, which encompasses the methodologies of Lean, Six Sigma, and Theory of Constraints. As I transition into the private sector, I have been reflecting on the valuable lessons I learned and would like to share them as a way to give back, just as my mentors taught me to pay it forward.

Cultural Roadblocks to Deploying Continuous Improvement

The road to pursuing excellence in continuous improvement within the Marine Corps has not been easy, and I had to unlearn some behaviors that were counter to what I now understand true continuous improvement to be.

The Marine Corps is, by design, a command-and-control, top-down structured organization. The resulting culture has posed challenges for continuous improvement professionals like myself. For example, in improvement teams, lower-ranking individuals are timid because they are not accustomed to voicing the true current condition, out of fear of retribution. The same is true in the classroom setting when talking about problems that hinder operational excellence.

A countermeasure I put in place was a set of Rapid Improvement Event / Project team meeting rules. These include:

1. Everyone on the team speaks professionally and with an equal voice
2. Respect all ideas and ideas, once verbalized, become the property of the team and not the individual
3. Check your rank at the door (in order for everyone to have an equal voice)

In addition, the one rule I establish before coaching a team is that I will not allow the sponsor to suggest "solutions." I have to be very tactful when having this talk with the sponsor who is usually a senior leader and who is used to making all the big decisions.

The reason for this rule is that it's disrespectful to tell an improvement team what to do. If the senior leader has an idea and will not budge, I tell them there is apparently no need for a cross-functional team and that he or she has no need for the team to solve the problem because the sponsor has the "solution."

This is a large organizational cultural change that must take place.

Also, senior leaders get too focused on results. Yes, continuous improvement will yield big results via problem solving, but there is another side to the coin that is equally important. The second reason for problem solving is to facilitate learning and build capabilities within the organization via the problem solving process.

Lessons Learned from Japan

I had the honor and privilege of working and living in Japan between 2005 and 2007. My time in Japan was long before I was ever exposed to continuous improvement, but there was something different about the culture of Japan compared to the United States.

Unfortunately, while practicing CI in the Marine Corps, I was never exposed to what "Respect for People" was. It was never taught in any of the training I went through. Even going through Black Belt training through the University of San Diego didn't introduce me to what respect for people meant.

It wasn't until I disciplined myself to a journey of self-learning through reading, listening to podcasts, watching webinars, reading blogs, and applying as much as I can, that I learned what respect for people was.

Now, I have a good grasp on the concept of respect for people based on the last two years of dedicated learning. Now, I can understand what the difference was between the culture of Japan and the United States.

First, "respect for humanity" is a better translation that more clearly represents what I was exposed to for nearly two years in Japan.

Some key takeaways I can still remember are:

1. An attitude that reflects a sense of pride, admiration, and es-

teem for others.

2. Pride in the community and country. I was taught not to spit, throw trash, or litter. When going to restaurants or certain homes, you were expected to take off your shoes. If given chopsticks, you were expected to use them.
3. Demeanor of joy and happiness in the workplace. While in Japan I went on several tours of factories and witnessed people on the front lines being delighted in their work.

What I have done based on these key takeaways are:

1. Create an environment which is conducive to sharing and implementing improvement ideas within all ranks of the organization. My CI team within the Marine Corps has created and implemented many great ideas based on Alan Robinson and Dean Schroeder books *Ideas Are Free*[57] and *The Idea-Driven Organization*[58] and Mark Graban's *Lean Hospitals*[59].
2. Make myself an equal to those who are of lesser rank when I feel it is hindering great ideas. I will put rank aside and talk person to person on a first name basis.
3. Go to the gemba, ask why work is being done the way it is, and show respect from a curiosity perspective. This allows for deep conversation about improvements.
4. Lead with respect by following a servant leadership model. The approach I take is "Follow me and we'll figure this out together."

Practicing Continuous Improvement

When I first started practicing CI, I was a "tool head" and ended up wasting my time and my team's time by trying to use as many tools as possible. But, over time, I have learned the problem solving process, and I only develop, test, and apply countermeasures to address the root cause(s).

---

[57]http://amzn.to/1PMCrBg
[58]http://amzn.to/1PMCtsF
[59]http://amzn.to/1WXHODj

Next, I had to learn the hard way that being a doer, a belt, and a facilitator hindered the growth and development of the problem solving capabilities within my organization. For the last two to three years, I have been working on being a teacher, coach, and mentor. I have learned to lead with questions, and only teach when I know the other person doesn't understand the mechanics behind a tool.

Also, I also had to learn that my inability to stop and listen and ask Socratic questions hindered the output of the improvement teams I was facilitating. Additionally, I feel that I have only scratched the surface of knowledge in the field of CI. I subscribe to Malcolm Gladwell's view of 10,000 hours or 10 years to mastery. As I continue to learn and grow in the field, I find Albert Einstein to be 100 percent accurate in which he said, "The more I learn, the more I realize how much I don't know."

Problem Solving Process

The Continuous Process Improvement journey for the majority of the USMC began in the spring of 2006. Secretary of the Navy Dr. Winter, with his industrial background, was the catalyst for transformation in the Department of the Navy using Lean Six Sigma. Given Lean Six Sigma was the approach, the scientific methodology that is utilized is Define-Measure-Analyze-Improve-Control (DMAIC).

Over the last six years, I have found people to get too wrapped up in the tools within DMAIC. Within the last year, a countermeasure I have taken and used within my organization is creating and implementing an eight-step problem solving process (very similar to the "Toyota Business Practice"), which works to help people think more holistically about problems. Additionally, the eight-step problem solving process helps people to think through DMAIC more cyclically versus the traditional linear model.

The eight steps are:

1. Define and break down the problem
2. Set a target condition
3. Grasp the current condition

4. Conduct root cause analysis
5. Develop and test countermeasures
6. Refine and finalize countermeasures
7. Standardize best practices
8. Measure process performance

I hope that everyone can take away something from my lessons learned.

Chapter Ten - David Haigh

David works at Johnson & Johnson Canada, the largest consumer healthcare company in Canada, and part of the Johnson & Johnson family of companies.

David started his career in the telecommunications sector, working at Research In Motion, and has worked in Lean and Six Sigma in the telecommunications, construction, automotive, consumer packaged goods, and healthcare sectors in Canada and globally since 2003.

David has a BASc in Mechanical Engineering from the University of Waterloo, an MBA from Wilfrid Laurier University, and his Lean Six Sigma Master Black Belt certificate from Villanova University.

David and his wife Cindy currently reside in Toronto, Ontario, Canada with their son. He can be found on Twitter @Leanlearnlead[a] and LinkedIn[b].

[a]http://twitter.com/Leanlearnlead
[b]http://ca.linkedin.com/in/david-haigh-3136812

Leadership's perception of what Lean is, and what Lean isn't, completely drives the success of Lean.

I wish I knew that when I first started my personal Lean journey.

Why do I start at this point? Because I've seen a lot done, and said, in the name of "Lean." I've seen it chosen from a smörgåsbord of tools to address a specific problem without sustaining a solution. I've seen it "deployed" (and later undeployed when its leader left). And, I've seen it live, and breathe, and grow.

Leadership's perception of Lean is always the starting point.

Lean From The Source

When I first started my personal Lean journey, I didn't have "a perception" of Lean. I was still a student, working at a summer job at Toyota Motor Manufacturing in Cambridge, Ontario. I had the benefit of having Toyota engineers take me under their wing while we launched the Camry Solara coupe. This was 1998. The Toyota Way by Jeff Liker wasn't in print yet.

At the employee orientation, the plant trainer stood at the front of the auditorium, where I, along with hundreds of other new employees, were given two very simple lessons:

1. If there is a problem, you must first ask: is it a problem with a) the part, or b) the specification?
2. If there is a problem, raise your hand and get help.

That was it. We weren't told what a problem is. We weren't told how to solve a problem. We were simply told to get help if there was a problem and determine if the problem was due to the part or specification.

There is a real beauty to that kind of training. The first instruction helped us sort out what kind of problem it was - design or execution. That helped with figuring out whom to talk with to get things fixed.

The second instruction was even more powerful. You might not start off as a strong problem solver. But, you work with someone who is. And they work with expert problem solvers. You will get the help you need to solve the problem. All you have to do is say there is a problem. At that moment, Toyota unleashed hundreds of new "problem finders" into their plant.

That didn't mean that they took the problem away from you - not at all! I took on problems, with my mentor's help, and I solved them. My mentor pointed me to other people to talk with, in maintenance, manufacturing, road testing, final inspection, suppliers. They asked me how I would solve the problem. They wanted my ideas. They encouraged me to experiment and to try things out in a safe environment. After all, we were dealing with expensive luxury vehicles with hundreds of complex and interrelated systems. Some problems,

I brought to solution quickly. Some problems took weeks. Others took months. But in the end, they were all solved, and I was asked to make a presentation to plant leadership. My mentors coached me through the A3s required for the presentation, which I crafted with scissors, white-out, and photocopiers through a dozen revisions. When I got the "ringi-sho" - the signature of my department VP on my A3 showing that they approved my work - it was humbling!

(An A3 is Toyota's version of a report on a page, although how you build an A3 is just as important as the content on the page. John Shook does it justice in his book *Managing to Learn*[60].)

That was my first perception of Lean. It was amazing! And what was Toyota's leadership perception of Lean? Smarter folks than I have attempted to describe it - but I will put it in the words of Taiichi Ohno: Lean is the Thinking Production System. It is about how you think, every day. That is what I witnessed and experienced at Toyota.

Isn't Lean Just a Bunch of Tools?

My first practice with Lean, on my own, was five years later at a small automotive manufacturer in Windsor, Ontario, Canada (call it "Company B"). I was joining as an "Organizational Improvement Specialist" - shorthand for "someone to assist the president with special projects." The president of this company had received advice that to sustain cost improvements and efficiency gains, there needed to be an in-house presence to help implement solutions, train employees, and ensure the strategy was executed. So, I was hired. When I inquired about their thoughts on continuous improvement, their response was simple: Whatever tools are needed to solve a problem, that's what should be deployed.

This company had already gone through a great change. Months before I arrived, they had relocated all of their manufacturing from Canada to Mexico. Globally, they were doing the same, moving production from Germany to Hungary and China. They were negotiating consignment deals with their suppliers to reduce inventory carrying

[60]http://amzn.to/1KVf9rF

costs. The Mexican production site was adopting the Toyota Production System (TPS) through "single-minute exchange of dies" (SMED), 5S, layered process audits, and one-piece-flow assembly lines.

When one of our customers approached us to participate in Six Sigma training, subsidized by them, we leaped at the opportunity. Our plant leadership saw it as a complement to their TPS culture. Our engineers and sales leaders were more skeptical - why were we being asked to participate from outside of manufacturing? Wasn't Six Sigma and Lean just a manufacturing thing? Our president, however, was keen - so we got on board.

When we started to apply Lean, we put our newly minted Six Sigma Black Belt, Matt, against our problem: Accounts Receivable. Certain customers, including the one that had trained us, were sometimes late with their payments, as long as six months. The project was selected because Matt had worked in customer service, and had a special talent for collections. As his mentor, I coached Matt on how to use the tools to frame up the problem differently, get buy-in for a new process, and create early visibility on collection issues. The Six Sigma trainers were thrilled, everyone was excited, except for one caveat...

We weren't getting paid on our oldest overdue accounts! No accounts were "aging" into that six-month overdue bucket. While the new process was working, the accounts that were already in that bucket before we started were still stuck there.

I can remember Matt approaching me, and saying, "Y'know David, I can clear out the old accounts, but it won't be through using any Lean or Six Sigma tools."

I had to give him credit – he had addressed the root cause of aging accounts, and made sure collections would never accumulate to six months again. But to clear a really old charge it would take a personal visit, lunch with a couple of beers, and some schmoozing, to get that cheque written by the customer and that old invoice off the books. There wasn't anything in the Lean or Six Sigma training about that!

When presented with this option, I was concerned - what would this tactic say about our Lean culture? Wouldn't we be compromising people's opinion about Lean when we solved a problem the "business as usual" way? Would they have the impression that Lean only works in theory? However, when the specific situation was explained to me by Finance and Sales - and trust me, I needed it explained a bunch of times - it really seemed like this was the best solution.

So we sent off our Black Belt, Matt, expense account in hand, and following a three-day road trip, he came back smiling with the paid invoice.

Did our problem get solved? You bet! The problem didn't come back either - the Lean process worked and good ownership ensured that. But, there was always a sense in the organization that the reason Matt was successful was due more to his strong customer relationship skills than Lean.

We realized that sometimes, to solve a problem, you have quick wins, 'Just Do Its' that you can execute without delay and significant investment. Our Lean work took on that flavour, which, in hindsight, was a good thing - it showed we had a bias for action and for getting things done.

On the other hand, for our Black Belt, Matt, there were side effects. Instead of evolving his reputation into a trusted advisor, someone who could work analytics effectively and problem-solve, the situation had reinforced his reputation as someone who can work his relationships, not someone who was strong analytically or as a problem-solver. When it came to the relationship aspect of solving problems, Matt did it best. But when it came to Lean, there were moments I thought we had made a bad choice in selecting him as our pilot Black Belt.

However - Matt didn't let that define him. The same techniques he used to get invoices paid and strengthen customer relationships, he also parleyed into effective engagement and change management skills. He was smooth! Matt could draw out quiet employees in work-shops, manage conflict really well, and with the charm of his smile convince folks of a solution and get their buy-in. It wasn't the skills they taught in Black Belt training (he still sought out mentoring when running a Design of Experiment or Hypothesis Test), but it's helped me to realize that the soft skills of being a Black Belt are just as important, if not more so than the analytical skills.

So the perception of our Lean culture had evolved from a tools-based approach to a problems-based approach. Lean was seen as a way to solve problems! We complemented our initial Lean work with what Six Sigma had to offer and it became the prototype that the headquarters leveraged when they wanted to deploy Lean globally. Did it become embedded everywhere, the de facto way of solving and preventing problems? Well, that took some more time...

Financial Waste Isn't Always Muda

Lean in an organization always evolves, and sometimes, that evolution is a validation of the good work that is done locally. After the successful deployment and Lean journey for the North America operations, the firm I was working for had promoted me and extended my scope to start a global Lean deployment.

I had been tasked to help spearhead Lean implementations at all of Company B's sites throughout six countries across three continents. Not only was it a fantastic way to earn frequent flyer miles, it gave me wonderful perspectives on different cultures, different countries, how getting manufacturing jobs can transform small towns and people's lives, and an appreciation of how good things are in Canada.

I got to see roads in eastern Europe, with potholes so big I could swear they would swallow a truck. I walked across borders where it felt like a sniper might be tracking my every step. I celebrated a job well done in Mexico and found out that, with enough tequila, I can sing folk songs in Spanish. I realized that I could have a real tough argument with a colleague, but afterward be treated to a beer and gain respect for holding my ground. And, I realized that everywhere you go, people want to do a good job, serve their customer, get paid, and provide for their family. For a young guy raised in rural Canada, it meant a huge broadening of my perspective.

One project involved setting up a new manufacturing site (a "green field" site) in Ukraine. The plant manager wanted it set up "in a Lean way." The plant had four walls, a floor, and a ceiling – we had to figure out where the equipment would be located, how material would flow, and how the plant would operate. We designed the shop floor layout from a blank slate and created a Lean material flow, including where to locate the loading docks for inbound and outbound freight to reduce unnecessary transportation waste. The work didn't stop with the material flow. We ensured that Lean training was part of every employees first day on the job, coached line leaders on problem solving, and helped employees spot waste wherever they worked.

One day, as part of the plant start up, our CFO approached me, filled with excitement. He had been negotiating the procurement of manufacturing equipment for the new site. He was thrilled that he had avoided a bunch of waste when negotiating the final agreement for the purchase. When I asked how, he proudly stated that he had saved thousands of dollars not buying spare parts for the equipment. A little voice in my head told me this could be a bad idea... but, before I reacted, I asked him to take me through why not buying spare parts was a good decision.

"Because we can get parts shipped to the site in 24 hours; our vendor has committed to it! We don't have to carry the cost of spare parts."

I paused – one of the longest pauses in my career – and thought about my options. There was no way I could influence this decision – it was taken, the vendor was paid. I knew in my gut that this decision was putting our operations and flow at risk, but it would be difficult to prove in advance. So, I decided to wait. Maybe it would work out.

The first breakdown happened during a ramp-up for a launch. The customer's clock was ticking - they needed our products to support a pilot build. The production equipment failed during the ramp-up. We contacted the vendor for the spare part... it turned out they didn't have it in stock. It would take them time to get it back in stock.

First 24 hours went by, then 48, then 72 hours. The part finally arrived but was held up in customs crossing the border. This dragged on and on. The customer was furious and threatened huge fines for being down during a pilot build.

Eventually, we got the spare part and were able to fulfill the order.

When I met the CFO the next time, to his huge credit, he was contrite and humbled. He remembered boasting about the amazing savings he had wrought for not buying spare parts. But, he had the presence of mind, and the personal accountability, to see the impact of his decision – he had traded off financial savings against satisfying the customer.

He chose to see it as an opportunity for learning – that eliminating waste always has to be in the eyes of the customer, not through a financial lens. He immediately wrote the cheque for the rest of the spare parts and had the courage to use this example about how he had personally learned about Lean, and what it really meant to eliminate waste. He would joke about it more than once over a beer and used Lean thinking when planning a huge ERP implementation so that it sustained the Lean processes already in place.

Lean had moved from a bunch of tools to a way to solve problems, to a way to keep our customers satisfied in the least waste way. That meant trade-offs; that meant putting the customer first; that meant making tough decisions; that meant going to the gemba* and raising the profile of our manufacturing plants. It also meant that we were relentless about describing the value-add of Lean, across many dimensions - the reduction of defects, shortening lead time, reducing operating expense, developing our employees and communicating all of that good work.

(gemba – shop floor – "where the music plays" and where all Lean activities should be initially focused)

You Can Use Lean to Grow

I had moved from being a student, to an internal champion for Lean, to a global champion for Lean, working across multiple sites and influencing leadership. Eventually, the benefit of earning air miles wasn't enough, so I decided to find another opportunity where I could work in Lean but stay closer to home. I found a great opportunity at my next job.

I was hired at a billion-dollar company (call it "Company C"), which had just been created from the merger of three multi-million dollar companies. The company leadership had already experienced some growing pains from the merger from a process perspective.

Something as simple as paying vendors on time had become a mysterious process. Invoices and receipts were getting lost and vendors weren't getting paid. The situation came to a head when the local power utility put a notice on the door, announcing that the electricity would be cut off that day. We were a billion dollar company that had forgotten how to pay a bill. The CFO realized the issue and leveraged my experience in sizing up the problem and driving rounds of improvement, including our first transactional kaizen blitz workshop*, to streamline our payment systems and get a handle on our accounts payable.

(For transactional processes, visualizing the process becomes very critical to help identify the waste; a transactional kaizen workshop first starts with that visualization, identifies waste, and then moves into identifying solutions and countermeasures to the root causes of the waste.)

From that learning, the president put the Lean team against every process in the company, asking what was our process landscape and what was the maturity of those processes? With steady rounds of input and feedback, we drove sustained waves of improvement to reduce cycle time, to improve quality, and to reduce rework and waste. The entire company was empowered to think about how to put their customer first and come together as one company. The merger realized its value proposition a year ahead of schedule.

When there were thorny problems in parts of the product and segment mix, the company president reached out to the Lean specialists to better understand and characterize the problem. That meant shining a light on parts of the business that generated loss and created waste, but no one wanted to talk about it. To the president's credit, he made the environment a safe one to share those issues and to help come up with novel solutions. I hadn't seen Lean used to drive growth in this way; it's opened my eyes to the possibilities of using Lean to create better plans, better serve customers, and grow.

Leaders transition, especially the good ones, and a new president joined our organization. His perception of Lean and the value proposition it brought was similar - however, he saw the opportunity in a more granular level. Gone was the burning platform of the merger;

improvements took on a more granular nature, focused on key pain points in the organization.

By virtue of this work, the president tapped the Lean specialists and empowered their employees to leverage Lean thinking whenever a massive undertaking was being started, to get the process thinking right, iron out the kinks, and put their customer first. IT upgrade? New channel to market? Involve the Lean folks to help understand the situation, get things right the first time, and make a bigger impact.

The president also supported taking Lean broader, to help engage customers in partnerships that made their processes more efficient. We got to delight dozens of customers and start relationships that thrive to this day. It also drove support for developing our employees - future generations of experts that could lead improvements in their areas.

Don't Forget Your Lean Value Proposition

Driving improvement, in that kind of environment, when you have so much leadership support, can mean that you take the value proposition of Lean for granted. I got behind the big initiatives, the big momentum, and employee development - but didn't put the results front and center. With the president at the time, that wasn't a big deal - he was fully bought in and supported it. But when, out of interest, I had shared with him the dollar impact of the work, he was stunned; it had totaled in the millions of dollars just on one initiative.

In hindsight, especially with future leaders, the financial impact was an area I would have continued to focus on.

Now, the pure Lean practitioners may cry out, Lean isn't just about cost savings; after all, I never saw a cost savings chart at Toyota. All true!

But as a practitioner of Lean, you have to read your culture. Some organizations have a very strong financial bent. Financial results, including cost savings and revenue, aren't going to suddenly stop being important simply because you're starting a Lean journey. Those results don't tell the whole story; but without those results, without the complete story being available and bought into, your Lean deployment is vulnerable.

And that's what the Lean deployment at Company C was. It was vulnerable to change.

In quick succession, two changes happened in the organization that exposed that vulnerability. Those changes were innocuous and can happen to any organization. First, we got a new president. Second, I was moved into a different department, one that aligned better, at least on paper, to the value-add Lean can provide (from Finance to Supply Chain).

But, with the new president, and moving the responsibility for Lean to a different department, combined with the vulnerability our deployment had around not keeping financial results front and center, the mold was cast.

Instead of a story being about sustained cultural improvement, results for our customers, financial benefits, and development for our employees - the story became about butts in seats for Lean training. Instead of a story about cross-enterprise impact, which was well embraced by leadership, it was a story about Supply Chain improvements.

Leadership's perception of Lean was open territory. Old perceptions and biases from other experiences with Lean came out of the woodwork and were accepted, such as "we're too busy to do continuous improvement," "these always turn into a make-work project," "this doesn't work in our department," "this won't help me meet my financial objectives," and then finally, the death-knell for any Lean journey, "this isn't a priority for us."

It's important, in those moments, to reflect on the bigger picture. I'm pleased to note that more broadly, Company C is reinvesting in Lean throughout the manufacturing organization. There are other really talented practitioners in the company who are making great improvements and customers are benefiting from it. There are new Lean leaders emerging every day, taking Lean beyond the borders of the organization and influencing customers, patients, and suppliers towards better outcomes. I've grown, in ways that traveling to other countries never would have facilitated.

Leadership's perception of what Lean is, and what Lean isn't, completely drives the success of Lean. That's the lesson I've learned - and I hope that you'll learn during your organizational and personal Lean journeys.

Chapter Eleven – Joseph Swartz

Joseph E. Swartz is the Administrative Director of Business Transformation for Franciscan Alliance, a group of 14 hospitals in Indiana and Illinois. He has been leading continuous improvement efforts for more than 20 years, including ten years in healthcare.

Joe is a co-author of the book *Seeing David in the Stone: Finding and Seizing Great Opportunities*[a] *(Leading Books Press)*. Joe has also co-authored the book, **Healthcare Kaizen: Engaging Front-Line Staff in Sustainable Continuous Improvements*[b], with Mark Graban, which was awarded the 2014 Shingo Research and Professional Publication award. He also co-authored *The Executive Guide to Healthcare Kaizen[c] (Productivity Press).

Joe consulted from 1993 to 2005, working in automotive engineering, semiconductor manufacturing, industrial product manufacturing, pharmaceutical manufacturing, and aerospace assembly.

Joe studied Electrical Engineering at Cleveland State University as well as Management at Purdue University, where he graduated as a Krannert Scholar for academic excellence in their master's program. He lives in Indianapolis, Indiana with his three children.

You can find Joe on Twitter[d] and on LinkedIn[e].

[a]http://amzn.to/1Se2Qyd
[b]http://amzn.to/1LewvA0
[c]http://amzn.to/1LewwUt
[d]https://twitter.com/joekaizeneer
[e]https://www.linkedin.com/in/swartzjoe

Go To the Coalface

Clouds of dust and chunks of coal were hurtling through the air. I was standing within a few yards of the coalface 800 feet below the surface. The coalface was lit with the brilliant light of high-powered bulbs. A big fan directing dust from either side of the coalface was blowing cold air currents from the depths of the mine across my face. The earth floor was shaking as the giant continuous cutter with large protruding carbide teeth, ripped at the coalface, sending seven tons of coal per minute to the shuttle car. Every few minutes, a 70-ton shuttle car filled with coal moved past, brushing perilously close to me.

As I stood watching the coal continuously flowing like a stream off the face, I reflected on how we ended up at the coalface. It was a Saturday morning, November 12, 1994. We were in shaft number 16 of the Sasol Company, south of Johannesburg, South Africa. Earlier that year, apartheid ended, Nelson Mandela was elected President, and the economic boycott was lifted. Suddenly, many South African companies, whose markets had been protected during the boycott, were faced with foreign competition. Sasol, which had been founded and supported by the former government to develop fuel oil from low-grade coal, feared an oncoming crisis as the country began importing low-cost oil. They needed to quickly reduce costs in order to be competitive.

I was fresh out of graduate school and had joined my dad, Jim Swartz, in his independent consulting business. Prior to consulting, he had been the general manager of worldwide production control for Delco Electronics (a General Motors company) and learned Lean from a variety of Japanese companies. He was modeling how to practice Lean, and I was taking copious notes. This was one of my first jobs with him and, more than 20 years later, this engagement is still viscerally imprinted in my brain.

The noise was deafening. Jim yelled at the site foreman, "When the cutter breaks down, how long might it be down?" Screaming back, the foreman said, "It can be down for hours. Just last week it was down for eight hours." Jim leaned into me, saying, "That's about 3,360 tons of coal that didn't get cut." Knowing the marginal return on a ton of coal, I said, "That's quite an opportunity cost."

Several months earlier, the managing director of Sasol Mining Operations appointed a team to find ways to reduce costs enough to warrant continued operations. After focusing primarily on supporting operations, the improvement team found savings of about $1.7 million, mostly in labor and inventory reductions. But, this was far short of what the organization needed.

We were in a weeklong rapid improvement event. During the first three days, we reviewed the work the team was doing to improve productivity by streamlining work and then they planned to cut employees. During the previous evening, we had dinner with the managing director at his home. He talked about the productivity improvement work and he mentioned that the mine could sell more if it could produce more and that his long-term objective was to increase sales dollars per person. Jim asked him numerous questions about his five-year plan.

After we left his house, Jim said, "That conversation changes everything. They're going down the wrong path." He said the work the improvement team was doing could harm the managing director's longer-term goals. He said that for the organization's best interest we have to change the improvement team's focus to increasing the rate at which they cut coal with the same resources. He added, "We need to go to the coalface first thing in the morning." It was our focus on continually searching for the highest leverage opportunities that lead us to where we were standing – at the coalface. This was the "gemba" – where the creation of value starts for Sasol.

A cutting operator stood before us. Jim said, "Is there a way to cut coal faster?" He replied, "Yes, we could. If leadership would just listen to us and trust us we could show them how to cut more coal." We brainstormed a plan with him and several others working in the mine to reduce downtime, and also to cut coal faster during the uptime.

"Did they get everything cleaned up?" a man said as he walked past us. "Yes, but it took awhile," the manager said. "What happened?" I asked. "We had an accident two weeks ago," the manager replied. "It was during a shift change and we had 84 people down in shaft 16 when a cutter hit a gas pocket and a spark initiated an explosion that depleted the mine of oxygen." He paused. "No one survived," he said. "It was one of the biggest disasters we've had."

Jim and I looked at each other with wide eyes. It was one of those moments you don't forget, as if a bus had just passed by inches from my head. I looked for the exit and all I saw were dark shiny mine walls in every direction. We politely got out of the mine as quickly as we could.

Once out of the mine, we discussed a new plan. In the analysis, we discovered that downtime averaged 13%. Analysis showed that 60% of downtime was caused by a lack of repair parts. Although they maintained a spare for every part they used, the repair cycle time was so long that 40% of the time, by the time a part broke, the spare repair part had not returned from being repaired at the machine shop outside the mines. An analysis of the parts repair process revealed that although average repair time per part was just four hours, the average part took 16 days to be repaired. By reducing the time to repair to two days, they would be able to increase uptime from 87% to 95%, thus increasing marginal return by $27 million per year, which was one third of the five-year goal the managing director was going after.

Not only did they recognize the impact that reduced downtime could have on the future of the company, they also found higher meaning because in order to achieve the savings in the supporting operations they were going to lay off people. With the new focus on reducing downtime, they could save jobs.

The improvement efforts were successfully implemented and six months later they had made a huge impact on Sasol and on the secure tenure of the managing director.

Lessons Learned:

- Go to the Coalface – where the value is being added – appreciate and ask those who work at the coalface to help create improvement opportunities.
- Continually search for, find, and focus on the highest leverage

opportunities.

We Didn't Have Insurance

The next week in South Africa, we were part of a weeklong event with a large insurance and financial services company. We couldn't get an audience with top management, as something urgent came up for them and they couldn't meet with us. The improvement team assured us it wouldn't be a problem and that top management would be okay with whatever the team came up with.

It turned out that top management didn't come to the report out. Our week was up and we had to go. We learned later that top management was not okay with what the team came up with. They felt the proposed improvement was too radical and risky. It was a great lesson for me – if you can't get leadership engaged early in your effort, then don't be surprised if nothing gets supported or implemented.

Lesson Learned:

- Leadership must be engaged from day one. Buy in must be lined up from the CEO all the way down through every reporting layer to the front-line associates who need to change their daily practices.

Touch and Feel the Output

Since the late 1970s, Jim has used a factory simulation game in his manufacturing improvement workshops. Toward the end of the workshop, he gives the teams up to an hour to come up with their final round solution. We've noticed that the teams that do the best in that hour are the ones that are quick to touch and feel the products being produced. They start with the product, which is composed of LEGO blocks, and break it apart. Then, they search for the best way to assemble it.

Whereas, the worst performers are generally those that spend a large part of their time analyzing the solution on paper or debating approaches. I kept track of how teams perform with the simulation for years. The worst performer in the simulation game I ever had was a group of "black belts" from a large industrial organization. They spent most of the session analyzing the data and debating solutions and didn't try to assemble anything until it was too late. I am reminded of this when I get too overly involved in analysis. If a group of very highly educated people can get stuck in analysis paralysis, then the rest of us can too.

Some of the answers are in the data, but more often than not, the answers are where the work is happening. You have to go see for yourself and touch and feel the product or service and ask lots of questions to really understand. This "touch and feel the output" concept generally applies in the real world also. We find that better solutions seem to come from teams that are quick to get grounded in the reality of the output they are producing.

In another example, a semiconductor fab was having a major quality problem and leadership asked me to help them resolve the problem. They reviewed the data with me. I then talked with a few of their engineers who had a number of hypotheses, but the solution had eluded them. Then I talked with operators in the fab. The clues that lead to the solution came from one of the test operators. She was seeing very small bubbles in the silicon on the bad parts. Random bubbles had always been there, but she had noticed that the bad parts had a few more bubbles than the good parts. I started asking, "What could cause bubbles?" That question lead to the solution.

Lesson Learned:

- Go see, touch and feel the products, services, and processes yourself.

Pride Cometh Before the Fall

Have you heard of the Fat, Dumb, and Happy Syndrome (FDH)? It's a term to describe complacent companies. However, I don't agree with the "dumb" term because, almost without exception, companies are made up of intelligent individuals. They may be "fat" and "happy," but are by no means "dumb". The real problem originates in the mindsets that creep into our heads, and it can happen to the best and brightest of us. It is a natural makeup of our human condition. Let's explore the mindsets that limit us.

Complacent companies are typically successful, sufficiently profitable, and they have done well in the past. I am reminded of Division X. The headquarters of a company we worked with, who will remain anonymous, sent Jim and me to help one of their manufacturing plants, Plant X, in a rural Kentucky community. This plant employed 350 of the highest paid workers in the county – a county that already had an unemployment rate that ranked them among the highest in the county. This was definitely a plant that you wanted to make sure performed well so it could stay open in the community.

We met with the plant manager and his direct reports for three days. On the first day, we had communicated the situation to him. A sister plant in North Carolina had been making more significant improvements year after year, compared to his plant. The danger was that headquarters could shut down his plant and move the production to the sister plant, which had freed up half of their factory floor space because of the improvements they had made.

The option on the table was to search for and find dramatic improvement opportunities in his plant and then implement them. We received permission from the corporate office to explain the situation with the plant manager and we were open and honest. When we told him that headquarters was considering moving the work to the sister plant, his response was, "They'd never do that to our community. They've blown smoke in our face before." He paused and continued, "It's their way to squeeze more money out of us." He was rationalizing away the warning signs.

After we understood their strategy and their business, we started to search for improvement opportunities with them. Each time we came upon something that had some potential, the plant manager would come up with a reason why it wasn't the right thing to do. In those three days, we heard about how great they have been doing and about the improvements they had made in recent years. It was impressive, as they had made good improvements in the past, and they were sufficiently profitable. He was quick to show us the two to three percent improvement in quality they had been making each of the last five years. However, he was also quick with all the excuses that we typically hear from complacent leaders.

Common excuses for not acting on the warning signs are:

1. We're too busy, and we don't have enough time.
2. These efforts will slow down production.
3. We don't have enough resources, in people, and money.
4. We already have a set of improvement initiatives ongoing.
5. We're different. That doesn't apply here.
6. We've already tried that here, and it didn't work.

No matter what we said, we couldn't convince him to act beyond their current plans. Regrettably, he either didn't trust us enough to believe us or refused to believe what was possible. After striking out, we sensed that improvements could be made because we saw a willingness to act from two of the plant manager's direct reports. We then negotiated with headquarters to spend another three days at the plant a few weeks later, unpaid.

This time, we convinced the plant manager to let us work with those two direct reports to find opportunities and help implement them. Within three days, the small team was able to increase quality by 10% by focusing on final assembly. Rather than see this improvement as beneficial to the company, the plant manager unfortunately somehow saw it as a threat to him and put a stop to it by pulling his two reports off the project.

We ended up walking away and, six months later, headquarters closed the plant and moved the production into the sister plant in North Carolina.

When people ask, "What are the biggest failures you've been involved in?" I tell them this story. It all centered on getting through the mindsets, mental models and measures of one man, and we were unable to do so. It reminds me of the danger each of us faces if we remain complacent, ignore the warning signals, assume that all is well, and don't act. When I tell this story to managers, they typically respond, that they are not like that at their plant. However, each of us, as a human, is susceptible to blinds spots and complacency. Like the old saying, "Pride cometh before the fall."

Complacent individuals and organizations tend to reject concepts immediately upon hearing them. When we get a concept in our mind, all other concepts that don't fit the ingrained concept are rejected as insignificant or wrong.

Those who are enlightened tend to dissect the concept, looking for the salient, beneficial, usable features, they tend to look at it from many different angles and ask lots of questions about it. They try their best to understand where the concept fits into their view of the world, and how it could be applied to make them better. As soon as they see an application of the concept with improvement potential, they are quick to embrace it and to spread the concept. The most enlightened have been hunted to near extinction, they have survived bloody battles that shook them to their core. They have been through numerous wakeup calls and fights of survival that forever changed them. Here are some better mindsets.

Better Mindsets:

1. We're busy, but we'll find the time if this is important.
2. We're squeezed, but we'll find the resources if this is important.
3. We already have a set of improvement initiatives ongoing, but we'll modify them to tie in with new initiatives if they are important.
4. We're different; however, if there is anything in the new concepts that will make us better, we'll make it work here.
5. We've already tried that, but this time we'll figure out how to make it work.

Lessons Learned:

- Discover if our current mindsets, mental models, and measures are blinding us to the warning signs around us.
- Become aware of the mindsets, mental models, and measures of leadership and team members. Help them see how those are or are not working for them. Then help them see better mindsets, mental models, and measures.

Oops, I Shouldn't Have Said That

One of the first events I facilitated on my own didn't go so well. I had a few years of experience in Lean, but I wasn't ready for this job. It wasn't the best setup because the corporate office had tried to help them, but didn't have much luck, so they sent me in to fix them up.

They were a manufacturer that made a unique set of parts that they provided to other OEM manufacturers. However, their operations were a mess. After some analysis during the pre-event discovery process, I concluded that the first high leverage area to focus on would be setup reduction at the welding operations. The manager disagreed, as he felt that no further setup reduction was possible. As I probed with the manager, he kept countering every possible opportunity to make an improvement.

I was getting a little frustrated because I saw so many opportunities. Then, he asked me how his operations stacked up against many of the others I've worked with. I said, "This is the worst operation I've ever seen." He got quiet. I was being honest with him. It was the worst I'd seen. After some awkward silence, he concluded that he didn't need my help. I tried to assure him that I could help him, but he wasn't willing to move any further.

It was a big lesson for me. I learned not to do that again. That was an honest comment, but it wasn't what I should have said. I didn't know the history. He may be a good manager stuck in a bad situation. All I saw was the bad situation. I learned that you don't say anything unless it will move the conversation forward toward the mission at hand. I don't believe he had any intention to work with me, but, if I had managed my conversation better, I may have been able to help him. Because of my lack of patience, I missed an opportunity to help make dramatic improvements to an operation that desperately needed help.

Years later, when I moved into healthcare, I learned to be patient and keep my mouth shut unless I could structure the conversation to move it toward accomplishing the mission at hand. I've avoided straying off topic and it has paid off.

Lesson Learned:

- All conversations, like activities, must be aligned toward achieving the objective.

These are a few of the early and scar-tissue-building experiences that have influenced how I practice Lean. Now I go to the coalface, I go touch and see for myself, I discover and influence mindsets, I engage leaders, and when I can't, I have learned to remain patient and persistent toward achieving what is wanted and needed, because I have experienced what can be accomplished by practicing Lean well.

Chapter Twelve – Cameron Stark

Born in Glasgow, Scotland, Cameron Stark graduated in medicine from the University of Glasgow in 1985. After working as a junior doctor in medical and surgical posts, he spent four years working in Psychiatry in the West of Scotland. Stark then trained in Public Health Medicine and has been an NHS Consultant since 1996, first in Ayrshire and then in the Highlands. He has professional qualifications in Psychiatry and Public Health and postgraduate degrees in Risk, Crisis and Disaster Management (University of Leicester) and in Public Health (University of Glasgow).

With research interests in public health, mental health and quality improvement, Stark has published over 50 papers in peer-reviewed journals. He has written four previous book chapters, co-edited three academic books and co-authored a recent book on the psychology of soccer coaching.

He trained as a Lean Leader with Tees, Esk and Wear Valley NHS Foundation Trust, and now coaches staff who are learning about Lean in NHS Highland. Stark is responsible for the quality assurance of Lean training materials used in NHS Highland and works with their Kaizen Promotion Office manager to arrange events and develop training.

Away from work, Stark is married with three children and lives in Inverness, Scotland.

Looking for Lean

Beginning work on service improvement is daunting. A Google search brings up any number of approaches. Published work ranges from formal academic papers to unquantified anecdote. Deciding how to start is difficult.

The purpose of this chapter is to describe my own journey and to identify transferrable lessons that may be useful for readers. Predictably, most of my lessons have accrued from failures, or at least partial successes. Five years ago, I would have been reluctant to write about them, for fear of looking foolish. I now believe that improvement efforts are only wasted if you do not learn from them or if you allow momentum to be lost.

Clinical Audit

My first exposure to improvement methods was to clinical audit. In audit, a standard is identified, and existing practice compared to the standard. Once you know the gap, you make a plan to close the gap, implement it, and re-audit the results. This is a Plan-Do-Study-Act cycle and is a building block of improvement work.

As a junior doctor in the 1980s, I was allocated an audit project by my Consultant (the most senior doctor in a clinical 'team' at the time). I worked in psychiatry, and I was asked to look at how often blood levels of lithium, used in mood disorders, were tested in patients on the treatment. This is important as lithium is effective in a fairly narrow range of blood concentrations. Lithium toxicity can be fatal, so knowing that blood levels remain stable is important.

There was an available national guideline that gave advice on how often levels should be checked. As often happens in audit projects, it became a paper chase. In a pre-electronic database age, even identifying who was prescribed lithium was difficult. I then had to obtain their case notes, look for the blood results section and check the date of the last filed lithium level.

The main finding was that about a third of people had their level checked later than the recommended time period. I talked to other junior doctors, probably in a coffee break, and came up with ideas about why this was. I decided that it was probably because there was no clear reminder of the time the next test was due, and because not all the junior doctors had the same view on how often blood should be tested. To tackle this, I designed a form that went into the notes and showed the testing schedule, and on which results could be noted.

I tried this in my own clinic and persuaded two colleagues to try it for six months. I then re-audited, and found that the number of people exceeding the testing dates had decreased to about 15%. This was a 50% decrease in the proportion of people missing dates and I was pleased. I presented it at an audit meeting and the other Consultant teams present agreed to try the method themselves.

I rotated back in the same hospital about two years later. A quick check found some aging forms in notes and none in the notes of patients newly established on lithium treatment. Enquiries to the current batch of junior doctors produced blank looks, although one did know that a junior doctor had been asked to do a new audit on lithium.

I suspect this experience was common. I was discouraged: I had put a lot of work into the audit, much of it in my own time and thought that I had made a difference for patients. I had no real idea why it had not worked.

Looking back at this with the advantage of subsequent experience, I had not defined the problem in detail; I decided on the cause myself and took the cause that seemed most plausible to me rather than quantifying the relative contribution of different causes. I also did not involve others in the problem identification, or solution generation, and this contributed to the failure to embed the changes in the system.

Service Planning

The more I saw of services, the more I felt that their design was lacking. Different services did not appear to mesh with one another and there were any number of issues that made no real sense to anyone but happened regardless. Clinical colleagues felt there was an amorphous and invisible "other" who controlled this. In retrospect, we were seeing systems that had developed over forty years, layer on layer, like an oyster laying down a pearl. As one system was established, previous systems and arrangements were often not reviewed – everyone was too busy, and felt this would not be a good use of time.

Largely as a result of this, I trained in Public Health Medicine, because I believed that this would let me into the design "engine room," if you will, where the big decisions on expenditure, services, and service structure were made. Public Health practice includes four areas of work – health protection, health improvement, health services and health information. For most of the quarter of a century that I have worked in Public Health, I have focused on health service Public Health and in health information.

Working on large re-design projects is interesting. The projects are data intensive, and can, at times, produce large-scale change. Establishing whole new services for excluded groups of people, based on need, is rewarding, as is replacing old hospitals. However, control is illusory. As soon as a service is established, it develops its own way of doing things. It meshes – or doesn't mesh – with neighbouring services.

Most service re-design is not on this scale. Rather, it produces incremental change, for example by adding a new procedure, a new test, or a new site. This does little to tackle pre-existing problems. Services very often optimise their own function and this often has limited fit with the overall service required.

I also came to realise that new or altered investment is at the margin of service delivery. Most services, and most of the money spent on services, changes little from year to year. The quality of the large bulk of existing services is at least as important as the quality of new or altered services. Building quality into day to day services, is the single most important health service activity.

Around this time, I had the chance to see a large commercial provider work in the area, looking at acute hospital flow. This was conducted largely with external staff, although local workers were interviewed, and helped to contribute data to the consultants. The information, analysis, and recommendations were fed back to a large audience in a lecture theatre. The breadth and depth of the analysis was impressive, but it left me unclear on how changes were expected to be achieved.

There were some modest changes in the months after this work, but my impression was that the work failed to embed. Reflecting on it now, I think that too few people really understood what had been done and how the analysis had been conducted. The link between the analysis and the proposed solutions was therefore not grasped as well as it might have been. The work left a legacy of improved information skills and started the discussion of service flow. There was, however, limited impact on the overall skills of the organisation.

National Collaborative

Realising this, I took on a part-time role as the Clinical Lead for the local part of a national Collaborative project. The Collaborative projects are designed to produce large changes in services across an area, region or country through the use of improvement methods, and by promoting learning across sites. Some, such as the Scottish Patient Safety Programme, have been very successful.

The collaborative I worked on was aimed at improving quality in mental health services. It had three main aims – to promote earlier diagnosis of dementia, to decrease anti-depressant prescribing, and to increase the availability of psychological therapies.

The structure was that there was a national office, with money being provided to each NHS area to employ at least a part-time project officer. The national office arranged training on quality improvement methods and arranged regional and national meetings to share learning from the different areas of Scotland.

The training was delivered over five or six days, spread over several months. It covered PDSA cycles, improvement metrics, and training on flow. The most striking event for me was a masterclass run by Richard Steyn, an English cardio-thoracic surgeon. He described how he and his colleagues had changed a service with long waiting lists into one on which people were scheduled for surgery the week following the assessment if surgery was required. They had done this with no additional resources, by redesigning the service to create standard work, and to improve flow. This opportunity to speak to someone who had collaborated to produce an enormous change in a live NHS service without additional resources was very important to my personal conviction that change is possible.

In the Mental Health Collaborative, my colleagues and I tried to apply some of these principles. We had a central challenge, as some of the national targets were not widely accepted. General Practitioners and Psychiatrists firmly believed that anti-depressant prescribing was not only appropriate in most cases but that a large number of people who could benefit from treatment passed through the net and suffered in silence. There was widespread support for increasing the availability of psychological therapies, so we focused on the two ideas of appropriate prescribing and psychological therapy access. Later research found that the increase in anti-depressant prescriptions was not driven by new prescriptions, but by increased maintenance prescribing, which was in line with national guidelines. In due course, the Scottish Government dropped the anti-depressant reduction target, retrospectively endorsing the clinical view at the time.

Information on all these areas, other than prescribing, was limited and we devoted significant effort to establishing mechanisms for counting performance, so we could respond to regular requests for data to be provided to allow a national overview to be taken by Government. This was useful, as it did produce some agreement on the nature of the problem, but the work was largely invisible to the people who delivered the services.

In this work, a bigger range of people contributed to identifying the problems and coming up with solutions. We undertook various pieces of pilot work and using PDSA cycles, and the work did result in some improvements. It felt throughout, however, as if we were doing things to people, as opposed to co-producing a system with them. We noticed that increased visibility of performance seemed to make a difference. Seeing waiting lists appeared to be important for staff and, after some initial anger and distress, focusing on current performance, instead of abstract targets, did have a positive effect. As soon as we moved on to different areas of work, however, the gains began to slide. Visual displays of information became less common and staff became less clear on the current performance. The rate of reversion back to business as usual was startling.

My reflections on this, with the benefit of hindsight, are that we addressed some of the weaknesses of earlier work and did actively involve more staff and some patient groups. Using information to plan, monitor, and react was not embedded in local ways of working. People were used to retrospective review of information rather than doing weekly, daily or hourly reviews. Managers tended to see the work as an improvement project, rather than a change to a new way of working – and to at least some extent, I did as well.

Knowledge Transfer Partnership

As part of the work on dementia in the Collaborative, we applied to the UK Government for a Knowledge Transfer Partnership scheme. It can take a long time for academic knowledge to move in to practice, and the UK Government established this national scheme to try to link academics to the practical applications of knowledge. Most of the awards were for technological links, for example between University Engineering Departments and commercial companies, but there was nothing in the rules to stop NHS applications. Our application was successful.

We partnered with an expert academic unit at the University of Stirling. From the Collaborative work, we had some idea of the areas of practice that troubled staff and had ideas from patient groups about things they saw as important. This was better than the previous projects in which we started with limited knowledge of staff concerns and of patient priorities.

The academic partners supplemented this by gathering experiences from patients and relatives on the use of services and the process of diagnosis and support (Innes et al 2014). This was done to the requisite academic standards. We also reviewed the previous academic literature to establish the current state of knowledge on diagnosis and support in rural areas (Szymczynska et al 2011). These pieces of work were both well received, locally and nationally. As a result of them and the information from staff, we developed training targeted to the needs of particular staff groups. These were again piloted, assessed by the academic partners, and then extended out based on the learning and the feedback from staff (Szymczynska and Innes 2011).

Overall, this was a more successful process. It built on academic knowledge, on the experience and feedback of patients and relatives, and on gaps identified by staff (Stark et al 2013). There was some joint creation of materials and the project was regarded generally as a success.

The main challenges were in the timescale and the impact. Our academic partners were internationally recognised for their expertise, as they brought experience, worldwide links and academic credibility. They also conducted their work to established academic standards. The project sought a win-win result and the University expected publications to arise from it, as did the funders. This meant, however, that work inevitably took time, particularly on a modest budget. Compared to previous academic projects in which I had been involved, this work was very nimble. It responded to wants from staff and relatives and it changed, or at least altered course, in response to feedback and demand. Our academic partners listened carefully and acted on our requests. In NHS terms, however, the timescales remained long and the work was still working towards its maximum impact at the time that the funding ended.

Finding Lean: Virginia Mason, Tees, Esk and Wear Valley, and NETS

Producing Change

It felt to me as if each piece of work had produced some impact, but I had an intense dissatisfaction with my part in the process. I was delivering work to the highest standard I could, but the impacts were clearly limited. Improvement work remained largely project based and rarely seemed to result in continued improvement when the pedal was lifted from the floor.

Around the same time, the Scottish Patient Safety Programme (SPSP) was beginning to report impressive and lasting successes. SPSP was a national leap in the dark – a belief that, if you took evidence-based "bundles" of good practice and applied them in very specific clinical situations, then process improvements would result in improved clinical outcomes for patients.

This was the same type of approach as our Knowledge Transfer Partnership, but on a grand scale. By identifying bundles of good practice that had to be undertaken every time to produce good results, then working out how to apply them on every single occasion, SPSP obtained astonishing results. The work was initially in very tightly defined areas, particularly intensive care units. Careful attention to detail reduced Ventilator Acquired Pneumonia and Central Line infections, for example (Morris et al 2011). The whole programme demonstrated beyond any reasonable doubt that if you took best practice, developed standard work, and then applied it consistently over time, then remarkable gains could be obtained (Haraden and Leitch 2011).

I was left with the question of how this translated to gains in less controlled settings, and in areas where there was no evidence to review. Many of the issues I saw day to day were on processes where there was no known "best way". Many processes were not widely transferable, but were still very important to the people who delivered them, as well as to the people who used the service. I was a man looking for a method of applying the methods of standard work and staff engagement found in the SPSP work to other improvement work.

The Highland Porter

While I was working on the Knowledge Transfer Project, NHS Highland's head of quality, Dr. Lesley Anne Smith had been awarded an Institute of Healthcare Improvement (IHI) Fellowship. This allowed her to travel to the US for a year to learn. Our chief executive had asked Lesley Anne to identify transferrable methods: Lesley Anne came back with Lean.

Through visits and presentations, she had seen work at the Virginia Mason Medical Centre, Cincinnati Children's Hospital, Thedacare, and several others. Her advice was they had obtained and maintained significant improvements using Lean methods.

On her advice, three senior members of staff from NHS Highland travelled to the Virginia Mason Medical Center. VMMC told a good story – it sounded impressive. Our then medical director had heard good stories before – he had worked for the Government at one time. He wanted to know that the stories were true. He especially wanted to know that their claims to have involved all staff were real.

During his visit, he took to walking around the hospital and asking staff about their experience with Lean. One of the people he stopped on an evening was a hospital porter, who proved to be from a small town in the Highlands, about ten miles from Inverness, where NHS Highland has its head offices. This was a coincidence. This man then gave our medical director a brief, but convincing, master class in Lean, standing in a corridor in Seattle. The porter clearly understood the principles, he had direct experience of contributing to improvement work, he knew metrics relating to his own work, and he felt involved.

As a result of this, and of other observations in Seattle, our medical director – a hard man to convince – returned with a view that, at the least, this was worth a try.

Training

Our chief executive and senior management team talked it over and discussed it with our board. They decided to find out if Lean could support NHS Highland's care delivery. Three senior managers were sent to undertake Lean training at the Virginia Mason Institute. This was a big decision. Like most publicly funded services, money in the NHS is at a a premium. Across the world, people want good services, but they also tend to want conspicuous frugality from people paid through the public purse. Sending three people from the UK to the US to undertake a training course was bound to attract attention and at least some public opprobrium. It was a risky decision.

My first contacts with Lean were when the people who had undertaken the classroom training in the US were beginning to conduct improvement events in Highland. I helped out at part of two events, by helping to obtain information needed for the improvement work. This was an important moment in my improvement journey.

The aspects I noted in the Lean approach were clarity about the nature of the problem and the scope of the current work. It felt very different from the very wide scope of some previous projects. There were clear metrics. The people delivering the service had been involved from the start and there was a patient at each of the workshops to offer direct input. There was a real sense of urgency. Most strikingly, the people working in the service were identifying and agreeing on the problems, coming up with the solutions. This felt very different than the approach I had seen and used before – contrast it with the way I undertook the improvement work in psychiatry.

Many of the things I had seen before were involved. The projects used data, they were based around PDSA cycles, and they included some of the flow issues that I had seen in Richard Steyn's work years before. This felt to me as if it tackled many of my previous improvement problems.

Sending people to Seattle was not practical at scale. Virginia Mason pointed us towards the North-East of England, where they had worked with a UK health system. We partnered with Tees, Esk and Wear Valley NHS Foundation Trust (TEWV) for local training and coaching, using the North East Transformation System (NETS) a package of Lean training materials developed by Ian Smith and colleagues in Gateshead.

I leapt at the chance of joining one of the courses run by TEWV in Inverness. The training included two blocks of classroom training, with various exercises and homework, followed by an examination. That then allowed me to undertake two supervised improvement events, with the coaching coming from Tees, Esk and Wear Valley staff.

The two coached events were revelatory. The TEWV / NETS system has a fairly constrained structure for these supervised events, with a scoping meeting and four planning meetings. Access to coaching was good. The two coaches (Maureen Raine and Keith Appleby) had led over 100 events between them, so they were confident and helpful throughout. Not much surprised them.

The experience was very different from my previous involvement in improvement work. The hardest thing, I found, was to move away from forming opinions early, from closing down options, and from making decisions for people. The experience of observing was new. I thought I had looked at processes in the past, but that had involved going to see people and asking them to talk me through what they did. This had been useful, but I was surprised at the richness of direct observation of practice. The coaches wanted deep learning and expected repeated observation of processes without comment. Being told to watch the whole process at least three times before I even started to record anything reflected an intensity of focus (on process) that I had not appreciated.

The NETS / TEWV method uses two external workshop leaders who facilitate the workshop for the local team and Virginia Mason uses a similar arrangement. The dynamic with the local team fasci-nated me. I was surprised at how quickly people stopped worrying about you being there. It was common for people on the teams to look at what you recorded, then asking to begin to undertake observations themselves.

It was clear that any change can be stressful. Respect for people was a core part of the approach which the coaches emphasised repeatedly. I was surprised, at first, at how defensive people could become at even gentle inquiries about process. The reason I found this odd was that it was often staff in the service who asked for the work in the first place, because they perceived problems.

I realised eventually that an abstract knowledge of a problem can feel very different from a painstaking description of the process that confirms problems in a process. It is very difficult for people to sep-arate what they do from what they are and to separate motion from value. The workshop leader, along with managers at all levels, has a key role to play in their response, to emphasise that the problems lie in the processes, not in the people who have been asked to operate it.

The amount of work that could be accommodated in a one-week event was remarkable. Staff who took part were engaged, energetic, and usually very positive about the likelihood of change. When we checked the metrics from our first twenty improvement events, 72% of the measures showed improvements. Some were enormous, like a Community Mental Health Team that reduced its average waiting time by many months.

What Now?

My recent work has focused on documenting the improvement processes we have established, and working with colleagues to teach others. Gavin Hookway, who manages our Kaizen Promotion Office, was an electronics engineer before becoming, in turn, an operating department practitioner, an operating theatre manager and then an improvement practitioner. His focus on process has been important. Improvement events are now largely predictable. We have expanded settings, working recently in a General Practice, for example. Generally, improvement events themselves work well (Stark et al 2015). Staff enjoy them. The patient representatives are positive about changes. There are usually a few sticky moments during the preparation phase and the improvement events, but Lean delivers.

The challenges are threefold: maintaining gains over prolonged periods of time; turning process gains into outcome gains, and embedding improvement.

Maintaining Gains

David Mann (2015: pg. 7) suggests, "so many Lean implementations fail because Lean is easy."

When you are starting out, this seems a preposterous statement. Getting your head around some of the Lean ideas is challenging – exactly how does level loading, or heijunka, work? Where does error proofing fit? With time and exposure, you come to realise that people can "do" Lean. It is common to see a staff member who knew nothing about Lean on day one of an improvement event coming up with, trialling, and implementing an improvement idea based on sound Lean principles by day four of an event. This happens so often, it ceases to be a surprise. It is what happens.

The immediate follow-up period is fine. The trick is maintaining gains at nine months, a year, or eighteen months. I can now recognise when this is happening. A unit we had worked with monitored their service routinely, but they asked me to help them with some other measurements for a one year review. It was the first time I had been in the area for at least six months. I noticed several changes, and it was clear that some of the processes established at the RPIW had been altered. I asked a nurse about it. She looked puzzled, then her face cleared.

> "Oh, we're always talking about things we can improve. It's just what we do. We worked out better ways of doing that process."

This unit, not surprisingly, had not only maintained improvements, it was obtaining better results than it had reported at its six-month review.

In another unit, an out-patient service, we took some people to look at some of their work, all of which had been done without the benefit of an improvement event. The unit "sister" (charge nurse) was excited to show us some new changes they had made since we had been there last, less than a month before. The changes had come from examining problems at their daily huddle, identifying causes, and introducing new ways of working to counter the problem, then embedding them as standard work.

This does not always happen. Virginia Mason reported repeating many of the Rapid Process Improvement Workshops (RPIWs) that they undertook in their first two years of their Lean implementation (Kenney 2010) because changes did not stick. In our first twenty improvement events, we counted four events that resulted in no meaningful impact a year after the event. Our percentage was better than that of VM not because we were cleverer than then them, but because we had the benefit of advice from them and from people they had trained who had themselves undertaken many events. We built on the hard earned experience of others, just as this book seeks to promote.

There were plausible reasons in each case of non-sustainment in our organisation – timing, changes in management, etc. but the overall reason is that we did not have necessary systems to support maintenance in every case. Mann (2015) and Kenney (2015) emphasise the importance of management engagement in Lean. In my organisation, there is excellent senior manager involvement – seven Directors have either trained as Lean Leaders or are in training – but in a large organisation, engaging everyone takes time.

My initial feeling was that I needed to offer some degree of Lean training to everyone. In fact, we ran introductory sessions for over 2,500 staff. I eventually stopped these sessions, because the yield from them was too low. When interested staff went back to managers after the event, they often encountered people who were not themselves familiar with many of the ideas. We are re-focusing this capacity on directing training to people in middle management. In the NHS, this group of people are very commonly health care professionals who have been promoted to management posts.

Following Mann's ideas, we intend to target the initial training on what this layer of manager needs to do to support services that are involved in Lean improvement work. Over the next few years, we then plan to return to this group and offer training in Lean approaches to matters such as value and waste, flow and error proofing. We will target the initial training on managers working in services in which a greater volume of improvement work is already happening so that there is an opportunity for immediate practice.

Turning Process Gains into Improvement Gains

Process metrics look good, as I explained above. Some processes show an impact on measures such as waiting times in particular areas, cancelled operations, and so on. The challenge is in aligning enough work to make a difference to entire value streams, such as elective surgery.

Our chief executive, Elaine Mead, is tackling this in one main way. She has begun to move to a "hoshin kanri" system, supported by advice from the Virginia Mason Institute. The basics of hoshin kanri are straightforward – agree on your organisation's "true north", and what its aims are; identify your key medium term priorities based on a review of performance figures, quality measures, and changes in your near and far environment; identify annual or at least shorter term objectives that fall out of the medium term priorities; consult with staff on these annual objectives, and through a process of "catchball," refine and agree on objectives, means and metrics. This then needs a process of continuous review at various organisational levels, accompanied by a willingness to problem solve, rather than blaming people when things prove difficult (Akao 2004, Jackson 2006, Hutchins 2008).

The general advice on this is that you cannot take a system off the shelf – you need to develop your own way of doing it, based on Lean principles. This takes time and effort.

As part of this work, her leadership team has identified three high-level value streams that are particular priorities. Each of these value streams now has a guiding team and their role includes working with staff to identify where improvement events are needed. This should increase the strategic alignment of improvement work with organisational priorities, making it easier to seek multiple improvements across a value stream. At the same time, they have decided to keep a proportion of corporate resource to support improvement work arising directly from staff interests.

Embedding Improvement

The hoshin kanri and middle management support discussed above should have some impact on embedding improvement. There is a potential hazard in the structure we have adopted, however, in that people may come to believe that improvement happens only as part of large, set piece improvement projects. Graban and Swartz (2012) argue that supporting staff to work on continuous improvement in their own service is key to success.

I plan to address this risk in three ways. We have had teams who have applied Lean methods to their own work with little or no external support, bringing considerable success. I plan to publicise their work as much as I can so that people in my organisation can see active examples of staff working with their own service with little or no external support.

Secondly, we have partnered with the University of Stirling, who train nurses on an Inverness campus. Inevitably, a large proportion of NHS Highland nurses come through this process. Michelle Beattie and Brian James teach an improvement course to nurse undergraduates and each nurse is required to undertake an assessed improvement project as part of their required work for their degree. We have worked with the University of Stirling to make the project approval process as straightforward as possible, ensuring that the internal NHS teaching aligns with the University teaching.

Thirdly, we need to make it clear in our middle management education that there is clear corporate support for improvement work within services and that external approval is not required.

Conclusions

Improvement is never ending and this is as true of people as it is of processes. Over a thirty-year career, I have been engaged in many pieces of work that aimed to obtain service quality. The external training available in the NHS improved steadily and there is now considerable emphasis on quality improvement. Despite this, I feel that I was a person in search of an improvement method. In Lean, I found a method that works in practice, is easily grasped, and can reliably produce improvements when applied by staff. I see the challenge for the next five years as making sure this produces the organisational gains that it has the potential to create.

Acknowledgements

Thanks to the people who contributed to the steps on this journey:

Improvement work in mental health – Brian Kidd, Tom Henderson, Marilyn Clarke, Lynda Forrest, Morag Bramwell, Michael Perera, Bill Cook, Anthea Innes and Paulina Szymczynska.

Lean – Anne Gent, Linda Kirkland, Gill Cooksley, Pam Cremin and Steven Bartley.

References

Akao Y. (2004) *Hoshin Kanri: Policy Deployment for Successful TQM*[61]. Productivity Press, New York.

Graban M, Swartz J E. (2012) *Healthcare Kaizen: Engaging Front-Line Staff in Sustainable Continuous Improvements*[62]. Productivity Press, New York.

Haraden C, Leitch J. (2011) Scotland's Successful National Approach To Improving Patient Safety In Acute Care. Health Affairs 30; 4: 755-763.

Hutchins D. (2008) *Hoshin Kanri: The Strategic Approach to Continuous Improvement*[63]. Gower Publications, London.

Innes A, Szymczynska P, Stark C. (2014) Dementia diagnosis and post-diagnostic support in Scottish rural communities: Experiences of people with dementia and their families. Dementia 13; 2: 233-247.

Jackson T L. (2006) *Hoshin Kanri for the Lean Enterprise: Developing Competitive Capabilities and Managing Profit*[64]. Productivity Press, New York.

Kenney C. (2010) *Transforming Health Care: Virginia Mason Medical Center's Pursuit of the Perfect Patient Experience*[65]. Productivity Press, New York.

Kenney C. (2015) *A Leadership Journey in Health Care: Virginia Mason's Story*[66]. Productivity Press, New York.

Mann D. (2015) *Creating a Lean Culture: Tools to Sustain Lean*

---

[61]http://amzn.to/1QkhPS5
[62]http://amzn.to/1n1kCar
[63]http://amzn.to/1QkhY85
[64]http://amzn.to/1R6Vw1W
[65]http://amzn.to/1QkihzF
[66]http://amzn.to/1n1kPdN

Conversations[67]. CRC Press, Boca Raton.

Morris A C, Hay A, Swann D, Everingham K, McCulloch C, McNulty J, Brooks O, Laurenson I F, Cook B, Walsh T S. (2011) Reducing ventilator-associated pneumonia in intensive care: Impact of implementing a care bundle. Critical Care Medicine 39; 10: 2218-2224.

Stark C, Innes A, Szymczynska P, Forrest L, Proctor K. (2013) Dementia knowledge transfer project in a rural area. Rural and Remote Health 13: 2060.

Stark C, Gent A, Kirkland L. (2015) Improving patient flow in preoperative assessment. BMJ Quality Improvement Reports 4: doi:10.1136/bmjquality .u201341.w1226

Szymczynska P, Innes A, Mason A, Stark C. (2011) A review of diagnostic process and postdiagnostic support for people with dementia in rural areas. Journal of Primary Care & Community Health 2; 4: 262-276.

Szymczynska P, Innes A. (2011) Evaluation of a dementia training workshop for health and social care staff in rural Scotland. Rural and Remote Health 11: 1611.

Dr Cameron Stark MBChB, MPH, MSc, MRCPsych, FFPH Consultant in Public Health Medicine, NHS Highland Honorary Reader, University of Aberdeen

---

[67]http://amzn.to/1n1kU0S

Chapter Thirteen - Harvey Leach

Harvey Leach is an independent management consultant based near Oxford, England, where he works with a group of close associates. He supports clients by applying his experiences of Lean thinking, change management and leadership development to help them solve complex operational problems and grow their internal capability to identify and implement improvements.

Prior to moving into consultancy in 2004, Harvey spent 27 years with Rover Group and BMW Group, where he gained an impressive reputation for implementing improved ways of working in every team he managed or was part of,covering areas as diverse as Product Development, New Product Introduction, Production Planning & Control and Production Strategy. Alongside this, he acted as a trainer for a number of internal programmes to grow the organisation's Lean capability – Total Quality Improvement, Leading Management and Coaching for Performance.

Since 2004, Harvey has applied and developed the skills he acquired to support clients in a range of industrial and public sector organisations, covering both operational and administrative areas. In addition to leading and facilitating improvement programmes for clients, he has developed and delivered a range of highly acclaimed public and bespoke training programmes.

"I don't know anything much about Lean!"

When I left my role at the MINI factory in Oxford in the autumn of 2004, I really didn't think I knew all that much about Lean. All I could see was what appeared to me as a huge gulf between the practices I saw around our factory and what I read and heard about

Toyota, especially as I'd recently conducted a number of ex-Toyota consultants around the plant who had made some rather unflattering comparisons!

My confidence in my Lean abilities didn't change much when I joined a locally-based consultancy group shortly afterward. Even when one of my colleagues said to me, "The problem you have Harvey, coming from the industry you do, is that you really don't realise how much you know," I struggled to believe him. I knew from my Rover and BMW Group experiences that I was good at making things work better, but did I really know that much about Lean? I still saw that gap.

It wasn't until I started working with colleagues who had some sort of formal Lean training and had worked in senior roles with respected companies like HP and Danaher that I began to think to myself, "Hey! This is the same stuff that I've been doing for years! Maybe I know more about Lean than I think."

Even so, it probably took me ten years to really contextualise my Rover and BMW experiences, underpinning that with more study of Lean principles through reading books by Jeff Liker[68], Mike Rother[69] and others and gaining confidence in applying that learning to a wide range of client organisations to get to the point where I think I've "got it" – if indeed one ever does. As Mark said in his opening chapter, the process of learning and applying always continues and it very much seems that the more I learn, the more I realise there is to learn.

So Mark's challenge to go "back to the beginning" and reflect on my "first year" came at a great time and encouraged me to look back at those early days with the benefit of considerable hindsight.

Like Mark, I could have picked more than one "first year," but I've chosen to go right back to the very beginning. My true "first year" - when I came across for the first time the principles that were to change the direction of my career - was before we even referred to "Lean." It was 1989 – a year before *The Machine That Changed*

---

[68]http://amzn.to/1SwzIBY
[69]http://www.amazon.com/Mike-Rother/e/B002AQBVLE/ref=sr_ntt_srch_lnk_1?qid=1457438468&sr=1-1

the World[70] was published and the term "Lean" started to be heard. Rover Group had started on a Total Quality Management programme a couple years before, initially working intensively with the executive team and gradually working downwards through the layers of management – interesting to note when compared with the way some organisations set about a Lean implementation today that often seems to believe that the senior levels can remain largely unchanged and that Lean happens much further down the organisation.

At the time I was working as a junior manager in Product Development, having moved out of the Research part of the organisation about a year before. I was aware of a number of managers sporting "TQI" (Total Quality Improvement) badges and was hearing great things about the Total Quality Management training programme that was going on, so was keen to learn more when my turn came.

An Industry in Turmoil

Before going further, I think it might be helpful for those unfamiliar with the situation in the UK automotive industry at that time to give a brief summary. It was certainly a time of considerable change that left the industry almost unrecognisable from the indigenous UK motor industry of the late 1960s.

Back then, foreign cars were a rarity on British roads, although the cracks were starting to show. The industry was dominated by four major players, having emerged from a period of consolidation. Three were American owned: Ford of Britain, GM (in the guise of Vauxhall Motors), and the former Rootes Group, now owned by Chrysler. Pretty much all of the rest of the industry had just recently come together to form the British Leyland Motor Corporation – incorporating great names such as Jaguar, Land Rover, Triumph, Rover, MG, Austin, and Morris, together with other divisions making trucks, buses, road laying vehicles, tractors and even armoured vehicles!

Twenty years on, the landscape looked somewhat different, as Ford and GM had both merged their British and German operations

---

[70]http://amzn.to/1UPwYQH

to leverage economies of scale. Ownership of the former Rootes Group had transferred to Peugeot Citroen as its US parent, Chrysler, struggled with its home operations. British Leyland had struggled to compete and been taken into state ownership for a period before, following a change of government, being manoeuvred into a takeover by British Aerospace. More significantly, sales of Japanese manufactured cars had grown significantly on the back of a growing reputation for value for money and better reliability than British made vehicles. Bringing the challenge closer to home, Nissan, Honda, and Toyota had all selected the UK as the base for their European manufacturing operations.

In the process, the Japanese had gained an impressive reputation for value, quality, and reliability that the former British Leyland, by now renamed Rover Group, was struggling to emulate despite its near ten-year association with Honda. The renaming was part of a deliberate policy to position the group's products upmarket from its mainstream European and Japanese rivals. All current cars were going through a process of "Roverisation" to improve both the perception and reality of quality, with new vehicles being developed in collaboration with Honda to enable Rover to bring new products to market more quickly and at lower cost, while at the same time learning from Honda's engineering and production expertise. Initially, Rover had assembled rebadged versions of Honda Civic derivatives, and the first vehicles from a collaborative development programme – the Rover 800 (known as Sterling in the US) and Honda Legend – had recently gone into production at Rover's Oxford factory.

The next new vehicle was the medium-sized car that would become the next generation European Civic for Honda and the 200/400 range for Rover. It was into this area that I was thrust, having been so far insulated from this strong Honda influence in the research division. Having done some work there on simulation of vehicle crash performance, I was now putting those skills to use in the development of the crashworthiness of these new vehicles.

As a support function, we were a little remote from direct contact with the joint Rover-Honda design teams. Stories had filtered through about different ways of working. We began to be invited to presentations about workshop and meeting formats with strange Japanese names like "Geba Kai" – what we'd probably now term a stage gate event – and were seeing single, faxed sheets of paper summarising design and development ideas with illustrations and descriptions that were surprisingly clear given that the text was in Japanese! With hindsight, this was an early introduction to the power of the A3 concept.

An Introduction to Some Different Thinking

It was with some trepidation that I received my invitation for my "Total Quality Management" training. Prior to the first day, I was required to interview my manager – itself a novel concept – on his experiences of TQM so far. Through that, I picked up three key messages. Firstly, that the main consideration is the quality of the product as experienced by the customer. Secondly, that the key theme is "prevention not detection,"; that quality is not achieved by having some rigorous checking process, and, thirdly, that products should be "right first time." An interesting side conversation to this third point was that we also need a place to get it wrong. In our case, this meant that Product Development as a whole needed to be able to experiment in order to truly understand what would work or not work when the vehicle hit production.

It is both surprising and pleasing, looking back at my notes of these sessions for the first time in many years, to observe how these key ideas still resonate today and sit at the core of what we might call "real Lean" thinking. In particular, I was struck by my note that we need "space to get it wrong." It seems that even now many can still struggle with this idea that freedom to experiment and "fail" is an essential component in making improvements and is a key part of the "scientific approach" associated with effective application of Plan-Do-Check-Act.

Armed with this basic introduction, I set off for my first day's training, where I discovered myself among a mixed group of junior managers from all functions of the company – Sales and Marketing,

Finance, Personnel, Production, Design, and others. Even today, in a world where "Lean" is still seen by many to be the province of manufacturing, this would seem like quite a bold move, so imagine how unusual it seemed almost 30 years ago!

Up until that point, my only real exposure to the wider business since my student training had been to other parts of the design and development function, so it was not long before my appreciation of the rest of te organisation had grown considerably. Alongside learning the "theory" about getting deeper into customer requirements, considering internal departments as customers and suppliers, root cause problem solving, statistical process control, team working and managing change, I came to appreciate the challenges faced by other areas of the business. Common themes emerged, most often simply poor communication between areas, with differences of understanding of what information was required that could be put right relatively easily just by making time to talk to each other.

The idea of improving communications and understanding of requirements was to become the key theme of that "first year." As part of the work between the formal Total Quality training sessions, we were encouraged to go and talk with our customers and suppliers. This activity proved highly enlightening to me and was to become a guiding theme of much of my subsequent career.

It's important to note that, at that time, vehicle crashworthiness was not seen as a significant topic in Europe, rather as a series of somewhat unwelcome, time-consuming and costly hoops that the company had to jump through to satisfy US safety legislation. Consequently, our team was seen as something of a "thorn in the side" of vehicle development programmes. Not surprisingly, they were reluctant to send expensive prototypes our way, as we tended to make something of a mess of them! Equally unsurprisingly, when vehicles failed the test, the necessary changes to design and need for retest would add significant time and cost to the vehicle programme, and somewhat late in the day. No wonder we were unpopular! I began to see the potential value of "up front work" at the conceptual design stage before basic designs were frozen and expensive tooling and production facilities were commissioned. Again, another theme that was to gain greater prominence in later years.

As a result of our TQM experiences, we began to talk as a department about how we could make things better. The department had only been together for a few months; previously those involved in computer simulation had worked very separately from those carrying out the actual tests, and the two sides eyed each other with some suspicion. Even now that we had been brought together in one department, the analysts and the testers were still two separate groups. Fortunately, our manager had some great ideas and we began to explore how we could build on the strengths of both methods and both groups – physical testing and computer simulation – to become better at "prevention" and less dependent on the "late detection" that was a physical crash test.

My conversations with colleagues in vehicle programme management, undertaken as part of my training, had proved most enlightening. It seems almost embarrassing to admit it now, but I don't think I had ever really thought about what we were doing from a "customer" perspective. Somehow, they'd always seemed a bit like an "enemy" who were preventing us doing our jobs well. Of course this was clearly not true, and the dialogue produced a far deeper understanding of the challenges they faced to deliver a vehicle on time, within budget and capable of meeting all its performance and cost targets. Their prime goal, as far as we were concerned, was a statement of confidence at each stage of the development programme, later followed by demonstration, that a vehicle would meet the necessary test standards. While, of course, using as few costly prototype parts and vehicles as possible.

Encouraged by these conversations, we explored how we could bring our experiences to bear more effectively at the early conceptual stages of vehicle design, working more closely with teams that were working to package Rover and third-party engines into structures that had been designed around a particular range of Honda engines. Often, a relatively simple decision about the location of an engine mounting or packaging of a particular component could make a huge difference to performance. To support this, we restructured our department into vehicle teams, bringing the testers and analysts working on a particular vehicle programme even closer. Gradually, respect for each other's skills and experiences began to build as we worked on problems together.

My memory is that this took considerable time. Too often, debates raged that the "prediction" of the result was "wrong" – meaning that the test results didn't match the model – or that the testers could observe what went wrong without being able to offer any conclusive insight into why.

Reflections

Reflecting now, a more deliberate focus on encouraging these de-bates to happen in a more productive way within the team might have helped us come together more quickly. However, happen it did, and through these dialogues clarity of the preventive actions we needed to take emerged. Our experience in the use of the simulations to understand and explain a particular test behaviour improved, and hence the models became better. We began to form clearer ideas on what we needed the simulation tools to do for us, which guided a well-structured programme to develop more advanced simulation methods that were really fit for purpose.

Alongside this, we began to exert greater influence on the design process as a result of our efforts, aided by the recent growth in awareness of vehicle safety issues in Europe as well as the US that, although it gave us some more challenging goals, also made the topic more significant to sales and marketing, and thus to the overall organisation, so we acquired a stronger voice.

One thing we didn't do, that now surprises me, is create much by way of standard documentation for how to go about all these things. We were still reliant, for some time, on maintaining the knowledge and experience within what was a relatively small team. Looked at with the benefit of hindsight, this would have been a prime candidate for the type of design checklist so beloved of Toyota. This was to take a couple more years as the team grew and we started to develop documented guidelines for approaching a new vehicle programme. At the time we hadn't heard of "standardisation," but that's what we were doing.

However, I'm now moving well beyond the "first year" I was challenged to write about. At the time, what we were doing didn't seem so remarkable, particularly in product development. However, looking back, I can see that it marked a turning point, both for the organisation and for me personally. Organisationally, it marked a move away from a culture of "firefighting" and a top-down, autocratic management style to one that was more engaging and focused on scientific method.

I believe we were very good at not just copying what the Japanese were doing, but rather took the time to understand 'why' they were doing it and adapting the principles to our situations, unlike so many organisations that often seem just to copy the method then wonder why it doesn't work. Personally, it opened my eyes to taking a wider perspective on my work that eventually led me out of product development into production control and then a number of strategic transformation roles. Alongside that, I was invited to become a facilitator for cascading the Total Quality Improvement programme to the rest of the staff in our function in product development, starting a trend that was to be a feature of the rest of my corporate life, running alongside my "day job," as I subsequently facilitated programmes in "Leading Management" (the Rover interpretation of Hoshin Kanri) and "Coaching for Performance."

However, I could forgive you for asking the question, was that all really "Lean?" If we were to look for the explicit presence of some of the "markers" that many practitioners today might cite – definitions of value, waste, flow and pull, application of visual management, 5S, standardisation, and so on – then you could argue that it wasn't. However, at a deeper level, I'm absolutely convinced that it was. Having studied and practiced what Mark might call "real Lean" for a number of years now, I can look back on those early years and reflect on the foundations that were laid for the work I do today, even though I didn't realise what was happening at the time. I still have, and refer to, the nine slim reference volumes for Total Quality Management that I received on that first training programme and, honestly, all of the key building blocks that we might think of today are there: focus on the customer, effective leadership, team working, observation and analysis, process management, root cause problem solving, engaging people at every level, and effective structures for continuous improvement. More fundamentally, I don't think I ever saw improvement activity as a set of tools, but more as a different way of thinking.

On reflection, I suspect that the company tried to cover too much ground too quickly as far as the training went, as I don't actually remember covering or using all of that material at the time. That said, I think that so much was done right; a focus on people and leadership as much as, if not more than the specific tools and techniques: the creation of a culture that valued prevention, real problem solving and continuous improvement rather than endless firefighting, a real attempt to value and engage people at all levels in the organisation. And those things are hard, multi-generational things to get right in a large organisation. If we look honestly at the MINI and Jaguar Land Rover businesses today – the descendants of the British Leyland I joined nearly 40 years ago – they are almost unrecognisable and vastly improved, yet would acknowledge that they still have a long way to go. After all, as Mark said in his opening chapter, real Lean takes time and constant practice.

At a personal level, looking at what few of my notes from the time still exist and reflecting on what I remember of what I was doing, I realise that a lot of my focus was on process – finding better ways of doing things and making sure they were followed. I was, and still am, an engineer at the core after all! While I recognised that building more productive relationships was important, I don't think I gave enough attention to developing this side of my skills and how that impacted on my effectiveness as a developing manager and leader of improvement activities. The more I do this stuff as a consultant, the more I realise how much is about people: engaging and motivating them, enabling them to understand each other's perspectives better, and finding more productive ways to work together. If I had my time again, I'd spend more time studying and practising these skills, particularly understanding in a deeper way those factors that impact on motivation and engagement.

That said, I believe that first year of Total Quality Management was hugely foundational and transformational and changed the course of my subsequent career. While I was never involved in a role that was specifically just about leading improvement projects as so many of the contributors to this book have done, moving into a role to improve the way a team or department worked became a guiding theme of the rest of my career with Rover Group and BMW Group and, eventually, to me leaving the organisation to focus exclusively on this aspect in my career as a consultant.

Chapter Fourteen – Andy Sheppard

Andy Sheppard helps businesses to transform their manufacturing operations and serves as a technical advisor to Lean specialists. He is the author of *The Incredible Transformation of Gregory Todd: a Novel about Leadership and Managing Change*[a].

[a]http://amzn.to/23gUgQk

Learning from Others

I wholeheartedly endorse the great hope for this book: that in reading it we can advance through the learning of others. The most significant learning I have to offer has its roots in a singular experience that set the course of my career. It concerns the approach to Lean transformation, although it also deepened and sharpened my understanding of Lean itself. At the time, I thought I already knew quite a bit about practising Lean. I also thought I understood the challenge of change management, and why it was so difficult to implement sustainable change. I had heard corporate reports of Lean transformations, but, as a British engineer, I tended to regard them with a healthy dose of scepticism (as I still do!). With hindsight, I had little idea how to kick start an organisation's Lean journey. I also had no idea that so much sustainable improvement could be delivered so quickly - until I saw it happen.

Fortuitously, this encounter was built on the learning of others. In 1991, just a few years after the term Lean production was first coined, Peter Willats co-founded the Kaizen Institute of Europe. He later recruited Blair McCallum into this earliest of Lean consulting firms. Blair had worked as a technical specialist for Toyota, implementing Lean in Toyota's European supply base. Through this experience, he had become a proponent of the Toyota Supplier Support Centre's systematic approach to Lean transformation. When Peter became Director of McKinsey & Company's Manufacturing Practice, he invited Blair to establish and run McKinsey's Production System Design Centre (PSDC). Its aim was to train engineers in a systematic approach to Lean transformation, to meet the growing need for this capability across the international consulting firm's clients.

In 1999, being oblivious to much of the debate about how best to introduce Lean to non-Lean operations, I became one of the first three recruits to the PSDC. The premise was to spend the first year with smaller "learning partners" who signed up to an agenda of transformation, rather than the tailored needs of more typical McKinsey clients that I would go on to serve. I thought I was reasonably well prepared. I had learnt aspects of Total Productive Maintenance (TPM) on oil refineries with Shell, who had sponsored me through university. I had studied Lean as part of my degree courses in manufacturing engineering at Cambridge. Thanks to the structure of these courses, I had also been able to practise Lean on varied industrial assignments, including value stream mapping at Land Rover and implementing kanban in a manufacturer of solar panels. I had then spent three further years as a production engineer in CarnaudMetalbox (now part of Crown Cork), where I had learned further intricacies of leading improvement groups and navigating change within a large corporation, albeit one with a well-established corporate improvement program. So, on the brink of our first PSDC assignment, I felt ready to contribute to a good 10 to 20% improvement in our learning partners' Key Performance Indicators, providing we would have good management support. With hindsight, I had never considered that, although personal experience can be valuable, it can also shape and limit our expectations - and with this, our own potential. Thankfully, under Blair's leadership, I was shaken out of my comfort zone from day one. Within four months, my expectations had been blown out of the water. Productivity had doubled, lead time had collapsed from two months to two weeks and two facilities had been consolidated into one. More importantly, the organisation was brimming with fresh verve, because of its collective achievements, to which everyone had contributed. They had come together and there was a strong sense that together, they could take on the world. The learning partner had been transformed and so had my horizons.

I have now been working out further transformations in diverse industries around the world while reflecting and building on this learning experience. I would say that the power of the approach lies in blending effective content for three ingredients: technical insight, practical change management and good leadership.

Before I go on to describe what I have learnt about each of these in turn, I would like to say something about alternative approaches to implementing Lean. In particular, I have met many people – particularly in the USA - who have learnt to implement Lean through a series of kaizen events. I have learnt a great deal from some of these people about how to organise and run effective improvement events. I appreciate the sense of urgency, bonding and drive to get things done that they can accomplish, and I wish I had benefitted from more of this when running improvement groups at CarnaudMetalbox.

However, most companies have systemic problems, especially concerning the flow of material and information through more complicated processes, which cannot be solved through a series of relatively independent events. I believe that most operations that have not already been shaped by Lean should first benefit from a more directive and systematic Lean design, applied to its end-to-end flows. This ensures maximum impact but also avoids creating an isolated island of improvement in the middle of a value stream. Blair always insisted that such an island is likely to be eroded over time by the surrounding waste. I believe that the appropriate role for kaizen events is for further improvement once Lean systems have been implemented. They can also be very effective in focusing people on a relatively contained problem, such as a loss in Overall Equipment Effectiveness (OEE). If this does not yet appear to make sense, I hope that the following sections may shed some further light on this argument.

Technical Insight

My first transformation initiative started with mapping the current-state flow through the entire operation, together with the learning partner's own agents. So far so good, although Blair seemed a little directive about the information he was after. It became evident that Blair was looking for data to confirm a vision he already had in mind for the business. This I was not so comfortable with: as an engineer, I wanted to start with the problem and it seemed like Blair was starting with a solution. He then began to farm out specific pieces of analysis, with instructions such as "prove that if we do one-piece flow, the entire assembly operation can fit into this amount of space." In our second learning partner the requests were different, such as "prove that if we process parts like this in that process, the maximum process lead time will be two days."

Technical insight requires more than Lean knowledge: it means discerning the key that can collapse the residual waste for a specific operation. This is what Blair was modeling, drawing on his Toyota training and the experience he had gained in transforming Toyota's suppliers. In most operations, his focus was the key needed to transform the specific end-to-end flow, since this would then tend to collapse many, if not all, of the seven wastes. It appeared Blair would never be satisfied with incremental improvement: he was always driving towards radical transformation. This resulted in transformed results so quickly that even sceptical leaders in other parts of a business were forced to sit up and take note. Furthermore, it also resulted in facilities that *looked* radically different. This emphasised the transformation to the workforce and helped to lock in the new ways of working, not least because processes had been bolted down in new locations.

The capability to redesign end-to-end flow for a specific operation is something that Blair appeared to pull together intuitively. Nearly all of the Lean literature for flow still seems to focus on designing flow for low-variation, high-volume components such as automotive components. For me, one of the most intellectually stimulating aspects of leading Lean transformations has therefore been working out how best to design collapsed flows for more complicated, make-to-order products – and how to teach others to do so.

A common principle for redesigning more complicated flows can best be illustrated with a distribution plot of production lead time. This can be computed from a representative sample of orders and a typical example is shown schematically in Figure 1.

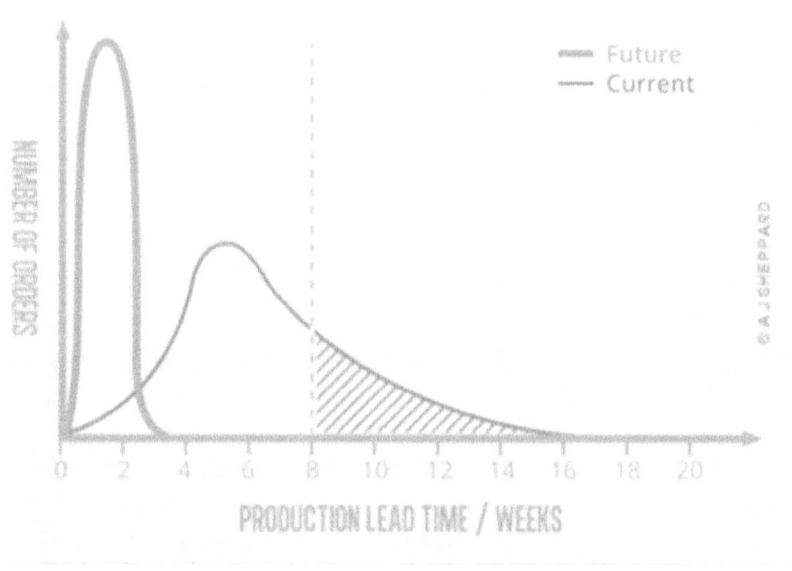

Figure 1: Schematic Example of Distribution Plot of Production Lead Time

The *current* plot shows a wide variation of lead time: a few critical orders may have been bullied through the operation within one week but the mode is currently around five weeks. The long tail causes the problem and typically results from orders which are delayed in successive processes (e.g., because they are rarer variants). Since the standard customer order lead time in this example is eight weeks, the orders in the shaded tail would be shipped late. If this is considered unacceptable, pre-production of unconfirmed orders would be a likely strategy. This would enable the operation to get a head start on orders, and it would entail *finishing* products to customer specifications instead of pure make-to-order production (from raw material). For example, although not shown on this chart, pre-production might then start ten weeks in advance in order to improve delivery performance. This would then lock in at least ten weeks of inventory. The key question to ask is what if the plot could be narrowed in the future as represented by the taller curve (i.e., by end-to-end flow design, which may feature value streams, First-In-First-Out or standardised every-part-every intervals)? This core question now informs my hypotheses in many types of make-to-order or finish-to-order operations. For example, if I judge from a bottom-up perspective that good Lean design across all processes can result in a tail that never exceeds five weeks, orders can be released five weeks in advance and we can return to make everything from scratch within this period, if appropriate. Doing so will halve inventory from ten weeks to five weeks, and all associated wastes can be collapsed. This can then form the spine of a significant, holistic transformation.

Interestingly, during general consulting training within McKinsey & Company, we were taught to become hypothesis-driven. The central idea is to form an educated hypothesis for a solution to a client's problem. This can then be tested with a fraction of the data that is typically available in a complex organisation. My reticence was overcome by seeing that the approach is rational because the hypothesis can be rejected or modified if the data disprove it. The benefit, of course, depends on the quality of the insight that instructs the hypothesis, but a good hypothesis can lead to benefits being delivered within a fraction of the time it would take to systematically analyse all the available data and opinions. Although Blair was also new to McKinsey, he had been modelling this core skill as well as any consultant I went on to work with within the firm. He had also clearly demonstrated the power of this skill in facilitating systematic transformation.

It is perhaps worth stating that I have been assuming all readers are somewhat familiar with Lean, as depicted in the Toyota Production System (TPS) house. However, to conclude this section on technical insight, I feel that it may be helpful to briefly make two clarifications.

Firstly, I have been using the term *flow* to refer to the *just-in-time* pillar in the TPS house. I normally try to avoid the term "just-in-time" because I have seen it misapplied so often. For example, I have heard people claim to have implemented just-in-time despite *increasing* waste in the supply chain by pushing the need for inventory upstream (albeit neatly organised in visual lanes or even in a supermarket.)

Secondly, while I have focused on flow design as the spine for a radical transformation, such a flow system must always be implemented as part of a broader Lean system. By this, I mean reinforcing the flow changes with the relevant application of "Jidoka" (or building in quality at the source, the second pillar in the TPS house) and supporting all changes with standard work, problem-solving skills, and performance management. The transformation should also be built on a foundation of stable processes and people. However, I would describe myself as a Lean pragmatist rather than a Lean purist. For example, I have heard it argued that a transformation should not be attempted until all processes have been stabilised. My view is that although a certain amount of stability is indeed required, other techniques can often be used to work around remaining instability. Otherwise, a business may never have the incentive or the patience to get its journey into proper Lean off the ground.

Change Management

Having the technical insight to know *what* to do in a specific operation is not enough. It is also essential to know *how* to go about implementing it, and how to work with the right people in the right way to ensure that the new systems can be sustained and further improved. This concerns the art of change management.

I joined the PSDC thinking I knew a bit about managing change. I had already learned how to work with people to develop sustainable solutions and I had learned the hard way to involve process experts from the outset if I wanted to improve it. This includes technical experts as well as those who run the process every day. For example, in CarnaudMetalbox I had helped a technologist go a long way towards developing a setup reduction device for a machine with multiple heads – only to be told by a line technician that it would not work because the heads were wearing at different rates. I had also learned the hard way not to develop anything without working with someone who had agreed to take ownership of it. For example, I feared I might have 'wasted' a summer developing a commercial database for Shell: users liked it but I had neglected to take the initiative to find someone to keep it updated. I also liked to think that my character, background, and experience had equipped me to work well with all kinds of different people.

With hindsight, I realise that on the brink of my first transformation I still had no idea how I could get multiple, complex changes done quickly and sustainably. Part of the issue was that I still had no idea how radical Blair's vision would be: it would require everyone within the scope to change the way they thought about their work and to change what they did all day, every day.

In McKinsey, I went on to meet other consultants who had worked for Toyota and who had good knowledge of Lean flow. Most were good at describing how a facility could and should operate differently. They were also good at describing the potential impact. However, among them, Blair stood out because of the capability he had built in *delivering* the impact. Most Toyota employees had worked in Toyota facilities that had been designed from Lean principles: they had never had the opportunity to transform non-Lean operations.

For example, how do you start by convincing a general manager that radical changes are worth risking, especially when their boss or board may not be demanding it? And how can you ensure that *every* manager and operator agrees with the changes enough to help develop and implement them, let alone to sustain them? In developing their non-Lean suppliers, Toyota's Supplier Support Centre is the one part of Toyota that has long been grappling with these challenges and learning how to overcome them. Blair brought with him a change management mechanism that had been born out of this learning.

After sixteen years of practising Blair's approach because of *how well* it works, I am still learning about *why* this is the case, and how to make the best use of the model. Just as good technical insight pulls the relevant *Lean design* together, so I see that the change management model pulls the relevant *people* together. It generates a spotlight to create focus, a process to engage, and an urgency to change. It is a bit like delivering the benefits of a kaizen event while enabling the more complex and holistic end-to-end transformation. The model comprises four phases as shown in Figure 2: Diagnose, Design, Implement and Refine. The simple words communicate how the organisation will be led and engaged through a natural problem solving process. The needs and opportunities must first be diagnosed before solutions are designed to meet them. The changes are then implemented, before provisions are made to refine them and to check that they will be sustained. The expert facilitating the process must tread a fine and challenging line: keeping his/her own immediate hypothesis private while guiding the team to develop their own similar yet improved design.

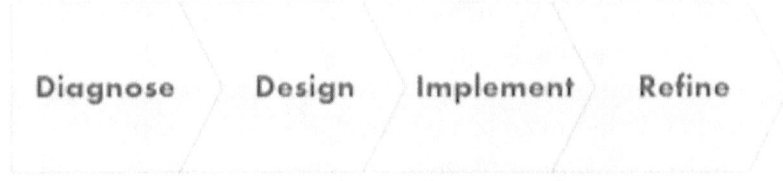

Figure 2: Four-Phased Approach to Managing Change

Typically, sixteen weeks is a good time for the entire process. This tends to be long enough to get into sufficient detail, to ensure that solutions will work for every product that goes through a typical scope. However, it is also short enough to create the sense of urgency required for change. It is good to have clear time limits for each phase, such as two weeks each for diagnose, design and refine phases, with the remaining ten weeks to implement. Without these deadlines, the diagnose and design phase will tend to overrun, because there is always more analysis that can be requested. I was shocked on my first transformation when Blair announced we would move assembly workstations on the weekend leading into the very first week of the implementation phase. Yet this shock demonstrated to everyone that substantial transformation really was happening: every day without such a shock would have preserved the status quo and reinforced inertia.

A lot of deep work is required to design detailed flows that will work for all products, and a deep level of coaching is required if everyone is to understand and be convinced of what they need to do differently. Given this depth, a good number of change agents should be freed up from the operation to be dedicated to a full-time change team. It is critical - but very difficult – for organisations that have already improved to free up the right quantity and calibre of people for this team. Therefore, it is normally necessary to limit the scope of the first transformation accordingly. The first transformation can then be billed as a pilot, to prove the approach and the benefits of Lean to the organisation. Since the scope should incorporate an end-to-end flow that can be collapsed, it tends to concern a narrow slice through the organisation. Hence the approach is described as "narrow and deep." In my experience, an appropriate level of resourcing can be suggested through a 1:5:50 guideline. This refers to one capable expert training and leading a full-time team of five change agents to facilitate a narrow-and-deep transformation in a scope that involves 50 frontline operators (although this might range from 20 to 100 operators, depending on an operation's labour intensity and the number of shifts involved).

An important principle is that although the full-time change agents do the bulk of the analysis and coaching, they should never make any decision by themselves. They must, therefore, work with the operation's chain of command, who must make all the decisions - especially the line manager or team leader in the relevant area for each set of changes. During my first transformation, this very quickly became the bane of my life but it helped to ensure ownership and sustainability, not to mention my focus on developing my influencing skills!

The process of change should be governed by a steering committee. Typically, this should be chaired by the most senior manager on site and incorporate others who have a particular influence, interest, or role in the likely changes and benefits. They need to be involved in preparing the pilot transformation and they should be seen to be leading the initiative as it progresses. Typically, the committee will meet five times during the four months: to provide direction, to ratify proposals presented by line managers, to monitor progress on the shop floor, and to solve problems or constraints that are limiting progress.

Leadership

During the first transformation, I was aware that Blair was preparing and coaching the managing director behind the scenes. He kept on emphasising that, without good leadership, an organisation's Lean transformation would fail. This much sounded pretty obvious, but most of my own learning in this field has come by doing: working out how best to prepare, support and coach leaders through the transformations that I have been facilitating on their behalf.

To some extent, all the issues described in the previous sections are also leadership issues, insofar as people can rarely grant themselves the mandate to drive a systematic approach or a cross-functional programme of change. Therefore, managers or change agents first need to convince their senior leader to grant them this mandate. This can be particularly tricky when the leader has already demonstrated their belief in Lean, through granting the mandate for an internal continuous improvement function, for example. The organisation is already doing Lean: why should it risk confusion and upheaval by doing anything differently?

In general, it is wise to look at any situation through the lens of the person you are seeking to engage. Empathy and a genuine ability to help a leader with their most pressing concerns go a long way towards making the case for a narrow-and-deep, cross-functional, systematic transformation initiative. I have only come across one senior leader whose motivation concerned methods: his goal was to do the right things in the right way, to reduce waste. It is more natural for leaders to concern themselves with outcomes and results. I normally avoid the term Lean because of the many misconceptions that can be associated with it. Instead, I tend to inquire about the business needs that the operation can help to deliver through targeted improvement.

I have also learnt to broaden this discussion by introducing what I call the 5Cs, as shown in Figure 3.

Figure 3: 5Cs for How Operations Can Impact Business Performance

These are five potential business needs that can be impacted by operations. I find that this helps to gently navigate beyond limited perspectives that can sometimes be held about operations. For example, one typical leader I worked with was initially focused on the need for his operation to reduce costs, as to help the business compete in markets that were generally in steady decline. He was unaware of the opportunity to design different systems for different products, but the discussion surfaced their recent success story with a new product that passed through some of the same equipment. They were already capacity constrained in this high-growth niche, so we discussed the opportunity to tailor a transformation for this need. By designing a tailored flow system with a special focus on OEE improvement, we were able to collapse lead time and liberate capacity to grow sales in this priority area without adding labour. This resulted in an exponential growth in profitability, not to mention boosting morale within the facility.

My personal goal for an early meeting with a leader in a new organisation is, therefore, to discern a potential scope and a tailored hypothesis to help them achieve the most from improving their operation. I can then seek to validate this and estimate the likely impact through initial observations on the shop floor.

Preparing a leader to *lead* the transformation is often more difficult. The minimum requirement is to provide good training on technical, change management and leadership aspects of transformation, and to prepare the scope and resources (including agreement for their own role and the time they would personally set aside for the initiative). I began to learn that the risk of all such training is that it can give leaders a false assurance of *knowledge* while failing to impart capability. After all, Blair had not shaped my own career as a trainer but as a role model: I had not been told what to do, I had been shown. This point was underlined when I was asked to train further McKinsey consultants about transformation, but away from client sites. If I had been in the shoes of these consultants, it might have reinforced what I thought I had already known, without showing me how to navigate the issues like Blair. Admittedly, the leader of a business does not need to develop the same capabilities as a change agent, but I find that similar principles apply. For example, I have found that without prior experience of transformation, ambitious leaders will often try to move faster down pitted tracks that seem like clever shortcuts. Eventually, it was this desire to *show* the accidents these pitfalls can cause, as well as to model the art of transformation that had been modeled to me, which led me to craft a management novel. By painting a picture of both good and insufficient role models, I wanted to offer more than knowledge: the aim is to offer a shortcut to *capability*.

One of the more subtle pitfalls I was keen to portray is the trap of a leader viewing their transformation as another initiative in need of their *support*. This default position is not enough. Neither will it be enough for a leader to *manage* the change program. A change program does, of course, have to be supported and managed. But, in my experience, a leader will not transform their business with this perspective. I need to help a leader to see their role as leading their organisation *through* a successful transformation. Otherwise, a leader will effectively be expecting change from *other people.*

Firstly, this can compound existing problems of mistrust or morale in the organisation. Secondly, leaders often do have to change their thinking more than anyone else, because it is likely that their thinking has shaped the current system and sustained the waste in it more than that of anyone else. In order to lead the business through a proper transformation, leaders will normally need to surface and solve institutional problems – including those that may have been buried for years, and those caused by systems they may have implemented themselves, albeit with good intentions. For Lean transformations, these might include decision making distorted by accounting protocol, contracts that prevent teamwork, bonus systems that reward unhelpful behaviour, a culture of fear that prevents people from surfacing problems, and an excessive focus on short-term targets that sustains variability in operating practices.

In the early stages of working with an organisation, I now try to diagnose hidden issues like those above that may constrain it later on. Generally, I think it is good practice to raise these issues with leaders sooner rather than later. Firstly, their response gives a flavour of the organisation's initial appetite to deal with the issues. Secondly, it also tends to make it easier to coach the organisation by dealing with an issue later on. However, it is also important to avoid too much emphasis on the costs and challenges of a systematic transformation. Otherwise, why would anyone choose to start? The balance is found through refocusing leaders on the much greater benefits that are within reach. This includes releasing the latent potential within their workforce and transforming their organisation's culture. It is a source of great encouragement to me that there are many leaders who are in pursuit of exactly this, which will always release the greatest business and personal rewards of practising Lean.

Chapter Fifteen – Mike Leigh

Mike Leigh is the President and Founder of OpX Solutions, LLC, a consulting company that specializes in helping manufacturers and other organizations pursue Operational Excellence through leadership development and process improvement.

Mike has spent most of his 30-year career in various operational leadership roles. Prior to starting his own business, he worked as a manufacturing leader and a Lean leader for General Electric, building industrial gas turbines and wind turbines for the energy industry. Before that, Mike served 10 years on active duty in the US Navy, specializing in surface warfare and nuclear propulsion. He eventually retired from the Navy Reserve as a Commander.

Mike has a B.S. degree in Computer Engineering from the Milwaukee School of Engineering, and anan M.S. degree from Troy State University in Human Resource Management. He also qualified as a Nuclear Engineer in the US Navy.

Mike and his family live in Roanoke, VA.

You can contact him at mike@opxsolutionsllc.com, or connect with him on LinkedIn[71].

A very lucky guy

I am a very lucky guy. Most people would probably describe my career as successful. After retiring from the military and doing well as a manufacturing leader, I've been able to build my own business helping organizations improve their processes and develop their leaders. But

---

[71] https://www.linkedin.com/in/leighmichael1

along the way, I had developed the mindset that I was a good leader (I must have been because I was getting promoted, right?) I also thought I knew everything I needed to know to start and succeed in my own business.

One day about eight years ago, I walked into my plant manager's office and told him I was quitting to start my business. To say he was shocked would have been an understatement. At the time, I was working for General Electric as an operations manager with a team of 180 people. I was on the "fast track" and, unbeknownst to me, I had been selected to attend a corporate leadership course for potential future executives. In my new business, I was going to teach others how to be good leaders, but I probably would have failed because it was the start of the great recession.

My luck started the next day when the general manager of our business unit visited our factory. His name was Tim, and he was someone I had known and respected for several years. I considered him a friend and mentor. He met with me that day after I announced my resignation and said, "Mike, I think you should stay with GE, and let me tell you why." I won't bore you with all the details, but he ultimately convinced me to stay when he offered to get me into a corporate Lean leader role. Although I knew almost nothing about Lean, the little I did know was fascinating to me, and the role would allow me to develop "consulting skills" that could prove useful in my future business. My Lean journey was about to go from 0 to 60 overnight.

My introduction to Lean occurred about two years earlier. It was my first day on the job in the operations manager role. The morning I showed up at the factory, the guy whom I was replacing (Jim, who was moving to a new role himself) met me at the front door and said, "We are having a kaizen event this week, and the kickoff meeting is about to start." I hadn't even gone to my new office yet, or set down my bag, as we walked into the kickoff meeting with about 60 people. There were five teams ready to go, two corporate Lean leaders, a consultant from Shingijutsu, and the entire factory leadership team. "You and I are leading a kaizen team this week", Jim said.

I had started with GE during their Six Sigma heyday and like almost everyone else, I was a certified Green Belt. Twice in my GE career, I was offered Black Belt roles (considered an essential career role back then), but I turned them down because I just didn't like Six Sigma. I had heard of Lean, but I didn't know anything about it. So for the most part, I was simply along for the ride during this kaizen event.

Our consultant that week was excellent. Every time he talked to our team, I thought, "This stuff is great!" But I couldn't fully enjoy the week because I was too busy worrying about getting started in my new role. So as soon as the event was done, I jumped into learning about all the production processes I was about to manage and began to lead in a way that had brought me success in the past. And for the next two years, my style continued to work. During my tenure, we conducted four or five more major kaizen events, each one exposing me more to the concepts of Lean. It felt right and natural to me, and I began to form ideas of how Lean could help our processes. But why make changes and take risks when you are already successful?

So my first bit of luck was having a mentor talk me into staying with GE as a Lean leader. My second bit of luck was becoming a member of a true learning organization with phenomenal mentors. I had become a Lean leader in GE Energy's corporate Lean office. In total, there were four of us who were led by a GE Executive named Mark. Our team's function was to help GE Energy factories implement Lean. We did this by providing consulting and mentorship to the leadership in each factory on the concepts of Lean, and we hired Shingijutsu consultants to support multi-team kaizen events and mentor us along the way. Mark wanted the four of us to first and foremost learn from the Shingijutsu consultants so we could increase our knowledge and improve our support to the factories.

When I first started, Mark said to me, "It will take you about six months until you become comfortable" to give advice and support the business. What!?! Wasn't I expected to have all the answers right away? It was the first time in my 20 years of leadership experience that I wasn't expected to jump in and take charge. And Mark was right. It took about six months before I felt comfortable giving advice.

Over the next five years, I supported 45 Shingijutsu multi-team, weeklong kaizen events in 15 different factories. Prior to each event, my role was to provide advice and support to the factory to scope the teams properly and conduct necessary pre-work. But during the events, I was with the consultant for the entire week (including dinner each evening). At first, it was humbling, but the more I learned, the more I wanted to learn. And I believe I learned what Lean and TPS is really supposed to be about. Most people do not get the opportunity to learn about Lean like I did. I was lucky.

During those years with GE, and subsequent years in my own business, I've learned a lot of lessons and key concepts (most of which fall under the category "If I only knew then what I know now"). I sincerely hope these lessons will pass on some of my luck to you.

Lesson 1: Leadership and culture is trump

As I began to be exposed to the concepts and philosophy of Lean, I was hooked. Almost immediately, I understood the concepts of standard work, jidoka, flow, and respect for people. I was excited beyond belief because here was this philosophy/methodology/toolset, that provided endless opportunities to improve manufacturing operations. So why wasn't everyone excited?

Early in my Lean leader role, I expected everyone to quickly under-stand and believe in the concepts of Lean. I became frustrated that manufacturing leaders across our business couldn't see the benefits. The leaders of several of the factories I worked with seemed to support Lean and kaizen. But, during the kaizen events, they were only seen at the kickoff and closeout meetings. Why don't they par-ticipate? Although the lack of participation by senior leaders usually did not have a big impact on the success of the kaizen event, over the long-term, those factories usually experienced limited success and sustainability.

In a select few businesses, it was different. During the kaizen events, the plant manager would block out the entire week, and either walk with the sensei or participate on a team. These leaders wanted to learn, and their participation communicated to the workforce that Lean was important. As you can guess, the long-term success of kaizen efforts in these factories was much greater.

Before I go further, I need to make an important point. As you read this chapter, I may sound very critical of GE. It is unavoidable for me to describe what I've learned on my Lean journey without describing some things I believe GE does incorrectly. However, you would be mistaken to believe that I hate or disrespect GE. There is a reason GE has been successful for so long and has a phenomenal reputation. They were a great company to work for, and they do much more right than they do wrong. I have nothing but respect for GE, and I was fortunate to work for them for 13 years.

It's probably not a secret to anyone reading this that leadership plays an important part in the success of a Lean journey. I quickly learned the same thing, and I got frustrated when some leaders wouldn't become more engaged. I admit that I once considered these leaders as "cement heads." But over time, I changed my attitude and developed a deeper understanding of why some leaders stayed on the sidelines.

A wise mentor of mine once told me, "Those who are most resistant to change are those most effective in the current system." Senior production managers and executives who lead GE factories (or lead any organization) have achieved success in their companies. At GE, leaders who could hit their numbers each quarter were valued and innovative risk-takers were only rewarded if they didn't fail. I imagine this culture is not much different from most companies. So it takes a unique leader willing to do something different. I call these leaders promotors, because in their mind, practicing Lean is not an option, and everyone knows it through his or her words and actions. I was not a promotor as an operations manager. Hit the numbers and don't take risks. If I only knew then what I know now...

I also learned that some leaders do not become more engaged in Lean because they simply do not see the benefits. Many of the leaders I worked with had not been exposed to the concepts (and benefits) of Lean. No one (leaders or others) will ever be highly motivated to work toward any goal or initiative unless they truly believe in the benefits. In one of the factories I supported, there was a production manager named Joe who was also the site Lean leader. He was innovative, dedicated, and a Lean promotor. With the help of our team, Joe accomplished some phenomenal results, including a lead time reduction from eight to five days for a major assembly. He used to complain to me because none of the other production managers would engage in kaizen activities. I had to explain to Joe that none of the other leaders understood Lean well enough to understand how practicing Lean could help them.

There is an excellent book called *Mindset*[72], by Carol Dweck, that describes the benefits of having a "growth mindset" instead of a "fixed mindset." A growth mindset is a belief that your qualities can be cultivated through effort, and everyone can grow through application and experience. A fixed mindset is a belief that your qualities can't be changed, and creates an internal need to prove yourself. Someone with a growth mindset wants to learn, and mistakes are part of the learning process. Someone with a fixed mindset is risk adverse and looks at mistakes as failures.

For those leaders who have a fixed mindset and are not willing to make changes, there is not much a supporting Lean leader or consultant can do. Although I am an optimist, and I never give up trying to help leaders develop a growth mindset, I learned it was better to spend my efforts with those who want to try, and learn, and grow. So our Lean team focused primarily on supporting those managers and businesses who had a Lean growth mindset. We created "model lines" and highlighted our Lean successes with the intent of helping those with the fixed mindset to see. It is difficult to change someone's mindset, and we only had limited success "creating" Lean promotors, but I believe it is always worth the effort because significant success practicing Lean cannot be achieved otherwise. Strong, promoting leadership trumps all other factors in determining sustained success practicing Lean.

Lesson 2: Be believable

For anyone who has tried to convince others of the benefits of Lean, or to motivate them to take action, you know it's not easy. I've been

---

[72]http://amzn.to/1U91mHE

trying to do this for many years, and I still haven't figured it out. But I have learned at least one thing about motivation. Another mentor of mine once told me, "Everyone wants something to believe in." If a leader can create a vision that others believe in, there is a much greater probability that action will take place toward that vision. But it must be believable.

Once I understood how Lean could transform a business, I became very excited and motivated to help others. Moving lines. One-piece flow. Rapid changeovers. I saw huge opportunity everywhere. "We can create a one-piece flow cell here and cut our lead time by 90%!" "If we reduce the changeover time by half on the PCBA line, we can reduce our batch sizes by half and get rid of a lot of WIP!" "Let's put a team together to get rid of all the crane usage on this line!" The responses I received ranged from mild acceptance to downright negativity. "That CAN'T be done," or "It will NEVER work" were heard often. So I started to respond in a mature, logical way. "No one is allowed to use the words CAN'T and NEVER during our kaizen efforts!" Why didn't everyone get excited like I was?

Then one day during a Shingijutsu kaizen event, I learned what my problem was. There was a team working to improve an assembly line layout and they suggested minor changes to the sensei. The consultant gave his approval and the team proceeded to make the changes over the next couple days. I was shocked. It was obvious to me how some major improvements could be done, but the consultant didn't push the team. Once we were alone I asked, "Sensei, it was obvious the team could have made bigger improvements. Why didn't you push them to make bigger changes?" He responded, "Mike-san, the team must learn to walk before they can run. Until they learn to walk, they won't understand or believe they can run."

No wonder why few people believed me. I was trying to convince non-runners that they could complete a marathon when I should have helped them to run a 5K. Why would anyone believe a press die could be changed in 15 minutes when no one had ever seen it done in less than 2 hours? It took me a couple years before I learned this lesson. But once I did, it was much easier to convince others to take action. I simply had to provide a vision of the next small step and keep the bigger vision to myself.

Lesson 3: Promote the journey – the results will come

Results are important. Ultimately, it's why we work on continuous improvement. But when it comes to practicing Lean, it really is about the journey, not the destination.

One of the key philosophies of Lean is to create a learning organization. In an earlier chapter of this book, Michael Lombard mentions the importance of quickly trying ideas over and over again to learn. Mark Graban frequently discusses the importance of having respect for people and promoting a culture of learning in his books and blogs. I couldn't agree more, and that's what I mean by the journey. But how do you convince business leaders and clients that it's OK if we don't get results right away as long as learning is taking place?

It's a fact in business that results matter. And GE was no different. Almost every business leader wanted results and ROI from kaizen events, and I would be lying if I told you I didn't hope for a "big hitter" at each one. Before every event, we ensured that each team had measurable goals to accomplish, and if ROI couldn't be demonstrated, we often had to re-scope the project – or select a different project altogether. One business leader would go so far as to demand that every team had to complete two safety and two quality improvements during a kaizen event, regardless if they were related to that team's scope. On the last day of a kaizen week, team members would be searching throughout the factory for safety and quality improvements unrelated to the scope of their project while missing out on more opportunities to learn from the sensei. Sheesh!

I haven't figured out yet how to convince some leaders that short-term benefits are less important than the long-term results that will be achieved by allowing people to learn without pressure to achieve measurable results on every initiative. This was nearly impossible at GE because most leaders were only in their roles for two or three years before moving on, and missing your numbers each quarter was unacceptable. But I've discovered that smaller companies, and those that are privately owned, are more likely to think long-term because their leaders are there longer. I now always set the expectation that the primary goal of kaizen is to learn. Eventually, the results will happen. As a consultant, it's hard to not promise short-term results. It's difficult to turn down work where the client's only priority is cutting costs. But I would be doing our Lean community a disservice if I did work that focused on the short term or only on cost.

Lesson 4: Promote the philosophy – not the tools

I love Mark Graban's L.A.M.E. acronym (Lean As Misguidedly Executed)[73] and I've begun to use it when I teach. Unfortunately, I think there might be more examples of L.A.M.E. these days than there are solid Lean applications. I believe the primary reason this has occurred is due to the prevalent thought that Lean is a "set of tools."

When I started practicing Lean, like most people I first learned the tools (value stream mapping, 5 whys, process at a glance, etc.). Due to early success using these tools, I quickly formed opinions on how they should be used and what they should look like. Lean tools should be standardized, right? But once again, I learned this was L.A.M.E. from my teachers. I would attempt to force a kaizen project into a tool, rather than adapt a tool to my needs. Over time, as I observed and learned from Shingijutsu (and my own mistakes), I realized that Lean tools were meant to be molded, altered, and even invented as the need arose. And the need arose from understanding how to apply the concepts of Lean to a problem. Let me try to explain.

During one of our big GE kaizen events, a team was attempting to improve flow through a series of processes. It was very complex. It was so complex that no one (including our sensei) really knew for sure what would happen if the ideas of the team were implemented. Due to relatively long cycle times and multiple variables, "try-storming" was not practical. It was a perfect situation for a simulation. Now the sensei knew this would be tough, so he asked me to join the

---

[73]http://www.leanblog.org/lame

team for the rest of the week to help them create a simulation and analyze the improvement ideas. I can guarantee you, there is no book or other instructional material in existence that teaches the "tool" we created. And there is no way I could have created this tool without spending many weeks learning the concepts of Lean from my sensei. When I started my tool-centered approach to Lean, I tried to convince my boss we should buy a computer simulation program. He gently coached me why that was a direction we didn't want to go. Our results that week were phenomenal, but not because we saved GE a lot of money. All of us on that team developed a much deeper understanding of Lean.

The emphasis on tools, and the misapplication of them that occurs because of a limited understanding of Lean, is what causes L.A.M.E. In Taiichi Ohno's book, *Toyota Production System – Beyond Large-Scale Production*[74], he wrote:

> "With a better tool, we can get wonderful results. But if we use it incorrectly, the tool can make things worse. Kanban is one of those tools that if used improperly can cause a variety of problems. To employ kanban properly and skillfully, we tried to clearly understand its purpose and role and then establish rules for its use."

You could substitute any tool for kanban in this excerpt and it would be correct. I wish I would have spent more time early in my Lean journey reading the writings of Taiichi Ohno, Shigeo Shingo, and W. Edwards Deming, and less time studying tools.

Final Thoughts

When I learned about this book, I made a commitment to myself to write this chapter. Not only did I want to help my fellow Lean

---

[74]http://amzn.to/1OldLG4

practitioners, but I knew it would help remind me of where I'd come from on my journey. Thank you, Mark Graban, for this book idea (even if you don't include this chapter), and your remarkable contributions to the Lean community.

One of my pet peeves in the continuous improvement community is the misguided emphasis on certifications. I'm all for training and education, and I encourage everyone to acquire more knowledge whenever possible. But I firmly believe that certifications in the Lean and Six Sigma communities have done more harm than good. Certifications promote a fixed mindset instead of a growth mindset and a learning culture.

At GE, my boss was asked to develop the requirements for a new GE Lean Leader certification. He didn't want to for the reasons I've just mentioned, but higher authority prevailed and a certification was created. One of the requirements was to participate in a Shingijutsu kaizen event. Once the requirements were communicated, and because our office coordinated all these kaizen events, we were bombarded by GE employees around the country who wanted to know how to participate. Clearly, most of these employees were only interested in padding their credentials. If it's necessary for you to get a certification to advance your career, then, by all means, go get one. But please consider it as merely a small step toward a lifelong learning journey.

I believe I've achieved the highest "certification" you can get in Lean, but it's not hanging on my wall. In fact, it's not written anywhere and I can't put it on my professional biography because almost no one will understand. But it means everything to me. This "certification" was achieved during the complex simulation event I described earlier.

During that event, our sensei from Shingijutsu was someone I had worked with for 12 weeks over a four year period. After I had led the simulation team for three days, he was very pleased with the results and he said, "Thank you Sensei Mike. You did a great job." It was the first time he had ever addressed me as a sensei, and from that point forward he continued to do so. We both knew the significance of that moment. I was lucky to have the opportunity to get to that point on my journey and earn his "certification." I sincerely wish everyone could do the same. Good luck on your journey!

Chapter Sixteen – Jamie Flinchbaugh

Jamie Flinchbaugh is a lean advisor, speaker, and author, who has advised over 300 companies on their lean journey, from the board of directors and C-Suite to the front-line. He is a co-author of *The Hitchhiker's Guide to Lean*[a]. You can find him online at JFlinch.com[b].

[a] http://amzn.to/2bNmujC
[b] http://www.jflinch.com

What's wrong with your pull system?

My first formal experience with lean was in the early 1990s. I was managing the materials process at Harley-Davidson, where we had one of the first comprehensive, end-to-end pull systems. It was called MAN, for Material-As-Needed. The manufacturing plant was fairly fully integrated to make motorcycles. We had rolls of steel to cut, stamp, and weld to form gas tanks. We had our own (and very old) chrome-plating operation and zinc-plating operation. We had what we thought was a state-of-the-art paint system until someone left a bay door open overnight and the place filled with bugs, causing system problems for several weeks. Everything was connected to the MAN system. And I ran around with my radio trying to hold most of it together.

The MAN system was part of the what could be called the Harley-Davidson Operating System. There were only three components, represented in a triangle: Material-As-Needed, Statistical Process Control, and Employee Involvement. Statistical Process Control wasn't groundbreaking but focused on building some stability in the process which was much needed. The success of Employee Involvement wasn't as obvious to me. There were spots where it was going well and other spots where it hardly existed.

Our operation wasn't doing terribly well at the time. Our "float," meaning the bikes that had been built, but needed some repair before being shipped, was the equivalent of a whole day's production by the end of the week, despite us working to repair them as quickly as we could. Unlike my time later on in an automotive plant, we couldn't store new bikes outside. So we had a find a place inside. We clearly didn't have room for that many bikes. So, bikes were put everywhere, but the only available space was normally used to store material. By the end of the week, my biggest problem was where to put material. A typical call on the radio was "the shocks aisle is filled with bikes, where do you want me to put them?" I'd walk over, and we'd end up putting them where we could, including the aisles, which would generally cause my next radio call to get them moved.

The real circle-of-life is that the primary culprit of bike repairs was missing components. As the bike went down the assembly line, a component would be unavailable, and we'd keep building the bike as well as we could. As long as there were wheels, and there usually were, we could at least put it on the ground and push it out of the way. The materials department wasn't blamed for all of them, as many times the parts had not yet been produced by another department in the plant, but I was always the first call.

The Boss

While my boss will remain nameless, he was not the most engaged manager. He had come out of accounting with no operational experience, and also managed shipping and receiving, in addition to my area. We had a long and narrow plant and his office was at one end, with the administrative building at the other end. Instead of walking down the main aisle, where someone might stop him to ask a question or bring up an issue, he would walk outside down the length of the plant, and not just because it was a nice day outside.

He would often complain that the material handlers with fork trucks were driving recklessly. Honestly, they despised him so much that I believe they often made mock runs at running him down when they could. They would never admit it, but it was fairly obvious.

This resulted in a story that is a bit off topic, but worth sharing under the heading "bad boss." Convinced they were driving too fast, he wanted me to prove it for them. I resisted, mostly because I thought it was stupid. Never mind that there was no reasonable way to prove it. Finally, he simply ordered me to do the following. I put down two pieces of tape on the floor. I then stood between them with a stopwatch. I was a speed trap and a rather obvious one at that. They knew it wasn't my idea but certainly had their fun with me. They would speed up to the line and then crawl through the zone at 2 mph. This certainly put my credibility back a bit, but completely destroyed the credibility of my boss.

Then came his next assignment. Knowing that our MAN system wasn't working terribly well, he wanted to scrap the whole system. He believed that manufacturing was a precise and predictable machine. He wanted a schedule that stated we would pick up this part at this time. It would be a detailed, precise schedule to manage all of material handling. Again, I resisted, despite knowing that our current system wasn't working. I already knew that resistance was not going to work, so I finally took on the task.

The pivot and the lesson

I set off under the guise of building his system, but with the true intention of proving him wrong. The idea that pull systems worked was far from a common belief at that point. But, I was sure that a precision-scheduled system would fail. If our system relied on picking up the exact number of parts at the precise time on a certain day, then both the demand (schedule) and supply (quality and so on) must have zero variation. Now, I'm all in favor of putting challenges into a manufacturing system in order to drive improvement, but I have yet to meet the manufacturing system with zero variation.

So I set out to meet two objectives. First, gather the data needed by my boss for his magic system. Second, learn why our pull system wasn't working.

I put down my radio and committed to observing every employee for an entire shift, spanning a few weeks. It turns out I was practicing a fundamental lean method, of going to the gemba and directly observing the work, although I didn't quite understand this at the time.

I did nothing but observe the work, the people, and the system. If I would have done it for just a day, I never would have learned what I ended up learning. In fact, it took well over a week until the patterns became clear. I think they only became clear because I kept an inquisitive mind the entire time (to which I credit whatever success I have experienced).

The pattern was this: everyone violated the system frequently, but always with good intentions. On the line, people would see the material handler coming and would grab a couple extra pull cards from their bins to give to them. In the supplying areas, people would make just a few extra parts while they were already set up. The material handlers, while picking up parts, would grab just a couple extra bins in addition to the number of cards, since the line would need them eventually anyway. And, the parts and accessories group, not large enough at the time for their own inventory, would come to the line to grab some parts that customers needed and, while they were there, would grab a couple months' worth instead of just what they needed.

Everyone thought they were being efficient and helpful. But, the net result of all of their behaviors was that the system didn't do anything it was designed to do. For example, early card pulls triggered early production of the wrong parts, consuming valuable capacity. Every small deviation had a cascading effect on the system, which was now unreliable, which in turn drove even greater behavior distortion and workarounds.

The solution

I'm not sure if I ever convinced my boss that he was wrong, or if he just didn't care anymore, but we never worked on his scheduling system. Instead, we focused on the behaviors. With a combination of educating people on the purpose of system rules and accountability for following them, we had a modest, but measurable, improvement in behaviors.

But, that was enough to see real changes in the stability and effectiveness of the system. And, because some of the old behaviors were workarounds, even slight improvement in the results caused further improvement in behaviors surrounding the system. For example, a new behavior was only pulling Kanban cards when you've actually consumed the material instead of when you see the material handler coming. Trust that the material handler will come back later, and know that violating that process will cause work to start prematurely. When just a few more people follow rules such as this just a bit more often, the stability of the system improves and so do the results.

Much more work was needed before we saw a substantial improvement in the motorcycle repair rate, but this, combined with other improvements, eventually improved our first-time right rate and, ultimately, the factory's output.

The learning

I was extremely fortunate to have this experience because I discovered very early in my lean learning journey that the tools do not make the system. It's not the process that matters most. It's not even how all the tools fit together. It is the behaviors that matter most. If you don't get the behaviors right, the tools, processes, systems, and the rest will fail. Lean is about how we think, with an emphasis on the "we" because it is the shared behaviors, consistently applied across the organization, that matter most.

This shaped most of my lean journey, although by no means was I able to articulate how at the time. It led me into the realm of systems thinking and organizational learning and I was among the very first to see the connection between organizational learning and lean. Organizational learning focused on important methods such as reflection and system dynamics. Reflection later became recognized as "hansei," a useful method in the lean toolbox. The organizational learning community, in particular, its standard bearer Peter Senge, recognized Toyota as the ultimate learning organization.

This experience affected my journey at Chrysler and, later, at DTE Energy, making increasingly more effective efforts at making people, behaviors, and learning central to a lean journey. Ultimately, that path led me to co-found a consulting and education firm with Andy Carlino, and write, with him, *The Hitchhiker's Guide to Lean*[75]. Our work and our book helped shift the lean community as a whole to be less about the deployment of tools and more about building a culture. At the time, we were considered contrarians. Lean was all about tools, especially highly promoted tools such as value stream mapping. One person told me that an organization wasn't lean unless they had a value stream map on their wall. A university professor who was deeply involved in lean suggested that if you design the system, people will operate effectively. These sound wrong today but represented the prevailing opinions 15 years ago.

I would claim that we were the first to make lean about behaviors, but I believe that Kiyoshi Suzaki who wrote *The New Manufacturing Challenge*[76] and *The New Shop Floor Management*[77] was certainly articulating a people and learning-centric model of lean, although too few learned from his teaching.

I believe I also learned a bit about Suzaki's quote:

"Lean is common sense...after the fact."

People with good intentions wouldn't be violating the system so much if it was intuitive. But many aspects of lean are counter-intuitive, which makes education and coaching so vital.

I learned a lot from my initial experience. Some of it impacted me immediately. Other aspects would take another decade to fully take

---

[75]http://amzn.to/2bNmujC
[76]http://amzn.to/2ccIu8p
[77]http://amzn.to/2cmFaGW

root. For example, I didn't have clear language to articulate any of this, but then I didn't have an audience to share that language with. But, I was very fortunate to have the experience I had and was mindful enough to learn everything I could from it. I've always put learning first, ahead of career, money, location, or working hours. That served me then and has served me since.

What's next?

For the most part, more practicing. I want to bring lean into new frontiers, such as the board of directors, and continue to find ways to make it less mystical and more accessible to everyone. I also intend to be a better practitioner in working on my own systems. I am refining my use of Kanban management systems with myself and various partners, I am building more deliberate daily experimentation, and I am continuing to refine my personal standard work. For example, as I plan my week, I determine my primary customer for three days of the week, meaning who am I trying to deliver value for. I then determine how I will deliver that value, and how I will evaluate that value, creating my hypothesis. And then I test.

And overall, I simply hope to keep learning through the deliberate practice of lean.

Chapter Seventeen – Lesa Nichols

Lesa Nichols has spent over two decades guiding organizations to improved performance by applying the principles of the Toyota Production System (TPS) and Lean.

As a key leader for Toyota North America, she led teams to analyze and solve the toughest operational problems within Toyota, including the preparation and launch of new vehicles, plants and production methods. After leaving Toyota, Lesa spent four years helping clients of the Greater Boston Manufacturing Partnership (GBMP) to achieve successful enterprise-level improvements.

In 2013, Lesa created her firm, Lesa Nichols Consulting (LNC). Currently, she and her team help companies understand how and why to utilize principles of TPS and Lean as a competitive operations management system.

Lesa lives in Louisville and can be found at Lesanicholsconsulting.com[a] as well as LinkedIn[b].

---

[a]http://Lesanicholsconsulting.com
[b]https://www.linkedin.com/in/lesanichols

I heard a quote early on in my career with Toyota that goes something like this:

> "Within three days, people think they can talk about Standardized Work,
>
> Within three months, people think they can teach Standardized Work,
>
> Within three years, people realize they know nothing about Standardized Work"

This has certainly been my personal experience.

Just like any journey to acquire a skill, there are the high highs and the low lows. Graduating from high school, I thought I had conquered the world and the path ahead in college would be more of the same. Until I realized that I was a lowly freshman. Stunned at how quickly I realized how little I actually knew, it was hard to keep the shock factor in check. But I did. It became a lot easier with the recognition that everyone around me was having a similar experience. This pattern has continued throughout my career.

In the interest of sharing lessons learned, here is a bit about my journey and the major stages of discovery, along with some painful, but formative, learning experiences.

1. Beware the documents – see the work

All I could see in the early days of my experience with Standardized Work was a bunch of documents. Capacity sheet, Combination Table, Chart, Time observation sheet, blah, blah, blah. For me, they were merely something you had to get through to work with the more glamorous tools of the Toyota Production System (TPS) i.e. jidoka, continuous flow, and kanban. Of course, I wasn't able to see how one concept fit to another and why Standardized Work always came first.

While I was with the Toyota Supplier Support Center (TSSC), I was part of a small team assigned to improve the productivity of a work cell. It took about 10 minutes of observation to feel a high level of frustration from operators, and yet we proceeded to document the current condition standardized work. I felt I was wasting time working on paper and couldn't see how standardized work analysis could possibly help the operators have a less frustrating day.

My mentor, who was leading the improvement strategy at this plant, saw that I, along with the rest of the team, had become too caught up in details of how to do time studies and fill in the documents. He called a halt. He explained, "You are not seeing the true condition. You are lost in the documents."

He redirected us to the line. We gathered around him while he intently looked each of us in the eyes and instructed, "Watch the movement of each team member's eyes as closely as I am watching yours. Then, you will see the truth of the process trouble." My eyes apparently were saying to him, "What the heck are you talking about?" which was exactly what I was thinking. I was not alone. He patiently explained, "The eyes are mirrors of our thoughts and concerns. When people are intently doing their work, they are not hiding anything. Please discover this on your own." Off we went.

With this newly focused lens, the team could see the furrowed brows and the squinting and darting of the operators' eyes. Our connection with the operators evolved quickly as we tried to pinpoint the reasons behind a variety of facial expressions.

In my case, I was observing an operator who appeared to be struggling with a bright light shining in her eyes while attempting to assemble a part. When I went to confirm this with her, she said, "Oh no, come here and try this." I went to her spot on the line, stepped into her position, and was able to really see what she was seeing. Or in this case, what she wasn't seeing. The light was not shining in her eyes, but in fact, she was working with an obstructed view of the area where she needed to attach two components to the main unit. She was attaching parts by feel, which explained the continuous darting and squinting of her eyes.

The other members of the team were having similar experiences. In taking this "eyes of the operator" approach, we were able to find and fix the specific struggles in each person's work. As we knocked these issues off, productivity improved.

This experience revealed an astonishing approach to Standardized

Work. Without the barrier of a stopwatch, documents, and clipboards, it is much easier to deeply observe the work the team member is doing.

Ultimately though, without transferring our experiments and learning into SW documents, there is nothing for worksite leaders to ensure those improvements will continue.

2. Standardized Work documents are THE WAY to lead to improvement – but only if they change

Rather than getting in the way of how we observe conditions, SW documents are intended to show us the way to:

- Hone in on the most important problems to attack
- Provide a gauge to measure the impact of improvement
- Pinpoint specific elements of a process that are causing trouble

I've had many opportunities over the years to use SW documents as a guide for successful improvement. Many times, it has gone well and then there are the other times that were off the mark, creating terrific but painful learning conditions. One of my worst improvement attempts turned into a lifelong learning experience for me and two fellow coaches.

The assignment was to develop the skill of five new leaders of Standardized Work for Toyota plants in North America. In this case, we needed to transfer the key technical factors of SW including takt time, work sequence, and standard in-process stock. A Toyota supplier was interested to be our training ground as they were struggling to achieve consistent output in an area of their plant.

My fellow coaches and I needed to vet the worksite to see if Standardized Work was truly what they needed to improve operations. As we went about our pre-training investigation, we gathered the following:

- Customer demand was amazingly consistent so we could easily establish takt time (pace of customer demand). This would give us the target line we needed to judge whether process cycle times (time for each person to start and finish their work on one component) were a problem or not.

- Each of the team members in the area had the skill to keep a repeating sequence of the assembly operation.
- Once established, the concept of standard-in-process stock would be helpful for the team members to stay in their work rhythm/sequence.
- There were many chances for our trainees to try out improvements aimed at creating smooth, repeatable work.

From the view of our coaching team, this area fits the bill despite some concerns we had with equipment complexity, isolation of the worksite (the only clean room in the entire plant), and having no designated person in the area to lead the quick troubleshooting needed.

Using the SW capacity analysis sheet, SW work combination table, SW chart, and a line balance graph, we could see improvements that would allow the team members to achieve the customer demand. We thought we were good to go.

Three weeks later, as we gathered the team members with our group for the actual kickoff, things had changed:

- Customer demand had spiked due to an annual event of building products ahead of the holidays to cover customers' sales during a week-long factory shutdown. This meant a new, temporary takt time was needed.
- The equipment complexity had become an obvious problem with the additional volume. The capacity analysis we had completed now showed a bottleneck on one of the most complex machines.
- Quality problems had increased due to people focusing on making the higher demand levels while dealing with frustrations of frequent equipment disruptions.

For me and my fellow coaches, this appeared to be a nightmare. We quickly confirmed our suspicions by calculating the gap between the number of products needed and their actual output of good parts. Only 60% of the time available in each shift was actually spent making products the customer had already purchased. Yikes! This was no longer a great time to develop SW coaches. What was needed was deep, technical problem solving.

Abandoning ship was not an option. We regrouped to focus on ensuring the stability of each process so that we could at least make a smooth work sequence. You can probably imagine how hard this was to achieve. We soon had frustrated trainees in addition to frustrated team members.

The good news is that some improvement was made. The bad news was that many quality problems and machine malfunctions continued.

As we reported out to the factory's upper management as well as our TSSC bosses, the questions were tough but the learning was deep. Looking back, this experience was quite formative for me.

My key takeaways:

- The shop floor is alive! Things change all the time. Given that, SW documents will only show the correct path to improvement if they represent the current situation. We, as coaches, should have re-confirmed the real situation of the worksite immediately before our work was to start.
- Learn to imagine the conditions you will face at the time you are planning to act. This leads to better discovery in the planning stage and allows you to prepare for any obstacles you find.
- When you have a concern about barriers that could get in the way, investigate. In this case, we could have gathered facts on machine-specific downtime, response time to calls for help with machine disruptions and facts to show us the most important quality issues. Armed with this real-world intelligence, it would not have been a problem to have a maintenance person assigned to our team and a quality person available as a go-to resource.

3. Even the best SW Documents aren't enough

On the heels of experiences like those shared so far, I concluded the only way to understand the "behind the scenes" factors making highly effective, sustainable improvement hard to achieve was to gain real-world operations experience. I broached the topic of a rotation into a production role with my boss/mentor at Toyota. He agreed, but teasingly pointed out that we first needed a brave plant president willing to take on an "operations rookie."

Nine months later, I held the position of Production Manager in one of Toyota's Powertrain plants. The assignment for me was clear from Day One:

First Year: Learn the current condition of operations, including the interdependencies of all functions under one roof, lead cross-functional problem solving to raise current performance in Safety/Ergonomics, Quality, Productivity, On Time Delivery, and Cost.

Second Year: Lead the area to launch a major product change, designing out the problems found in the original "current condition." This involved significant change to the way components were machined, assembled, and conveyed.

Third Year: In the aftermath of the model change, stabilize the new work methods and kaizen to raise Safety, Quality, Productivity, On Time Delivery and Cost – yet again.

My original intention was more than met – to understand the real-world issues that make sustainable improvement hard. I still feel that experience was worth five times more than my college degrees. Going in, I had a strong theoretical understanding of the Toyota Production System. What I came away with was an understanding of the connections between the theory and practical application.

These years were tough, yet exhilarating. Many times, I laughed when I thought of my theoretical understanding of TPS with its aim of balancing Quality, Productivity, Lead Time, and Cost. In my daily life, it felt like those aims were in a blender that had somehow gotten stuck on the "Liquefy" setting – with me right in the mix.

Summarizing the SW lessons learned from this period is hard, but here is my Top 5 list:

First: The amount of energy required just to make quality products, safely, day after day, is incalculable. Time to work on deep problem solving and intensive improvement activities is hard to find. It took every ounce of my creative, strategic strengths to continuously carve this time out for the organization.

Second: If there isn't any human motion involved, there is no meaning to creating SW. Rather than Standardized Work, there are Operations Standards that clarify expectations of the equipment. These are invaluable decision-making aids for the people running, fixing and maintaining the machines.

Third: SW is the bridge to practically connect the team member making the product to the customer using the product. There are many ways this happens, including:

Takt: Takt time is truly a great balancer of work. When people have a disagreement about how work is distributed across processes, it is often a losing battle. One supervisor says it is fair, another disagrees. This can go on endlessly.

Because takt time is based on actual customer sales, it removes the element of "supervisors' whim" and focuses the discussion. Actually, it changes the communication from a debate to a problem-solving activity.

Work Sequence: While there are many factors to consider in developing the best work sequence for each process, the guiding light comes from the people who designed the product for the customer. Any important design factors that a team member can influence are captured in the SW. A familiar example of this is a specified sequence of assembly to avoid interference between components.

Job Breakdown Sheets: These are critical to helping each team member understand the importance of each individual work element they perform. When team members know the critical quality aspects of their job and the specifics of why they are important, the nature of training changes. We begin to shift from telling people what to do to answering their curious questions about how things work and why.

Job Instruction Training, Standard in Process Stock, and the list goes on. Really.

Fourth: SW is not just for assembly. Although it definitely looks different in machining, casting, painting, etc., the guiding principles of SW can be applied in processes that people typically think of as "craftsman" jobs. Many of the well-known tools of SW are not the same, but the concepts of takt time, work sequence, standard-in-process stock, and others apply, bringing the same benefits that SW does to assembly work.

Fifth: SW is an emotional thing. People feel strongly about the way they want to do their work. They have intense opinions about their own techniques. Some people want to have the loosest of structure identified, while others believe the movement of each finger should be clarified. To get on the same page from one team member to the next, one shift to another can be a messy process.

As difficult as this sounds, TPS is a brilliant system. People may disagree with this and that, but we are always pulling back to the same things: takt time is given by the customer (no debate), what is the best practice sequence of the process given the competing factors of quality, safety, ergonomics, and productivity, what is going on to cause the cycle time change from one hour to the next... I would much rather spend time managing these issues than the general world of human drama.

At the end of my job rotation in Powertrain, I developed a summary of my experience as a production manager and how I would use this to shape my future direction. In preparing the summary, I got input from several of my peers, shop floor leaders and mentors. The big discovery was how much I had learned about SW as an operations management system, not only for improvement projects.

This recognition was illuminated one night about a week before I left Powertrain to rotate back to Toyota's North American Toyota Production System group. Mr. Ano, one of the most valued mentors of my life, pulled a chair up to my desk and sat looking at me intently, with a slight smile, but serious eyes. This was a man that intimidated many without meaning to. As a veteran Powertrain leader in Japan, and now the US, he carried vast knowledge.

To me, he was a tough, but fair, leader and a mentor I respected beyond business. He was my coach of human nature and the one who gave me the confidence to bring my real, unvarnished self into the workplace.

I was all ears as he said, "You are such a lucky person. So many mistakes and challenges you have had. No one can pay for this experience." A bit disappointed with the perceived dig, I asked, "What are you worried about? That I won't carry my learning into my next job(s)?"

His eyes lit up and he replied, "This is why you are a strong manager. You read behind the words and want to hear the real truth. My request to you is to take every painful experience from here and apply it in your new life. Please give all your effort to the real world struggles of man (human) management.

Do not be surprised when you leave. Everyone will ask you to focus on productivity again. You have learned through these tough days, that when you fix the safety and quality struggles of the team member, productivity comes."

As he walked away, it hit me that Standardized Work would be the main mechanism to guide me from my Production Manager life to my TPS Manager one.

And it did.

Chapter Eighteen – Summation

By Cameron Stark (author of Chapter Twelve)

The Habits of Lean

The combined experiences of the contributors to this book range over decades, industries, and continents. From people who have worked on Lean for many years, to people who have started their Lean journey more recently, the accounts include many variations. Some people worked in organisations with active support for Lean, while others were expected to deliver improvements with little support.

When reading the accounts as a whole, it is the similarities, rather than the differences, that jump out. Lucas and Nacer (2015) tried to identify the behaviours that are important to improvement work in health care. The present book provides an opportunity to look at themes recurring in many and varied accounts of Lean work in different settings.

Approach

Assertions on the nature of Lean are common – "Lean is about efficiency" or "Lean doesn't touch on errors or variation," for example. By contrast to these incorrect broad brush statements, this book's contributors are remarkably consistent about the nature of Lean. Authors unite around a focus on value to the customer; reduction in waste; attention to flow, reducing errors and delivering quality. Unlike the statements on some book jackets and websites, the contributors see no conflict between efficiency, quality improvement, and error reduction.

The accounts are also united in rejecting the common notion that Lean is a set of tools that can be picked through as required, with other aspects being ignored. To obtain and maintain significant

improvement, the way organisations are managed, and the way organisations engage their staff, are also essential elements of the approach.
Quite a few authors described their experiences in organisations that
treated Lean as another blade on a Swiss Army knife, to be pulled
out for a particular problem. Most contrast this with the greater
improvements gained by organisations that took a whole system
approach to Lean.

Several authors go on to argue that Lean techniques are of limited
value if they are applied by rote. Examples of enthusiastic but unhelpful application of 5S are often discussed, and some examples are given
in this book. Clarity on the purpose of methods is important, rather
than seeing them as "must dos" that have to be applied relentlessly in
every situation, regardless of context.

Improvement Cycles

People who see Lean as a collection of techniques might find it
surprising that authors generally make only passing mention of particular methods within Lean. This relates at least in part to the
widespread discussion of the engagement of people, and the attitudes
that support it. The technique that seems to come up with the
greatest frequency is one of the most basic: improvement cycles. In
several chapters, the contributors emphasise the value of rapid cycles
of change, measured appropriately and compared to the original
predictions. One author notes the value of running experiments "for
the sake of learning."

Respect

Mark Graban gives examples, separated by a decade, of people in
industry and in healthcare telling him that they are "expected to
check our brain in at the door." This is a terrible waste of human
potential and expertise and, across the board, the Lean practitioners
in this book reject it. Rather than seeing staff as people who don't care,
don't try and do as little as possible to get through the working day,
their experience is of people who want to do a good job, and often

blossom as soon as they are given the chance to express opinions, look for solutions, and make changes to their work for the benefit of their customers.

Several authors used variations on the Toyota theme of "go and see, ask questions, show respect." People working in industries or services are not unthinking automatons who just need to do what they are told. When harnessed, the experience and enthusiasm of staff can make an enormous difference to error identification, problem solving and the delivery of quality.

This isn't to say that everyone will embrace Lean. The case studies make it clear that some people don't enjoy the approach, or have a career that has developed in such a different system that they do not manage to make the leap to a new approach. This doesn't make them bad people, and several chapters illustrate how the same person who is initially hostile to Lean may become a convert over time. For some people, this doesn't happen, and they may decide to move to an organisation with the more traditional approach that they find more sympathetic to their views. Again, this decision needs to be treated with respect.

Humility

Combined with respect for staff, most authors counseled humility. People who discover Lean often become very enthusiastic indeed. In the urge to help improve systems, it is easy to slip from respect for staff into a more directive approach. This is discussed further in relation to coaching, but also comes up in the context of lifelong learning. Despite decades of experience in some cases, contributors are generally reluctant to describe themselves as experts. This seems to be because they know what they don't know. Many chapters describe learning Lean as a lifelong process. There are always things to learn, and people to learn from.

Taught courses are important, but mentoring, on the job training and practical experience are all discussed by various authors. Conferences, site visits, podcasts, books and videos all feature in the accounts of different authors. The overall impression is of a widespread acceptance that you never "know" all of Lean and that you can always learn something new. This book is an example of that process.

Go To The Gemba

Theory is a wonderful thing. Scientists use theoretical frameworks, as long as they are useful for a particular problem – but another group of scientists, or sometimes even the same scientists, actively try to disprove the theory. In management, where this second group may not exist, it is easy to treat theory as fact.

Theories on what happens in a factory or service, what problems occur, why they occur and what approach might improve the problem, are common. In Lean, the chapter authors assert, you need to go to see what is happening, rather than to assume that you already know. Learning to see is not easy, but you can learn the skill, particularly if you combine it with respect for people.

Coaching

Management consultancy models, where an expert comes from outside, looks at your processes, and tells you what to do, are common. In some cases, it even works to help with a particular problem. The challenges from this model are that changes may not be implemented; when they are implemented and have an impact, they may not be maintained, and that it may do little to prepare your workforce for the next problem they encounter, other than to teach them that they need an expert to come to sort it for them.

In the descriptions in this book, by contrast, contributors do not paint themselves as heroes who fix a problem. In some cases, they understandably started out with this approach in their enthusiasm to spread Lean methods, but without exception, they moved to an approach where they seek to help people develop their own problem analysis and problem solving skills, using Lean methods. This relates back to the themes of direct observation – the people who do the work generally know what is happening – and respect for people. The experience of many of the authors is that if you support people in developing the skills in on-the-job coaching, then they can continue to make changes over time and, in turn, can become coaches in their own right, who demonstrate a way of working to their own colleagues.

Culture

Workplace culture is a theme in several contributions. Organisations develop ways of doing things, and people often have a collective view of what has been tried, and what has worked, in the past. If respect for people is lacking, and workers are not expected to notice problems or contribute ideas, then it can be very difficult to persuade people that anything is going to change. The things that managers pay attention to are usually the things staff prioritise.

A learning culture, where people identify problems and tackle them without fear of being blamed, is an important asset. If you don't know where the problems are, it is very difficult to tackle them. In a workplace where people are asked for ideas rarely and where most management attention is associated with problems and probably criticism, beginning to move the culture to a willingness to talk about problems, discuss solutions and try things out can be challenging.

Several authors discussed this, including identifying quick wins and starting small with staff ideas, rather than tackling a huge issue straight away. Other people report working on major issues from the start, but usually where they can obtain good management commitment to change, and to the use of the relevant methods.

Conclusion

The book contributors come from diverse backgrounds and work in many different settings. What unites them is stronger than what divides them. A commitment to core ideas on Lean, respect for people, understanding that no matter what you know, there is always more to learn, and that people achieve more when you support them to learn, are common themes in these accounts.

The authors report working in organisations with different degrees of receptivity for Lean ideas, and the accounts indicate that some organisations find it easier than others to adopt Lean. The cross-setting applicability of the ideas are clear. While detailed approaches vary by setting and organisational context, the importance of career-long learning in Lean comes across. By sharing experiences, we can see ways of getting better at Lean, together.

Reference

Lucas B, Nacer H. (2015) The Habits of an Improver. London, The Health Foundation.

Chapter Nineteen – Related Posts from LeanBlog.org

This chapter contains some blog posts that were originally published at www.LeanBlog.org[78] with the themes of "L.A.M.E" or "Practicing Lean." Some are posts that were referenced in my first chapters.

Lean or "L.A.M.E."?

Originally published March 21, 2007[79]

Many of the "anti-Lean" stories I hear sound like descriptions of situations or methods that I would hardly describe as "Lean." There are many problems with the word "Lean," but we're pretty well stuck with it.

1) "Lean" is often used in a negative sense that has nothing to do with the Toyota Production System, as in "we have a very lean staff," meaning "we don't have enough people to get the job done."

2) There is no official 'keeper of the Lean" to officially bestow the "Lean" title on any practice or behavior. We're free to describe pretty much anything we like as "Lean," the only downside might be getting mocked in the lean community, but that's not much downside, is it?

For example, the "5S" program in the UK that was described as "demeaning." From the news reports, this didn't sound very "Lean," in terms of doing anything much to reduce waste or improve things for employees. Does this give "Lean" a bad name or does it give the consultants and the managers a bad name? People tend to blame "Lean."

When companies use Lean methods to drive layoffs[80], something most lean consultants (myself included) say you shouldn't do since it

---

[78]http://www.leanblog.org/

[79]http://www.leanblog.org/2007/03/lean-or-lame/

[80]http://www.leanblog.org/2006/04/is-merck-getting-lean-right-this-time/

understandably drains any employee enthusiasm for Lean, does this give "Lean" a bad name or that company a bad name? People blame "lean" and say that "Lean" led to their layoffs.

When this guy[81] got the idea, somewhere, that Gemba walks led to more bureaucracy and paperwork. If that the was the case somewhere (and it shouldn't be if a Gemba process is implemented properly, would "Lean" get the blame for wasting managers' time?

We need a phrase that describes these "bad" or misguided attempts at Lean, things that give Lean a bad name.

How about this:

LAME: "Lean" As Misguidedly Executed

Lean As Mistakenly Explained?

Can you think of a better phrase? We need something to describe what bad managers do when they purposely distort or accidentally misunderstand Lean. Maybe this will catch on, or maybe it's lame. This way, when we see a "Lean horror story," we can refer to it as the "LAME method" instead of a "Lean method."

Read more "LAME" posts and stories via LeanBlog.org[82].

This WSJ Article (as do Many Organizations) Misses the Point of 5S

Originally published October 27, 2008[83]

Blogging about this article:

Neatness Counts at Kyocera and at Others in the 5S Club – WSJ.com[84]

I'm going to violate a rule I have to try not to blog when I'm frustrated or angry. Here goes...

Today's front page (argh, front page) article in the WSJ probably does more to give 5S a bad name than anything I could imagine. Of

---

[81]http://thecorporatecynic.wordpress.com/2007/03/13/gemba-schmemba-how-goofy-can-you-get/

[82]http://www.leanblog.org/tag/lame/

[83]http://www.leanblog.org/2008/10/this-wsj-article-and-many-organizations/

[84]http://online.wsj.com/article/SB122505999892670159.html?mod=todays_us_page_one

course, people don't read newspapers anymore.... but articles like this will make laughingstocks of those of us who try to teach "real 5S" not "LAME[85] 5S" (or Lean As Misguidedly Executed). Remember this story from the UK about "Lean Office" efforts[86]? This article brings us more 5S insanity.

Note: The UK Lean Office story follows in this chapter

It's too bad the WSJ couldn't have bothered to call Jim Womack on this (instead of calling him for every auto industry article), because I bet he would have set them straight.

I'll try to defend the good name of the TPS and Lean practice of "5S":

Hey, neat freaks with nothing better to do.... quit telling me what family photos or knick-knacks I can have on my desk. You're a waste of a paycheck, you people who want to depersonalize the workplace. You suck. "5S Cop"? Get a real job title, something that adds value to customers and isn't just a corporate drain on shareholder resources.

That's obviously not what Womack would have said. That's what I say. And I'll stand by it. Maybe the WSJ will start calling me for interesting quotes.

Here is the WSJ video[87].

---

[85] http://www.leanblog.org/2007/03/lean-or-lame.html

[86] http://www.leanblog.org/2007/02/bad-lean5s-hits-uk-media

[87] https://www.youtube.com/watch?list=PL41110EFA581A9D40&v=AUaJ9roHj2s

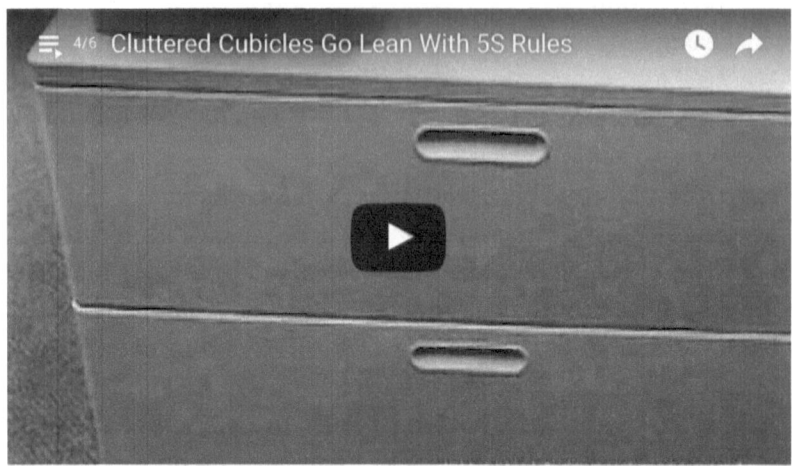

The article gets off to a decent start, with a stock description of 5S:

> "5S is a key concept of the lean manufacturing techniques that have made makers of everything from cars to candy bars more efficient. The S's stand for sort, straighten, shine, standardize and sustain."

Notice how they said "more efficient." That's supposed to be the key point – efficiency, not neatness. Or maybe, better yet, effectiveness.

I wish the WSJ had belabored the point that 5S is about identifying and eliminating waste, not being neat freaks for neatness sake. But then they wouldn't have been able to document the corporate (and hospital) buffoonery that's in the rest of the piece.

The article then starts to talk about the new "corporate initiative" that starts terrorizing people into having neat desks:

> "Kyocera's version of 5S, which it calls "Perfect 5S," not only calls for organization in the workplace, but aesthetic uniformity. Sweaters can't hang on the backs of chairs, personal items can't be stowed beneath desks and the only decorations allowed on cabinets are official company plaques or certificates."

You can't hang sweaters on the back of chairs? What? Where are people supposed to put them? A taped off section of a drawer labeled "outerwear"? Wouldn't a more significant reduction of waste involve NOT running the A/C so cold inside that people are forced to wear sweaters in July?

Not having a personal item on your cabinet is supposed to "impress visitors." What? The only impression that it would make on me is "this is a cold, heartless, impersonal workplace.... I bet the employees are beaten down and don't put much effort anymore into quality... just survival."

An "expert" (a "leadership expert" – where do they find these people?) chimes in:

> "While that may sound authoritarian, it's not the initiative that's important, it's how managers communicate it, says Gary Hayes, managing partner at Hayes Brunswick & Partners LLC, a leadership advisory firm in Bronxville, N.Y. "If managers clearly explain why they're doing something, I think most people will understand the rationale. But if you say, 'We're doing this because 14 efficiency experts say it increases productivity,' then it becomes kind of Dilbert," he says, referring to the comic strip of satirical office humor."

Authoritarian?? You betcha!!! I don't read much of anything in the article about explaining "why" desks need to be clear (other than the spurious "visitors" reason... what if you work in an office with no visitors?). Of course, it's more than "kind of Dilbert." It's Dilbert, absolutely. And it's L.A.M.E.

> "Mr. Brown, the manager of Kyocera's production technology center, has tried to inject some humor into the process. He recently posed for a photo wearing a white T-shirt and flexing his biceps, Mr. Clean style. The picture will be posted to the company's internal Web site along with tips on maintaining a clean desk."

Is Mr. Brown a waste of a paycheck?? Sorry if that's not keeping with the "respect for people" principle of Lean. It's probably not Mr.

Brown's fault. He's just following orders from corporate. The insanity must stop somewhere, though.

Mr. Brown targets employees who dare hang seasonal decorations (it's worse than the political correctness people who don't want to you hang "Christmas" decorations).

Mr. Brown and Kyocera further waste time by focusing on "5S compliance scores" (oh, yet another distraction from actually paying attention to serving customers, improving quality, and making money):

> "Employees in the main Kyocera office have been pretty good, achieving a total 5S compliance score of 88.9%. But people in the wireless-phone division in La Jolla haven't been as quick to embrace 5S. That division showed improvement during a separate audit the prior week, but it scored just 61.1%. "They're more loosey-goosey," Mr. Brown says. "They bring their surfboards to the office."

There won't be much solace when a company goes under and their corporate obituary reads "but they had really clean desks....."

In case anyone misses my point – I'm not anti-5S. I used 5S in manufacturing. I teach it and help implement it in hospital and healthcare settings. It's a wonderful tool, but ONLY for the sake of improving operations.

If tools and supplies are hard to find – let's say, nurses are searching around the clinic for one of the few available thermometers.... the 5S solution would include making sure the tools are available where needed (in each exam room, which might involve spending $$$) and that their standard location is standardized and clearly marked and labeled.

Jon Miller of Gemba Academy disagreed with me on this[88] (and I respectfully – emphasize respectfully) disagree with him. In my book, I made the case that 5S shouldn't go overboard or be taken to extremes. I made the point that a heavy printer that sits on a cabinet is not likely to go missing, get moved, or get lost. So why put tape around

---

[88]http://www.gembapantarei.com/2008/10/part_2_of_qa_with_mark_graban_author_of_lean_hospi.html

it? My argument is that there's enough "Real Waste" to be found and eliminated that putting tape around a printer trivializes 5S and seems silly because it's not solving any problem (the printer never goes missing).

Virginia Mason Medical Center (seen as one of the leaders in Lean Healthcare) is using 5S... for good and for what might be a bad application:

> "After Virginia Mason Medical Center in Seattle imple-
> mented 5S in 2002, doctors, nurses, and assistants now
> share desks grouped in pods so they can work more closely
> together and reduce the time they spend trying to find one
> another. That means each person is expected to keep his
> desk neat because someone on the next shift will be using
> it."

That's great – reduce the time spent trying to find one another, that's solving a problem. When people share desks or workplaces, the idea of keeping things in standard, consistent locations makes A LOT of sense. But when it's a single employee using their own personal desk (as at Kyocera), then it makes less sense (unless you plan on firing that person and replacing them with an interchangeable cog... no, not a good idea).

But some other VMMC practices make me think:

> "Employees created new places for everything to eliminate
> the need to hunt for things. But doctors and nurses in Mr.
> Boze's pod kept hanging the stethoscope in its old place on
> a hook, instead of putting it in the drawer marked "stetho-
> scope." "Eventually," says Mr. Boze, "we had to remove the
> hook."

I could challenge this approach – if a stethoscope is used very frequently (and it is, which explains why it hangs around most doctors' necks – that and for a status symbol identifying them as docs), then the stethoscope should be EASY to reach. Why dig inside a drawer? Maybe it should be on a hook where it's easily accessible? Of course, that violates some requirement (who gets blamed for this frequently –

the Joint Commission) that says things have to kept put away because patients might hurt themselves. Might be, but "removing the hook" seems top-down authoritarian.

It should be no surprise that your typical non-Lean command-and-control organization would LOVE 5S because it gives them another authoritarian thing to beat up employees about. CLEAN YOUR DESK!! Um, how about you give me an organized workplace and the tools to allow us to better serve customers? NO CLEAN YOUR DESK – CLEAN EVERY NIGHT.... CLUTTER – VERBOTEN!!!

We can do better than this. Those of us who have used 5S in constructive ways need to speak up about how 5S helps employees, rather than belittle them or antagonize them. Share your stories... let's share the real stories of how 5S helps.... what do you have?

And if you're Mr. Brown (or someone like Mr. Brown) who is offended and won't read the Lean Blog again.... I'm sorry. Go tidy up your desk.

Updated: There is a video[89] that actually gives a decent explanation of WHY factories would use 5S (waste less time looking for parts). There's one example in the video of what I think is an error. There's a hole punch in a copy room with tape around it. That's OK, if the hole punch can be moved. But when they pick up the hole punch, you just see a tape outline... so what was supposed to be there? All we see is that something is missing. Instead of putting the label on the hole punch (who doesn't know what that is??), put the label on the table, showing where it goes. It should be done in the way that's shown in the "freeze frame" photo of the video that shows before you hit play, not the way it was done in the video with a different item.

Click for the video[90].

---

[89] http://www.wsj.com/video/cluttered-cubicles-go-lean-with-5s-rules/ 08C6384E-D821-4E06-8D3C-7127672621CF.html

[90] http://video-api.wsj.com/api-video/player/iframe.html?guid=08C6384E-D821-4E06-8D3C-7127672621CF

Screenshot from WSJ Video

Bad Lean/5S Hits the UK Media

Originally published October 12, 2007[91]

A few weeks back, the British media was having a field day with reports of and complaints about what sounds like a horribly misguided "office lean" effort at a British government office.

The picture below is from one newspaper article[92] (with my added labels). It shows a desk where every item's location is marked with black tape. Read more[93] (in a later post) about why this image is labeled as "Bad 5S."

[91]http://www.leanblog.org/2007/02/bad-lean5s-hits-uk-media/
[92]http://www.thejournal.co.uk/news/north-east-news/tale-of-the-tape-4540105
[93]http://www.leanblog.org/2014/07/its-awful-when-the-person-teaching-lean-doesnt-get-the-bad-5s-joke/

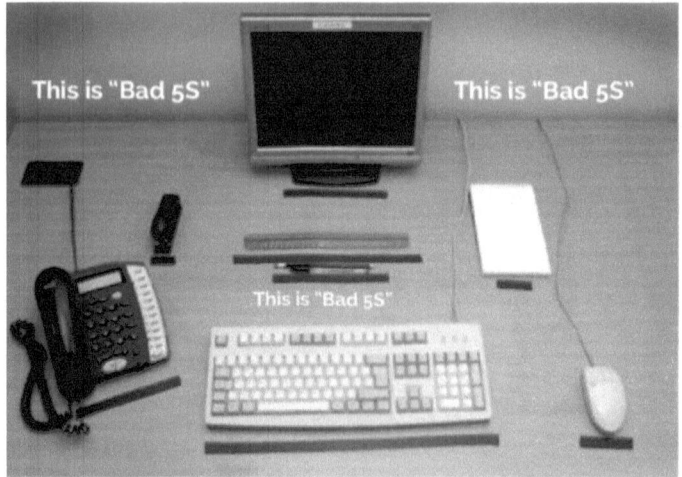

This is Bad 5S

The article explains:

"The exercise, which involves markers for items including computer keyboards, telephones, and stationery, is designed to improve efficiency by making desks neater.

However, one worker last night described the system, being implemented by logistics company Unipart, as "demeaning.""

This is a classic example of bad 5S and bad Lean efforts. Stuff like this is all too common and it really gives Lean a bad name. As we've talked about in other posts, 5S is about reducing waste and making abnormal situations apparent.

What waste is prevented by marking where the phone goes? None, probably. Is there anything to be gained by seeing that the phone is two inches too far forward? No, not really. Seems like this 5S effort isn't doing much, but antagonizing folks.

This article calls it "madness" in the headline and adds:

According to the Daily Telegraph , the programme has been so far reaching that one member of staff was asked whether a banana was 'active' or 'inactive', in other words, whether it was going to be eaten immediately, which was acceptable, or whether it was for later, which would mean the fruit would have to be cleared from the desk.

An HMRC spokeswoman said the programme, which was devised by consultants Unipart to improve performance, would help ensure that office space was efficiently used and would also support working relationships.

The consultants had good intentions. 5S *can* be a powerful method in a Lean company. But, marking the location of items is just one aspect of 5S and 5S/Lean have to be done the right way. The article also said:

> "... employees were allowed to move items into zones that suited them best."

If the consultants asked each accountant where they wanted their items, that might have been one positive sign – showing the slightest bit of respect for people in that sense, perhaps. So why did employees find it degrading? Probably because the consultants didn't explain "why", as Toyota would tend to do[94].

What if two employees who shared a desk (as happens in these British offices) disagreed with where items went? They wouldn't pick up and move the tape constantly, would they?

I could go on and on about how that effort gives "Lean" a bad name. If you're just antagonizing people with putting tape around stuff, please stop. Trying using Lean methods to solve real business problems (such as slow cycle time, defects, cost, or employee safety).

Lean, done right, won't feel "demeaning" to people.

How My Blog Rant Helped Keep an Office 5S Initiative from Being "L.A.M.E."

Originally published August 6, 2015[95]

---

[94] http://www.leanblog.org/2005/10/nummi-tour-tale-3-power-of-why/
[95] http://www.leanblog.org/2015/08/throwback-thursday-how-my-blog-rant-helped-keep-an-office-5s-initiative-from-being-l-a-m-e/

I referenced this post in my recent Keith Olber-Lean parody video[96]... the post goes all the way back to 2007, the early days of Lean Blog:

"Bad Lean/5S Hits the UK Media" (as referenced earlier in this chapter)

It's not the only "bad 5S" story that I've featured here, situations that are arguably L.A.M.E. (Lean As Misguidedly Executed) because the use of 5S in those office settings only annoyed the employees while adding no value to customers (and not even preventing any waste).

Lean is not about banning bananas from people's desks or banning sweaters hanging on chairs.

We should be solving problems that matter, for customers and employees, through Lean. We should be engaging people rather than throwing silly top-down mandates at them.

I tend to get on a soapbox and rant about the "bad office 5S" examples... but I got an email this week that made me smile because it helped an organization avoid the L.A.M.E. office 5S trap.

The email, shared with permission:

> I worked for a company that was very focused on implementing Lean concepts into all areas of the business, and that eventually grew to include support functions in the office area.
>
> When management gave the directive to implement concepts like 5S into our work, some well-intentioned people in the office took this quite literally, and I was part of discussions deciding things like:
>
> Should external monitors be on the back right or left of each cubicle? How many pens or pencils were ok to keep out on your desk at a given time? Should we standardize desk calendars, or allow people to choose their own? Should we leave room for a personal item, like a picture frame?

[96]http://www.leanblog.org/2015/07/parody-video-keith-olber-lean-and-the-worst-persons-in-the-lean-world/

As luck would have it, I had recently discovered your blog, and a post around that same time on the topic of office 5S caught my eye . This was shared around the group, and we all agreed that we were on the verge of stepping into the realm of LAME: "Lean" As Misguidedly Executed. Our attempts to 5S were based on the tool, as opposed to the principles behind 5S.

Circulating the blog post led to a lot of questions. In an office where everyone used the same desk every day (people rarely changed seats), would standardizing the placement of monitors have any real impact on quality or productivity? None that we could see. And removing personal items from the desk? Not exactly respectful of people, in our opinion.

Instead of directly copying the version of 5S that had worked so well in the manufacturing area of the business, we started asking questions about what areas of our work would benefit from 5S. This eventually led to several positive changes: how we name and manage files on the server, how emails are handled by the team, and an aggressive redesign of common areas like the supply cabinet and copier areas.

As with many other Lean tools, the transition from manufacturing to service/office work means the tools may change, but the same principles still apply.

I'm glad they came to that realization for focused on the key question of "what problem are you solving?" (as John Shook advocates[97]) or "how are you better serving the customers and employees?" instead of just blindly copying a tool.

Bad office 5S implementations helped inspire this video that I created[98], which now has almost 150,000 views on YouTube:

---

[97]http://www.leanblog.org/2014/01/video-john-shook-and-the-lei-lean-transformation-model/

[98]https://www.youtube.com/watch?v=t8IfQp4A4ZI

Be Lean, not L.A.M.E.! Have you had any near misses with bad office 5S or near-L.A.M.E. that you avoided or quickly changed?

Run Fast if You Ever Hear This Phrase from a "Lean Six Sigma" Instructor

Originally published May 16, 2014[99]

I sometimes torture myself by watching webinars given about "Lean Sigma." I hear a lot of claptrap about Lean… things that are just demonstrably wrong. These aren't differences of opinion. These are statements that are factually incorrect and can be proven as such.

If you ever hear somebody say some variation of this phrase:

"Lean is all about efficiency"

or

"Lean is only about increasing speed and reducing cost"

Then please just stop the video or run, don't walk, out of the room via the nearest exit, to avoid being further misinformed by the speaker.

Normally, I would say "safety first" and mean it, but this case might be an exception.

---

[99]http://www.leanblog.org/2014/05/run-fast-if-you-ever-hear-this-phrase/

There's a dangerously incorrect notion that is accepted as gospel truth in Lean Sigma books... that **incorrect** construct says that:

- Lean is for speed and efficiency
- Six Sigma is for quality

Again, that's false.

The truth is Lean and Six Sigma both can (and should) accomplish both goals at the same time. Lean and Six Sigma can work together, but to say "you need Six Sigma for quality" (as I often hear) is incorrect. Toyota's factories don't "do Six Sigma," as I've been told by Toyota people at the plant here in San Antonio. They teach everybody how to use basic statistical tools, but they don't train "belts."

Lean is about both quality and flow. Speed and quality. And safety, cost, and morale.

I asked my NUMMI-trained plant manager back in 1996 which thing our plant had to fix first – quality or productivity.

He wisely said "Both. They go hand in hand."

Lean and the Toyota Production System are focused on:

- Flow (just in time)
- Quality at the source (jiodka)

You can read about this directly from Toyota and their corporate website[100]. Please read that.

Whenever you hear somebody say or imply that Lean would somehow promote to inadvertently lead to "making bad stuff faster," you should point them to that Toyota page. Oh, and run away.

Watch this video clip[101].

---

[100]http://www.toyota-global.com/company/vision_philosophy/toyota_production_system/

[101]https://www.youtube.com/watch?v=79BrN2CYrw8

This speaker said:

> "Go ahead and use Lean on that quality problem... you'll
> speed up your quality problem and make bad stuff faster."

When people say outrageous things like that, the record has to be corrected.

Why would Toyota or any organization that practices Lean want to "make bad stuff faster?" That's ridiculous and it would only be said by people who don't understand Lean.

Where does this notion come from? It's right on the cover of the seminal book on "Lean Six Sigma[102] (2002)" that says:

> "Combining Six Sigma Quality and Lean Speed"

There you have it, "Six Sigma Quality and Lean Speed." It's hogwash. If people are just repeating what they've been taught, I guess we can't blame them.

---

[102] http://amzn.to/2h7t8oT

Can't Always Believe Somebody Saying "Toyota Would Tell You To..."

Originally published January 12, 2016[103]

In my experience, you have to be cautious when somebody says either, "Lean says you should...." or "Toyota would tell you to..." because those statements, even if stated authoritatively, can be wrong.

At a recent speaking engagement (I won't disclose where), a professor (one who teaches about Lean) made a curious comment that I'd put in the Lean As Misguidedly Explained (or L.A.M.E.) category.

The professor made a point that, when working in healthcare, we have to be careful about applying all methods and tools from Toyota. I agreed with that part of his statement. We're not literally hanging "andon cords" or putting tape around every piece of equipment just because a factory does it. We have to be solving hospital problems and not just copying tools. I get that.

His example, though, was a bit off base.

The prof talked about "takt time" (or the rate of customer demand) and how we balance the service or production time to match up with takt. Again, that's correct.

In his hypothetical, he said let's assume that a doctor's office is supposed to be seeing a patient every 20 minutes. What if the patient has been in the room for 19:59 already.

The prof said:

> "Toyota would tell you to kick the patient out of the room at 19:59 because you have to keep on takt time."

NO!

I think we were in agreement that you shouldn't kick a patient out of the room as if a timer bell went off. There's going to be variation in healthcare and we have to plan for that and make sure patient care comes first. We need to have a reaction plan for how to try to get back on schedule (and part of that approach could be to have buffer times

[103]http://www.leanblog.org/2016/01/where-do-hospitals-get-the-idea-that-lean-is-only-about-cost-reduction/

for charting during the day instead of doing all of the charting at the end of the day).

I explained, to the professor and the audience, that Toyota would do no such thing and there's no Lean principle that says kicking the patient out of the room would be appropriate.

Even on a Toyota assembly line, with relatively low variation and highly-engineered repetitive jobs, a worker might have 60 seconds to complete their work (based on takt and balancing the "cycle time" of the line to that).

If, in a particular job cycle, there's a problem with a part or the worker drops a bolt – let's say they can't get their work done in the schedule 60 seconds.

The worker is expected to reach up and pull the cord. The team leader comes to help. And, if the problem cannot be resolved, the LINE STOPS. You don't kick the car out because its time is up.

If the work really took 90 seconds for that particular car, you'd take 90 seconds. Quality comes first.

Interestingly, a tour guide at a Toyota plant I visited said they SOMETIMES let a problem move ahead in the line to be fixed later, that this is sometimes a judgment call depending on the problem and how it would get fixed for a particular car. This is certainly not the Toyota orthodoxy on "quality at the source".

Now, if a problem is occurring frequently, I think it's safe to say the team leader and production worker would try to fix the root cause of the problem using the Kaizen approach. It's important to understand WHY the problem occurred so you can prevent it from happening again.

Either way, you wouldn't kick the patient out of the room.

Where Do Hospitals Get the Idea that Lean is Only About Cost Reduction?

Originally published June 4, 2013[104]

---

[104]http://www.leanblog.org/2013/06/cant-always-believe-toyota-would-tell-you-to/

I had a bit of a new year's resolution about being positive and not fretting about organizations that don't "get it" when it comes to Lean. But, resolutions are meant to be broken, I guess.

It's very frustrating when I hear people in healthcare complain that their hospital or health system has equated Lean with cost savings – only focusing on cost reduction or primarily focusing on it. Hospitals that say to their staff that Lean is just about cutting costs (or demonstrate that) will fail to engage their most important asset – their employees.

I visited one hospital recently where standardized metrics boards in the hallways of different departments had a sheet of paper that summarized their Lean efforts... it simply listed the number of improvements (projects or other ideas) and the cost savings. It was millions of dollars. So, good for them. What was missing was anything equating Lean to safety, quality, patient satisfaction, patient flow, or other meaningful measures.

One can argue that it's an ineffective strategy to focus only on cost. By the way, that's been a very traditional healthcare management focus and hospitals can do cost cutting without even bringing the word "Lean" into the discussion. Health systems have been cutting costs by laying off staff for the longest time. Lean is a great alternative to that cost cutting approach.

I'd also argue that it's not Lean at all to focus only on cost cutting. A hospital's leadership can choose to focus on cost cutting... just please don't call it "Lean."

Lean comes from the Toyota Production System, whether we are practicing Lean in manufacturing, healthcare, or other industries. The core definitions of the Toyota Production System that come straight from Toyota emphasize that Lean is focused on improving flow and improving quality[105]. Cost reduction is an end result, not a primary goal.

If an organization is only focused on cost... and they're calling that Lean, it's disrespectful to Toyota, for what that's worth. It's also disrespectful to their patients and to their staff, which is more

[105]http://www.toyota-global.com/company/vision_philosophy/toyota_production_system/

important. Saying Lean is only about cost is a classic case of L.A.M.E. – Lean As Misguidedly Explained.

I wonder, "How do hospitals get the idea that Lean is primarily about cost cutting?"

There is a consultant out there who peddles Lean as a cost reduction strategy. There's probably many of them. There are traditional healthcare "cost cutting" consultants who have latched onto the Lean buzzword, but they're not really teaching Lean.

One hospital I visited recently is about two years into their "Lean journey." That journey is off to a bumpy start because they've focused primarily on cost. They had a national consulting firm "helping" them with this. They're now trying to adjust their strategy (at least that's some high-level PDSA at work).

It's also possible that healthcare leaders have an existing bias toward cost cutting. When they learn about Lean, they are maybe only learning about tools... so they think about how to apply those tools to cost reduction. They're probably doing so because they haven't learned that Lean is also a philosophy and a managerial approach.

I can't imagine anybody has gotten the impression from my blog or my book **Lean Hospitals**[106] (2nd edition) that Lean is only about cost cutting.

In the second edition, the word "cost" appears on 89 pages.

The word "quality" appears on 115 pages. "Safety" on 86 of them.

It's intentional that the word cost is not in the subtitle: "Improving Quality, Patient Safety, and Employee Engagement."

Even if people haven't bought and read my book, I make the first chapter available as a free PDF on my website. I wish we could get that PDF into the hands (or iPads) of every healthcare leader and manager in the world.

Relevant Excerpts from *Lean Hospitals*:

Dr. John Toussaint says, in the foreword:

"These [Lean] improvements all lead to better quality and lower cost–in other words, better value."

In various parts of Chapter 1 (which you can read for yourself[107]),

---

[106] http://www.leanhospitalsbook.com
[107] http://www.leanhospitalsbook.com/chapter-1/

it says:

"In today's world, the "need" for Lean in healthcare is very clear in terms of quality and patient safety, cost, waiting times, and staff morale."

...

"Lean is very different from traditional "cost-cutting" approaches that have been tried in multiple industries, including healthcare." ...

"Lean is a tool set, a management system, and a philosophy that can change the way hospitals are organized and managed. Lean is a methodology that allows hospitals to improve the quality of care for patients by reducing errors and waiting times. Lean is an approach that can support employees and physicians, eliminating roadblocks and allowing them to focus on providing care. Lean is a system for strengthening hospital organizations for the long term–reducing costs and risks while also facilitating growth and expansion."

...

"In 1945, Toyota set out to improve quality, while improving productivity and reducing costs..."

...

"Rather than reducing spending by slashing payments or rationing care, Lean methods enable us to reduce the actual cost of providing care, allowing us to provide more service and care for our communities. A hospital that saves tens of millions of dollars by using Lean methods to avoid costly expansion projects is a hospital that costs society less, while providing the same levels of care, if not more."

Good Quality Costs Less

Hospitals do have many opportunities, however, to improve the quality of healthcare delivery methods and processes in a way that also reduces costs. Across all U.S. hospitals, there is a large cost-savings opportunity from preventing errors and improving quality. For example, preventable adverse events from medication errors are estimated to cost hospitals $4 billion per year.

David Fillingham, CEO of Royal Bolton Hospital NHS Foundation Trust in the United Kingdom, has said, quite simply, "Good quality costs less." This was proven to be true as a result of Bolton's Lean improvements; the hospital reduced trauma mortality by 36% and reduced a patient's average length of stay by 33%. ThedaCare documented similar results in cardiac surgery; mortality fell from 4% to nearly zero (11 lives saved per year), with a length-of-stay reduction from 6.3 to 4.9 days, and 22% lower cost. It might sound too good to be true, but many hospitals are proving that you can simultaneously improve quality, access, and cost.

Lean teaches us to see quality improvement as a means to cost reductions, a better approach than focusing directly and solely on costs. Bill Douglas, the chief financial officer at Riverside Medical Center (Kankakee, IL), summed it up as the hospital began its first Lean project by saying, "Lean is a quality initiative. It isn't a cost-cutting initiative. But the end result is, if you improve quality your costs will go down. If you focus on patient quality and safety, you just can't go wrong. If you do the right thing with regard to quality, the costs will take care of themselves."

In another sense, Lean is proving to be an effective methodology for improving patient safety, quality, and cost, while preventing delays and improving employee satisfaction. It can be done. Lean is working; it is effective. Lean helps save money for hospitals, while creating opportunities for growth and increased revenue. Lean methods can benefit everyone involved in hospitals. Understanding Lean principles is just a starting point. The real challenge is finding the leadership necessary to implement these strategies and to transform the way your hospital provides care.

...

Lean Lessons

*Quality improvements are a means to cost reductions. *Productivity improvements and cost savings can be accomplished in ways other than layoffs or headcount reductions. *Lean is focused on patient safety, quality of care, and improved service, not just efficiency, cost, and productivity.

Why is the "Lean is about cost cutting" mindset fairly widespread? What can we, as a Lean community, do about this?

If you have stories to share about your own experiences, please post a comment (which can be anonymous) or contact me[108] (anonymity

---

[108] http://www.leanblog.org/contact-us/

assured).

The Emperor's Sacred Cow's New Clothes – "Flexing" Hospital Staff

Originally published December 7, 2009[109]

Since moving into healthcare in 2005, I've been surprised by a number of things in the hospital environment. The first time a skilled medical professional (a laboratory medical technologist) said, "they just want me to check my brain at the door" (true story), I was stunned. That's what GM assembly line workers said to me in 1995. It was sad then and even more heartbreaking to hear in a hospital in 2006.

Another thing that surprised me was the fairly common practice of "flexing" staff, including nurses. This typically means sending staff home early when the expected workload isn't there.

I saw a question on the online HME (Healthcare Management Engineers) group[110] about flexing, asking in a non-judgmental way about hospitals' practices. After a few days of general silence on the rights and wrongs of the issue, I chimed in, saying (at the risk of sounding sanctimonious, I realize):

I'd argue that "flexing" should really be called something more brutally accurate like "sending staff home because we view them only as direct labor."

There's such a lost opportunity in healthcare – nurses or other staff are sent home early... yet everyone says staff has no time for root cause problem solving or any continuous improvement efforts. There are studies that show that flexing really hurts morale[111] because staff feel less than fully valued as professionals.

Toyota never sends hourly workers home early when there are parts shortages or other situations that mean there's no direct work

---

[109]http://www.leanblog.org/2009/12/the-emperor%E2%80%99s-sacred-cow%E2%80%99s-new-clothes-%E2%80%93-%E2%80%9Cflexing%E2%80%9D-hospital-staff/

[110]http://health.groups.yahoo.com/group/hme/

[111]http://www.nursingcenter.com/Library/JournalArticle.asp?Article_ID=781841

to do. Supervisors engage their brains in improvement activities. Why can't we do the same with highly skilled nurses?

My source on the Toyota "never" statement comes from a discussion with John Shook. Has Toyota ever done this, sending people home early? Maybe, but my discussion with John:

Mark: "If a Toyota line were going to be down for the rest of the day, due to parts shortages or something, would Toyota send all of the production workers home?"

John: (without pause): "No."

Toyota would train people or have them work on improvement activities. Their system supports that and people are trained how to do so.

It seems to have been taken as the new conventional wisdom in healthcare that being "efficient" means low cost, which mandates "flexing" and sending staff home early. I've tried challenging that a few times with hospital executives and I get a lot of blank stares. It's like I've grown a second head (one of which you are tempted to send home early for being unproductive... or maybe both of them!).

Now, I realize staffing to demand is a good thing. We shouldn't be always overstaffed. But we need SOME capacity and time for improvement, not just doing work.

Hospital demand and patient needs are hardly ever level loaded. It's hard to bring someone into the laboratory for a three-hour morning shift and it might seem cruel to send a nurse home four hours early when her cost of commuting for that unexpectedly short day is just the same as a full shift.

I'm not opposed to staffing properly and I'm not opposed to cross-trained staff that can be shifted ("flexed") to another department that needs additional staff based on patient needs. But, just sending people home early... that seems to violate the "respect for people" pillar of Toyota's management system. It also seems to violate the need to drive improvement into the workplace.

Many hospitals are trapped in this cycle (roughly, a "reinforcing loop" to the system dynamics crowd[112]):

---

[112]https://en.wikipedia.org/wiki/System_dynamics

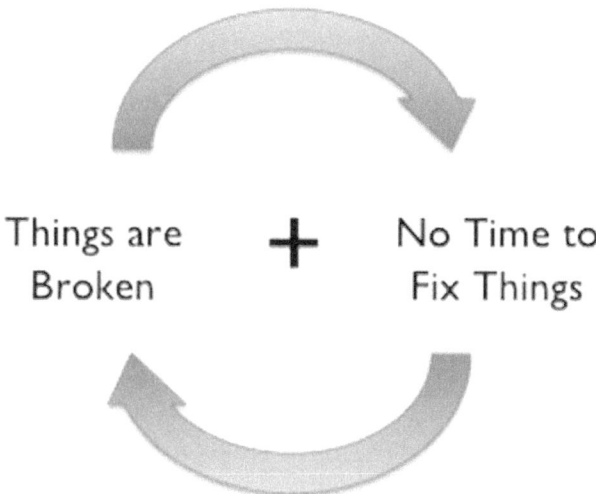

Things are **+** No Time to
Broken Fix Things

There's too much waste in the normal daily process, which inter-feres with proper patient care. For example, nurses can't quickly find needed equipment and supplies. But, there's no time for kaizen or continuous improvement activities. So things don't get fixed, better processes don't get put in place. Things remain broken (or get MORE broken).

When I teach hospital leaders about Lean improvement systems and employee suggestions, the first response is usually, "That sounds great, but we don't have time!!"

Maybe we would have time if we didn't rush to send nurses home the minute patient census drops. Maybe leaders are focusing too much on that sole labor productivity metric of Worked Hours Per Unit Of Service? We have labor productivity, but at what cost to quality, safety, and morale? How does length of stay suffer from this laser focus on labor cost?

Yes, I realize that labor costs are often 60 to 70% of a hospital's costs. I'm not saying to ignore labor productivity.

One follow up email on the HME discussion said this often happens:

*In the mid afternoon, patient census is low (after discharges), so RNs are sent home early (flex!) *Then the ED has patients to admit, but there aren't enough RNs to admit them, so patients wait and care/admission is delayed

So you've saved a few hours of labor, but at what cost to the overall system? I'm sure the root of this comes down to measures and silos.

Imagine, instead, a world where RNs and Techs take time that's available when census is low to work on improvement work – little "just do its" or simple process mapping exercises. 30 minutes here, an hour there – you can actually get a lot done in small chunks of time if you do the following:

*Track improvement opportunities and staff ideas in a visual way (see my book or David Mann's[113]) *Train staff and managers on Lean principles and teach them how to analyze and improve work (see the "Job Methods[114]" program from Training Within Industry, used in healthcare circa 1945). *Train managers on how to properly inter-act with staff to encourage continuous improvement (see the "Job Relations[115]" TWI program) *Measure results (not of each individual improvement activity) but long-term measures of the department (and broader value stream) that matter.

The alternative to "send people home" shouldn't be "let them stand around." We need to train and motivate people (or, as Dr. Deming would say, NOT de-motivate them) and allow them to drive improve-ment... that's how you break that cycle and start making things better in a workplace.

Who says it can't work in healthcare? Is someone reading this willing to challenge "flexing" in their own hospital – finding the leadership required to do the training so front-line staff can start doing this?

When I worked at GM, an old UAW guy didn't want to participate in improvement efforts as he said, "I was only hired for my back and my arms." Isn't it sad if the same is sort of true for nurses, where their brains aren't used for continuous improvement? As one person said in the discussion, "The workload is more than just direct care."

---

[113]http://www.amazon.com/gp/product/1563273225?ie=UTF8&tag=markgraban&linkCode=as2&camp=1789&creative=390957&creativeASIN=1563273225

[114]http://www.trainingwithinindustry.net/JM.html

[115]http://www.trainingwithinindustry.net/JR.html

Be Careful With "No Waiting Rooms" Just Like "Zero Inventories"

Originally published June 13, 2016[116]

For decades, manufacturers have been tripped up by the simplistic idea that Lean is about "zero inventories." It probably didn't help that one of the earliest and most prominent books about what many used to call "Japanese manufacturing practices" had that exact title: *Zero Inventories*[117]. It was published in 1983, well before "Lean" was a term used for this.

Not even Toyota has zero inventories. They don't have zero raw materials. They have non-zero buffer inventories in between parts of their assembly lines. And it's not hard to see INVENTORY of unsold cars at Toyota dealers (realizing those are independent businesses and the inventory's not on Toyota's book, but still...)

Being able to have low inventory levels – low raw materials, low work-in-progress (WIP) and/or low finished goods inventory is an end result. It's a function of a number of things, such as:

*Stable demand and/or leveled production *Suppliers that are located nearby *High equipment or machine uptime *Short changeover times and the ability to produce small batches *Low variability

When I was a grad school intern at Kodak in 1998, I worked for six months in their Microelectronics Technology Division. They made semiconductor-based image sensors for scanners, early digital cameras, the Mars Rover, etc. The "cycle time" through the semiconductor fab was measured in months, meaning it took that long to go from a raw wafer to finished chips (see an example in the photo, at left).

A previous general manager had erred in thinking they could (or should) be "Lean" by intentionally draining down their finished goods inventory levels (of finished sensors). This turned out to be a really bad mistake. They couldn't meet customer demand, given they had long cycle times, highly variable cycle times, and highly variable quality

---

[116]http://www.leanblog.org/2016/06/be-careful-with-no-waiting-rooms-just-like-zero-inventories/

[117]http://amzn.to/1THr6Fl

yields (hence my master's thesis[118]).

It was a huge mistake because the lack of image sensors became a bottleneck in the production and sale of Kodak Professional Digital Cameras that were being bought by photojournalists for $15,000 a piece... except Kodak couldn't make enough of them. Oops. That's not Lean at all to not meet customer demand.

Later, when I was consulting for a software startup called Factory Logic, I had a chance to go visit a manufacturer of enormous cranes. This was 2003 or so. The company, who would have been quick to say "we don't build cars!", had made a similar error in getting inventory levels down too low.

I was traveling with a Japanese consultant who was helping the startup and he shook his head at the situation.

He said very clearly, and it's a lesson I'll never forget:

> "Job one... meet customer demand. Job two... low inventory."

Too many companies made low inventory the primary goal. The goal is more like the lowest inventory level required to meet customer demand today. Over time, you can make improvements that ALLOW you to reduce inventory levels. You don't put the cart before the horse and just lower inventory below required levels.

You might "lower the water" a little bit to "expose rocks" as the Toyota / Lean cliche goes, but you don't drain the swimming pool completely before jumping in.

Let's Avoid This Mistake in Healthcare

It's possible that a hospital or health system could make a dangerous error by thinking it's "Lean" to cut inventory levels of supplies or medications too much. In manufacturing, you might accept that the line occasionally goes down because you ran out of parts. That's a cost of doing business that's lower than making sure you have so much inventory so that production NEVER stops.

In healthcare, we need to err on the side of slightly too much inventory since lives might be at stake. Some medications might expire (but not if we properly rotate our supply over time).

---

[118] http://dspace.mit.edu/handle/1721.1/9779

The parallel to inventory in healthcare is not just the physical supplies... we can draw a parallel to waiting rooms.

Waiting rooms are like warehouse space, basically. Why do clinics and emergency departments have waiting rooms? It's because of poor flow or it's due to an imbalance between capacity and demand. Today's process (and level of variation) requires a certain amount of waiting room space.

Over time, you can take actions that improve flow and better match capacity to demand... which means you could reduce the size of the waiting room. Look at Sami Bahri DDS, the "world's first Lean dentist." He doesn't have patients use his waiting room, but he improved his processes in a very systematic way. He didn't just open a new office without a waiting room, trusting he could quickly figure it out. He didn't put the cart before the horse. By the way, the 2nd edition of his book *Follow the Learner* is now available from LEI[119].

So, I wasn't happy to see this tweet recently, referring to a scale model of a new hospital that will be built (I'm using a picture of the tweet to avoid calling the person out by name)... she wrote this directed at me:

@MarkGraban Philosophy/construction of hospital is lean no waiting rooms, no inpatient beds, everything quickly transforms to patient need

3.18 PM - 18 May 2016

Lean doesn't mean "no waiting rooms" as an absolute.

I'm not sure what she meant by "no inpatient beds." Maybe it means beds/ rooms that are flexible for different needs (such as ICU vs regular rooms?)... that doesn't sound bad on the surface.

But let's talk about "no waiting rooms." That's likely to be a big disaster unless they have the processes and capabilities in place:

*Leveled patient demand *Matching staffing and capacity to demand at different times *Predictable process times *Slightly excess capacity for exam rooms

---

[119] http://www.lean.org/Bookstore/ProductDetails.cfm?SelectedProductId=259&ProductCategoryId=viewAll

Be careful about absolutes. Lean means no waiting rooms? Only if that's possible given a Lean process.

Saying "Lean means no waiting rooms" might be an example of L.A.M.E. or Lean As Mistakenly Explained.

Even in the most Lean of processes, we might still need waiting space. I was talking recently with an allergist who said, "We need a large waiting room."

I asked, "Why?"

The allergist pointed out the need for some patients to wait 30 minutes to check for a bad allergic reaction. Maybe that's a required inspection step... either way, having "no waiting space" would mean that patient clogs up an exam room and hampers patient flow. Having some waiting space makes sense.

And isn't that what it's all about? Making sense, making incremental changes, testing things out, and seeing what works instead of following Lean dogma?

Is it Lean's Fault or the Old Management System's?

Originally published March 17, 2014[120]

It's easy for an organization to say they are "doing Lean" or they have "started a Lean transformation." They might hire a consultant or put out a press release... or maybe there's an optimistic (but premature) news article about how the hospital or health system is going to turn around with Lean.

The problem is the culture doesn't change overnight. Leaders have years or decades of old habits (bad habits) that run counter to Lean thinking. They might be (might!) be trying to change, but people will still fall back into old habits, especially when under pressure.

I hear complaints (in recent cases) coming from different provinces in Canada that say things like:

---

[120]http://www.leanblog.org/2014/03/is-it-leans-fault-or-the-old-management-systems/

*Lean is causing hospitals to be "de-skilled" by replacing nurses with aides *Lean drives a focus on cost and cost cutting, including layoffs or being understaffed *Lean is stressing out managers by asking them to do more and taking nothing off their plate *Nurses hate Lean because they aren't being involved in changes

All of those comments get blamed on Lean. But, having studied and practiced Lean for 20 years, none of those complaints sound like Lean at all.

It sounds like what I call "L.A.M.E." – Lean As Mistakenly Explained or Lean As Misguidedly Executed. If those things are really happening, it's not "Real Lean," as Bob Emiliani calls it[121].

In all of the books I've read about Toyota... in all of the coaching I've received from former Toyota people (in both manufacturing and healthcare settings)... and my own books about Lean healthcare[122], nobody teaches that Lean should be used to drive layoffs. In fact, we strongly caution against it for many reasons... because layoffs are demoralizing and they're not usually the right long-term fix.

Read this hospital CEO's blog post on this topic[123]. The old traditional management thinking is to cut costs by laying off staff. There's a lot of that going on, unfortunately, in healthcare these days.

Lean is the ALTERNATIVE to layoffs. Being cheap or understaffing or not working together with people... that's the OLD management thinking that's been taught and practiced for decades.

So, let's say an organization has started on their "Lean journey." Old habits are hard to break.

What happens if a hospital hits a financial crisis (such as significantly lower Medicare and Medicaid reimbursements in the U.S.) just six months into this planned "Lean transformation?"

The Lean people (the consultant, the director of process improvement) might argue strongly against using layoffs and other short-term cost cutting. But, the senior leaders fall back on old habits and hire a non-Lean consultant who tells them how many people to fire

---

[121] http://www.bobemiliani.com/
[122] http://www.markgraban.com/publications/books/
[123] http://www.leanblog.org/2013/10/a-health-system-ceo-gary-passama-blogs-about-lean/

(based on spreadsheets and benchmarks). The non-Lean consultants tell them to fire nurses and hire more aides because their "ratios" don't look good compared to the benchmarks.

Let's say they do all of this (and layoffs and deskilling) without actually studying the work or engaging the people.

Can we blame things like deskilling, stress, and layoffs on Lean?

NO! Those things were happening long before Lean.

On the topic of "de-skilling" – in a Lean approach, we talk about the "waste of human potential." This includes the waste of not engaging people fully in improvement (such as through Kaizen). It also means that we shouldn't have people consistently working below their job level, education, and certification.

We'll study the work being done in a unit (including nurses, housekeepers, aides, unit secretaries), etc. to see who is doing what work – as part of a "standardized work" analysis. A key early step is to ask "who is doing what and who should be doing what?" If nurses are too busy (and they usually are), one thing we can do to free up time is to make sure aides are doing work that aides can do. This allows nurses to focus on the patients – it's compassionate to do so for many reasons, including better quality and patient safety.

We then have to make sure that the aides aren't overburdened, with too much work to do. We can remove unnecessary tasks from their plates (i.e., waste) or we can maybe actually hire more aides. The goal with Lean isn't headcount reduction – the primary goal is doing the right work the right way and making sure we have the right staffing to do so. That's Lean... and how it's different than spreadsheet-driven "de-skilling."

Also see Paul Levy's post on this topic from a few years back[124].

Lean doesn't do anything good or bad... Lean is just a set of principles. But these principles, as powerful as they can be, are often misunderstood (reading one book or taking one class doesn't make you a Lean expert) or they are just ignored. We can't blame Lean or a lack of Lean... we can really only blame the senior leaders.

I know, you're thinking, "But you say blaming people is cruel and

---

[124]http://runningahospital.blogspot.com/2012/03/dont-blame-lean-learn-together-from-it.html

counterproductive. Didn't Dr. Deming teach that?"

Yes, but Deming also taught that quality starts in the boardroom (or in the government, if it's public healthcare) and Deming certainly held them accountable for their policies and decisions. It's fair to do the same today, I think, if leaders are making decisions based on traditional thinking that get in the way of Lean and quality.

"Has Lean Ever Been Fully Implemented and Not Worked?" What About Yoga & Veganism

Originally published November 2, 2016[125]

I was interviewed today by a reporter today who is doing a story on Lean. I'll post what he's writing about when it's published... don't want to "scoop" him by saying who or what he's writing it on.

We talked about Lean being adopted in various industries and settings.

He asked a very interesting question, basically:

"Has Lean ever been fully implemented and not worked?"

I replied...

No organization that's really embracing and practicing Lean would ever say they're "done" with "implementing" Lean. Culture change is hard. Nobody is ever perfect. All organizations that many would label as "Lean" are going to be continuously re-inventing and improving themselves.

There ARE organizations that have given up on Lean. I wrote about one earlier this year[126], related to a hospital that had a new CEO kill their Lean program for unknown reasons.

If an organization reaches the conclusion that "Lean didn't work here," we'd have to ask why.

Did they think "Lean" meant just running a bunch of projects? Did they just train and certify frontline staff on Lean tools and tactics?

---

[125]http://www.leanblog.org/2016/11/has-lean-ever-been-fully-implemented-and-not-worked-what-about-yoga-veganism/

[126]http://www.leanblog.org/2016/04/why-would-a-new-healthcare-ceo-kill-a-lean-program/

If so, I would expect that they wouldn't get outstanding results.

I'm full of questions... so I'd also ask:

Were they not engaging everybody in continuous improvement?

Were they not managing differently at all levels?

Were they not trying to changing the culture?

Were they not adopting the Lean philosophy?

The writer had asked about scenarios involving engineers, staplers, and managers forcing them to put tape around their staplers... I've blogged about situations like that before and that sounds like a "Lean Failure" in the making to me.

I tried making a parallel... not that I'm practicing yoga or veganism. I said...

Imagine if somebody said they started practicing yoga and became a vegan.

It's possible that person might GAIN a bunch of weight and become LESS healthy.

We'd have to ask "why?"

What if they were just laying on the ground and stretching a bit? Is that really yoga?

Maybe they were avoiding meat, cheese, and milk, but were eating a lot of sugar and processed foods? Is that really being a good vegan?

Would that person give up and say "I tried yoga and being a vegan and it didn't work"??

Would we, as observers, criticize yoga and vegan? Would we say those methods are bad? That they don't apply to some people?

Or would we say, "They probably didn't really learn properly about yoga and veganism"? Would we say, "It's a shame they didn't have a good yogi or nutritionist to help them"?

What do you think about my answers to that question and that analogy?

Fighting Against "The Way We've Always Done It" – Before Lean or With Lean

Originally published November 9, 2015[127]

Through our practice of Lean, we're looking at processes and our management system, looking to identify waste and opportunities for improvement.

Lean is about engaging people to have them ask why we do things a certain way or if things could be better (it's not about finding fault from on high and telling them what to do).

The answer to why we do something a certain way is often:

"We've always done it that way."

Frontline staff often say that. Managers and executives say it.

The fact we've always done something that way doesn't automatically mean it's a bad practice. But, we should be willing to challenge things to figure out if we should reinvent that process or tweak it. The same question applies not just to the value-adding frontline work, but also to management practices.

Asking why is a powerful Lean practice.

Why do we spend a ton of time on annual budgeting? We've always done it that way?

Some organizations challenge that, via the "Beyond Budgeting" movement[128].

Why do hospitals so easily send nurses home early when census is low? We've always done it that way?

Some organizations challenge that, choosing to engage staff in daily continuous improvement, as paying people to work on improvement can save more money than strictly focusing on reducing labor costs.

As an organization embraces Lean (or as an industry has seen widespread adoption), it's easy for aspects of Lean to become the new "way we've always done it."

---

[127]http://www.leanblog.org/2015/11/fighting-against-the-way-weve-always-done-it-before-lean-or-with-lean/

[128]http://bbrt.org/

There are some Lean practices that almost become dogma.

I hear it more in manufacturing, but some people advise, in a quite prescriptive way:

"Always start with 5S"

There are plenty of references to this phrase online.

I think a statement like that should really become a question:

"Always start with 5S?"

If somebody makes an absolute statement (look for the words "never" and "always"), you should be able to ask "why?" Why start with 5S?

If the answer is "well, I've always done it that way" or "my sensei taught me that," we should be willing to challenge the way it's always been done (even if "always" is just a few years).

There might be a good reason why somebody suggests to start with 5S. I wouldn't say "never start with 5S." 5S can be helpful. But, I think we should be focused less on the question of "what tool should I start with?" and more on the question of what problem we're looking to solve.

I wrote about this a few years back:

Lean in Hospitals: Which Tool or Which Need[129]?

Taiichi Ohno, credited as a creator of the Toyota Production System, said simply in a book[130]:

Start from need

John Shook, of the Lean Enterprise Institute, asks:

What problem are we trying to solve?

See more about John and the LEI Lean Transformation Model[131].

---

[129] http://www.leanblog.org/2015/11/fighting-against-the-way-weve-always-done-it-before-lean-or-with-lean/

[130] http://amzn.to/1NkL8Ss

[131] http://www.leanblog.org/2014/01/video-john-shook-and-the-lei-lean-transformation-model/

Am I being too dogmatic in saying "always start by asking 'what problem are we trying to solve?'" Maybe.

Either way, if "the way we've always done Lean" is becoming rigid or is no longer helping, we need to ask why... we need to improve. There's a reason Toyota people call TPS the "Thinking Production System[132]."

We should be thinking. Asking "why?" Challenging things... not just accepting dogma.

Do you see other examples of "Lean dogma" or "the way we've always done Lean" that could be questioned?

---

[132]http://www.leanblog.org/2005/04/thinking-production-system/

Thanks for Reading the Book!

I hope this book has been interesting, helping, or entertaining. Or maybe all of the above. Thanks for taking the time to make it this far.

Please consider leaving a review on Amazon.com[133].

Again, all author royalty proceeds are being donated to the Louise H. Batz Patient Safety Foundation[134], a Texas-based non-profit that does excellent work in educating patients and hospitals about patient safety improvement. Their publications, like the Batz Guide for Bedside Advocacy[135] are really making a difference in the lives of patients and staff.

Over $1000 has been donated from sales of this book, as of December 2016.

If you would d like to donate, please visit their website[136].

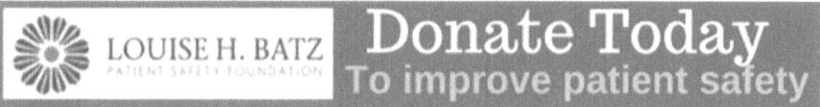

Mark Graban[137] Mark@MarkGraban.com

---

[133]http://amzn.to/2i7w7iQ
[134]http://www.louisebatz.org/Home.aspx
[135]http://www.louisebatz.org/patient-education/the-batz-guide.aspx
[136]http://www.louisebatz.org/
[137]http://www.markgraban.com

www.ingramcontent.com/pod-product-compliance
Lightning Source LLC
Chambersburg PA
CBHW020857180526
45163CB00007B/2533